VENGEANCE IS MINE

The Scandalous Love Triangle that Triggered the Boyce-Sneed Feud

VENGEANCE IS MINE

The Scandalous Love Triangle that Triggered the Boyce-Sneed Feud

Bill Neal

Vengeance is Mine: The Scandalous Love Triangle that Triggered the Boyce-Sneed Feud is Number 11 in the A. C. Greene Series

University of North Texas Press
Denton, Texas

Permissions:
University of North Texas Press
1155 Union Circle #311336
Denton, TX 76203-5017

The paper used in this book meets the minimum requirements of the American National Standard for Permanence of Paper for Printed Library Materials, z39.48.1984. Binding materials have been chosen for durability.

Library of Congress Cataloging-in-Publication Data

Neal, Bill, 1936–
 Vengeance is mine— : the scandalous love triangle that triggered the Boyce-Sneed feud / by Bill Neal.—1st ed.
    p. cm.—(A.C. Greene series ; no. 11)
 Includes bibliographical references and index.
 ISBN 978-1-57441-317-5 (cloth : alk. paper)
 1. Boyce-Sneed Feud. 2. Boyce family. 3. Snead family. 4. Sneed, John Beal—Trials, litigation, etc. 5. Vendetta—Texas—Texas Panhandle—History—20th century. 6. Triangles (Interpersonal relations)—Texas—Texas Panhandle. 7. Violence—Texas—Panhandle—History—20th century. 8. Texas Panhandle (Tex.)—History—20th century. 9. Texas Panhandle (Tex.)—Biography. 10. Texas—History—1846–1950. I. Title. II. Series: A.C. Greene series ; 11.
 F392.P168N43 2011
 976.4'05–dc23

                              2011018204

Vengeance Is Mine: The Scandalous Love Triangle that Triggered the Boyce-Sneed Feud is Number 11 in the A. C. Greene Series.

In memory of my loving parents,
Overton (Boots) Neal and Katharine Barnes Neal:
The cowboy and the lady.

"Vengeance is mine! saith the Lord."
But in Texas He has always had plenty
of help!

—*C. L. Sonnichsen*

CONTENTS

"Where It All Happened"

Author's collection: Map designed by Hanaba Munn Welch.

LIST OF ILLUSTRATIONS

✐ ACKNOWLEDGMENTS

Many acknowledgments are in order. First, and foremost, to my wife and companion, Gayla Neal, who is also my secretary, research assistant, and the doer of all manner of other unglamorous tasks. Thanks are also in order to Katherine Hinkebein for her insightful suggestions on manuscript improvements and to Hanaba Munn Welch for her research assistance and map drawing. I need to say "thanks" once more to a couple of college classmates of yesteryear for their unfailing help and encouragement: Mike Cochran, veteran newspaper reporter for the Associated Press and the *Fort Worth Star-Telegram* and Dr. David McPherson, retired University of New Mexico English professor and Shakespeare scholar. I must also say thanks for much appreciated support and encouragement from that ever-cheerful and uplifting history scholar, Dr. Garry L. Nall, editor of the *Panhandle-Plains Historical Review.* A couple of my courtroom friends from my pre-retirement lawyering years should also be thanked: the Honorable Judge John T. Forbis of Childress, Texas, retired judge of the 100th Judicial District Court for sharing with me stories of colorful lawyers of yesteryear, and my friend, Earl Griffin, Esquire, of Childress, Texas, with whom I crossed swords in more than a few criminal cases, for his research help and support. Also for my son, Monte Neal, for his manuscript suggestions and photographic assignments and to Allen Kimble for his photographic assignments.

Also appreciated are Tai Kreidler, Monte Monroe, Lynn Whitfield, and the staff at the Southwest Collections/Special Collections Library at Texas Tech University; Warren Stricker, research center director at the Panhandle-Plains Historical Museum; Donaly Brice and John Anderson, Texas State Library and Archives Commission; Cathy Spitzenberger at the University of Texas at Arlington Library Special Collections; Jill Henderson, librarian at the Taylor County, Texas Law Library; Patrick Lemmelle, University of Texas at San Antonio's Institute of Texan Cultures; and personnel at the Jamail

Center for Legal Research at the Tarleton Law Library, University of Texas at Austin.

Thanks also to court clerks in Fort Worth, Amarillo, Vernon, Memphis, Quanah, Benjamin, and Seymour.

ALMOST HALF A CENTURY AFTER the Boyce-Sneed feud erupted in bloodshed in 1912, one Texas historian, Lewis Nordyke, decided to write a book about it. But he had to abandon the idea: nobody would talk to him. Another chronicler of Texas feuds, C. L. Sonnichsen, commenting on the reticence of "mind-your-own-business" Westerners—especially Texans—to discuss local feuds, wrote in 1951 that it was "too soon to talk about the Boyce-Sneed affair."

It wasn't until the taboo of silence was finally breached in 1985 that anyone dared speak its name. The Amarillo High School graduating class of 1935 held its fiftieth class reunion that year, and one graduate, Lillian Blanche Brent, a Sneed family descendant, approached a classmate, Albert Boyce, a Boyce family descendant, extended her hand and said: "Albert, this thing has been going on a long time and neither one of us had a thing to do with it. I think it's time it ended."[1] They shook on it.

Still, the story of the Boyce-Sneed feud would simmer beneath the surface for yet another fourteen years before any public mention of the tragedy appeared. Clara Sneed, great-niece of John Beal Sneed, finally persuaded descendants on both sides to open up family archives and share their stories, photographs, and documents, including letters written almost a century earlier by all three of the principals of this star-crossed love triangle as well as by others caught up in the unfolding tragedy. With this treasure trove of feud history, Ms. Sneed was able to cobble together an insightful article describing this classic saga of passion, violence, and revenge; of retribution but never redemption.[2]

From my research of court records and from the lengthy newspaper reports filed daily during the sensational murder trials—reports that quoted much of the testimony of witnesses as well as a detailed description of the trial lawyers and their tactics and strategies—I had already shaped a fascinating tale. Yet, as a result of Clara Sneed's revelations, I acquired a greater understanding of the players in this drama. This, in turn, helped me to flesh out the principals—for which I am much indebted to Ms. Sneed.

When my tale was finally told, no screenwriter could have concocted a more dramatic plot or enlisted such an all-star cast of larger-than-life characters to propel it. What more could a director have asked for: a torrid sex scandal at the core of a love triangle featuring Lena Snyder Sneed, the high-spirited, headstrong wife; Al Boyce, Jr., Lena's reckless, romantic lover; and John Beal Sneed, Lena's arrogant, grim, and vindictive husband who responded to Lena's plea for a divorce by having her locked up in an insane asylum. The chase was on after Al rescued Lena from the asylum and the lovers fled to parts unknown—Canada, as it turned out when John Beal Sneed and his pack of hired bloodhounds eventually ran them to ground.

And that's when the killings began.

Yet there was even more stuff to add tang to this tale. This was not some squalid, sordid, low-life, back-street affair; the principals in this drama were the descendents of three prominent and close-knit families—the Snyders, the Sneeds, and the Boyces, all of whom had bonded in antebellum times on the Texas frontier.

No one who knew the vengeful John Beal Sneed doubted for a moment that he would go after his wife's lover with murderous intent. But that was not enough blood to satisfy the enraged husband's blood lust. In an unimaginable twist to this tale, for good measure Sneed assassinated Al's aged and unarmed father, Colonel Albert Boyce, a wealthy Amarillo banker who had been the general manager of the huge XIT Ranch in the Panhandle during the late nineteenth century.

Headlines splashed on the front pages of newspapers across the nation and Canada predicted that the upcoming murder trial of John Beal Sneed for killing Colonel Boyce would be the "greatest legal battle ever fought in Texas Courts."[3] It would prove to be an apt description of the drama that was played out in a Fort Worth courtroom—no hyperbole, no exaggeration, no headline-grabbing sensationalism in that forecast. The trial judge, noting that the case was receiving worldwide publicity, told the jurors that the defendant wasn't the only one being tried in his court: the State of Texas itself was on trial.[4]

Later, after three more sensational murder trials, one editor put this wrap on what has to be one of the most bizarre, true-crime tales in Texas history: "no other case . . . has occupied so much space in the public print of the country."[5]

In the end, when at last I laid pen aside, I realized that I had written three separate, yet interwoven stories. First was the story of the scandalous love triangle, the bitter family feud it triggered, and then the revenge killings that followed. This, in turn, resulted in the second story: the four sensational murder trials. Yet in the telling of those first two stories I realized that I had told a third story: a story of the culture of that time and place—1912 Texas. Indeed, for the reader to make sense of the first two stories and to understand the motivations, beliefs, and actions of the principals and the public's reaction to the scandal as well as the machinations, strategies, and the jury arguments of the lawyers during the courtroom dramas, the reader would have to filter it through the lens of that society. That third story is told, not by burdening the narrative with some academic discussion of the culture, but rather by quoting the spoken words and written letters of the characters, by quoting the comments of the reporters covering the unfolding tragedy, by including related anecdotes and news items, and by analyzing the trial tactics that were so carefully crafted to resonate with the jurors.

At the turn of the nineteenth century, the Victorian values and lifestyles of the Old South and the folk laws and customs of the western frontier still greatly influenced Texas society. It was also a time when justice administered in court under the written laws of Texas was struggling to gain ascendency over justice administered by Judge Winchester and Judge Lynch as well as by the self-help justice condoned by the Honor Code's unwritten laws. Only by illuminating those contemporary Texas mores could the personal conflicts and romances, the crimes of passion, and the courtroom dramas be understood and brought to life. Conversely, there is nothing quite like a crime of passion played out during the courtroom drama of a sensational murder trial to illuminate the social history and the contemporary mores of any given society.

✑ PROLOGUE

FOR FOUR MISERABLE DAYS the two would-be assassins sweated in the heat of early September. The small house they had rented for their intended ambush had no air-conditioning, but then nobody had air-conditioning in 1912 Amarillo. Still, most folks at least opened their windows to catch an occasional breeze. But not the assassins. They nailed the shades over all the windows, leaving only a narrow space for a peephole at the bottom.

When, several days earlier, John Beal Sneed heard that his prey had come to Amarillo, he and his deputy assassin, Beech Epting, caught the next train to town. Already anticipating his prey's arrival, the leader had grown a full beard, and now, instead of wearing his usual business suit, he donned a pair of faded overalls. Adding to this disguise a rather bizarre touch, he wore, as one witness subsequently described it, "a pair of blue goggles." Then, under aliases, he had Epting rent what would later be referred to as "the death cottage" along a street they knew their target would have to walk, sooner or later, en route to the downtown area. Ironically, the death cottage was just across the street from a venerable Amarillo landmark—the Polk Street Methodist Church.

The gunmen themselves were an odd couple, to say the least, and cut from entirely different cloth: the leader, a college-educated, wealthy pillar of his community; his deputy, a poorly educated tenant farmer. Nevertheless, they were united now. Both dedicated to their kill-dead mission.

The days dragged slowly by one . . . two . . . three . . . four days. Still nothing.

But the leader was patient. And he was determined. Perhaps, as the long hours of waiting gradually turned into days, he reflected on the strange turn of events that led him—a card-carrying member of pioneer Texas cow-country royalty—to this ironic juncture in his life. Already indicted for one murder, he now was hell-bent on committing another. Worse, his intended victim, Al Boyce, Jr., had been a friend from childhood. Philosophical reflection, however, was not John Beal Sneed's long suit, and the word "irony" was probably not in his working vocabulary. He was totally focused on the bloody mission ahead.

He was well aware that Al Boyce usually went armed, and he was also aware that his target was widely reputed to be a crack shot—one of the best in the Texas Panhandle. Therefore, the assassin had devoted considerable time of late to practicing his marksmanship. Even so, in a fair fight he would likely come in dead last. He knew that. But then he had no intention of fighting fair.

He did, however, have every intention of winning. That, or any other contest. Whatever it took.

Finally, on the fifth day, when John Beal Sneed squinted through his peephole, the manhunter sighted his target strolling towards him down Polk Street—unaware of the surveillance. Unaware, as yet, but not unarmed. Al Boyce had a loaded, semi-automatic Luger pistol tucked in his belt.

The hunter grabbed his twelve-gauge automatic shotgun. It was loaded with buckshot. Then he opened the cottage door and walked into the street.

The Three Families
Settling in Antebellum Texas

BY HAPPENSTANCE, the Sneed, Boyce, and Snyder families all settled in the same place, a wild and sparsely populated area a few miles north of Austin around the central Texas village of Georgetown. The three families were bedrock Texans, all arriving before the Civil War—some even before statehood in 1845. During those early years, the families shared the same struggles and hardships in that harsh, dangerous, and unforgiving frontier where there was the constant threat of Indian depredations. They also shared many of the same qualities. They were intelligent people and reasonably well educated for that day: ambitious, bold-spirited, hardy, independent, and, most of all, determined—determined not only to survive, but also to prosper. They were a religious people, devout Methodists. All three families, years later, joined to help found Southwestern University in Georgetown, a Methodist-sponsored college that received its official charter in 1875. Over the years, the lives and destinies of the three families became intertwined.

The first Sneed who came to Texas was a pioneer circuit-riding Methodist preacher named Joseph Perkins Sneed. He was among a small group of men who laid the foundations of Methodism in the brand-new Republic of Texas. When he arrived by horseback on February 8, 1839, he carried with him a letter of introduction penned by the Methodist bishop who had appointed him. Addressed to the superintendent of the Texas mission to whom he reported, the letter declared: "We have sent you Brother Sneed, a man who is not afraid to die or sleep in the woods." Parson Sneed devoted much of his ministry in antebellum Texas to black slaves—far more than any other white preacher. He became widely known among his Methodist brethren as "the old Devil fighter," and during his ministry he founded several churches, including the first Methodist Church in Waco.[1] Reverend Sneed prospered not only as a preacher but also as a farmer and rancher.[2]

The Snyder brothers, Dudley Hiram and John Wesley, were born in Mississippi in 1833 and 1837, respectively. Twenty-one-year-old D. H. was virtually penniless when, in 1854, he arrived at Round Rock, a small village located between Austin and Georgetown. D. H. persuaded his grandfather, Dr. Thomas Hade, a pioneer merchant, to let him collect delinquent accounts for 10 percent of the amount collected. His brother, J. W., followed in 1856, and they became partners.[3] Another Snyder brother, Thomas Shelton Snyder, soon joined D. H. and J. W. in Texas, and he too settled in the Georgetown area, purchasing a ranch near Round Rock. Years later—on July 20, 1878—under a live oak tree on his property, Tom Snyder witnessed a dramatic piece of Texas history. There Snyder discovered the famous outlaw Sam Bass, fatally shot, the result of a gun battle with Texas lawmen who had been tipped off, by one of the outlaw's own gang, about plans to rob a bank in Round Rock. Bass was taken back to Round Rock where the twenty-seven-year-old bandit died two days later. He soon entered the outlaw hall of infamy, celebrated in countless stories, legends, and songs.[4]

The family patriarch of the Boyce clan was Albert Gallatin Boyce, born in Texas on May 8, 1842. His father, James Boyce, born in 1800 in Tennessee, had moved to Texas in 1839, settling along Gilliland's Creek near Austin in Travis County where the Boyce family was soon initiated into the dangers of frontier existence. Comanches, Apaches, Lipans, and other tribes roamed the area stealing horses and cattle and occasionally killing or kidnapping settlers.[5] The hideous appearance of one of James Boyce's neighbors, Josiah P. Wilbarger, gave mute testimony to the barbarity of the Indian attacks. In August 1833, Wilbarger was a member of a surveying party that was attacked by Indians near Pecan Springs about four miles east of the site of present-day Austin. Savagely beaten, stripped, and scalped, he was left for dead. But he wasn't dead. Next day a neighbor, Reuben Hornsby, discovered Josiah, unconscious but still alive, and took him home for treatment. Although he managed to survive for another eleven years, wearing a knitted cap to cover his bare skull, he never completely recovered.[6] In the 1840s, Albert Boyce's older brother, Jim Boyce, was killed and scalped by Indians near the family home on the banks of Gilliland's Creek.[7]

If the plight of the families in the antebellum wilderness of Texas had been perilous, life got even more dangerous during and immediately after the Civil War. Albert Boyce was nineteen years old when the Civil War erupted. He enlisted in Company F of the 18th Texas Regiment. Soon thereafter he was captured, but then released in a prisoner exchange. Later, during the Battle of Chickamauga while serving under General Braxton Bragg, he was wounded. After he recovered, he served the remainder of the war under General Ford's command on the Rio Grande.[8] Although Albert Boyce never rose to the rank of colonel during his military career, in deference to his service and his commanding presence, he was commonly referred to as "Colonel Boyce" or "Captain Boyce."

It was the worst of times. Post-Civil War Texas was the most disastrous period in Texas history. Chaos reigned. The three families were threatened not only by Indians, but now also by an influx of outlaws and embittered, hardened, and starving stragglers from the war-ravaged South. Precious few effective, honest lawmen were left to protect them, and the court system was in shambles. The task of merely surviving was a challenge to even the hardiest of settlers. Destitute people struggled over meager supplies; feuds were common, and the economy had withered to almost nothing. Dollars were scarce, the money supply almost nonexistent, and the state and local governments struggled to provide a few basic services.[9] Still, the three families were as determined as ever not only to survive but to prosper. While others saw only destitution and disaster ahead, the family elders astutely recognized a great opportunity. Although the families had little financial capital, there were two assets available that could be had for very little financial investment: land and cattle. The State of Texas owned millions of acres of land that could be purchased at giveaway prices and with very little money down. However, a pioneer really didn't have to buy land to use it, since much of Texas was unfenced and already well stocked with cattle, and those were available for nothing more than a lariat, a saddle, a cow pony, and a hard-riding hand who knew how to use those tools. Large herds of wild, unbranded cattle had multiplied on untended Texas rangelands during the Civil War. Some estimated that by war's end in 1865 as many as five million head roamed free on the vast unfenced prairies. According to one observer, cattle were so numerous in South Texas as to never be out of sight of a cross-country traveler.[10]

And a good market for cattle existed—as much as $35 per head for those critters, a veritable king's ransom in Reconstruction-era Texas. However, there was a problem. Those markets were not located in Texas. They were located far away near large population centers in the North or burgeoning, gold-rich California. The problem was how to get all those cattle to the distant markets. There were no trucks. There were trains, but as yet no railroad tracks connected Texas to those markets. A solution was available, although an arduous and time-consuming one: round up a large herd of Texas cattle, and then hire enough Texas cowboys to drive them to a distant market.[11]

The Snyder brothers, D. H. and J. W., saw the opportunity and recognized the solution to the marketing problem even before the Civil War ended. During the war they obtained contracts to deliver cattle to the Confederate army. For two decades after the Civil War D. H. and J. W. Snyder drove thousands of Texas cattle to markets in Kansas, Colorado, Nebraska, and Wyoming, becoming among the most famous of Texas trail drivers. In one year, 1877, they drove herds totaling approximately twenty-eight thousand head to Colorado. In addition to the usual hardships of driving the large herds through storms and across vast, largely unwatered plains, until the mid-1870s they were in constant peril of Indian attacks. In an 1869 drive to Abilene, Kansas, the Snyder outfit came under an attack in the Indian Territory and had 140 head stolen before the attackers were repelled.

The Snyder brothers were unique as trail drivers of that time in one respect: true to their strict Methodist moralistic code, they laid down these three rules for all their cowboys.

1. You can't drink whiskey and work for us;
2. You can't play cards and gamble and work for us; and
3. You can't curse and swear in our camp or in our presence and work for us.[12]

Although there were some financial reversals over the years, the two trail-driving Snyder brothers thrived and prospered, and they bought large ranches with their earnings, including one 128,000-acre spread in the West Texas counties of Lamb and Hockley. The other Snyder brother, Tom, meanwhile, continued to prosper, ranching in the Georgetown area.

Colonel Boyce also gained fame and fortune as a trail driver. In the 1867–68 season he drove a herd of Texas cattle numbering approximately three thousand all the way from Texas to California. In succeeding years he made trail drives to Kansas and Wyoming. During those years he worked and traded with D. H. and J. W. Snyder.[13]

In 1870, Colonel Boyce married Annie Elizabeth Harris, and they had six children, including Al Boyce, Jr., as well as his brothers Will, Lynn, and Henry, and his sister, Bessie.[14] Al, Jr., shared some of his father's qualities. He was straightforward, hardheaded, and fearless. But in other ways, he was not at all like Colonel Boyce. The Colonel was loud, blustery, humorless, straitlaced, teetotaling. Al wasn't. Instead, he resembled the typical carefree, reckless, devil-take-the-hindmost, fun-loving, western cowboy type. And he certainly made no pretense of being a teetotaler. He also liked to smoke cigarettes.

Tom Snyder was the father of four daughters: Pearl, Eula, Susan, and Lenora, known as Lena. Lena would prove to be quite a contrast to her rigid, straitlaced, humorless father. She would grow up to become an enigma, and a very bewitching one.

Joseph Tyre Sneed, son of "the old Devil fighter" Parson Sneed, became the father of two prominent and aggressive entrepreneurs, Joe Sneed, Jr., and John Beal Sneed. The business interests of both sons included ranching, farming, land dealing, and banking. Both were astute and successful wheelers and dealers. John Beal Sneed was brilliant, humorless, and, more than anything else, determined. He would achieve much notoriety in his time. But it would be very different from the kind of fame earned by his old devil-fighting grandfather.

Migrating To A New Frontier: The Texas Panhandle

By the 1880s the three families began to shift some of their business interests to the north and west, most especially to the Texas Panhandle, a vast, unsettled frontier consisting of approximately seventeen million acres—large enough to swallow up Massachusetts, Connecticut, and Rhode Island plus chunks of New Hampshire and Vermont. The land itself is a flat, treeless unbroken plain of lush, protein-rich native gramma and buffalo grasses. Standing anywhere near the center of the Panhandle, the pioneer could turn his gaze for 360 degrees across an undulating ocean of grass without observing a single break in the horizon. When Francisco Vasquez de Coronado crossed these featureless plains in 1541 in his vain quest to discover those fabled, golden "Seven Cities of Cibola," he was unimpressed: no gold and precious little water. There were, however, immense herds of buffalo, and the buffalo, as well as the Comanches, the Kiowas, and the Apaches, found the land much to their liking.

Almost three centuries later the first Anglo-American explorer, Major Stephen S. Long, ventured across those limitless, windswept plains and pronounced the land to be an "unfit residence for any but a Nomad population." This region, he concluded, was the

"Great American Desert"—a denomination that would stigmatize the region for decades to come in the minds of folks back east.[15]

In 1849—almost three decades later—a dutiful young U.S. Army officer, Captain Randolph B. Marcy, came, saw, and agreed. "Llano Estacado," he reported back to his superiors in Washington, was "the great Sahara of North America . . . a land where no man, either savage or civilized permanently abides . . . a treeless, desolate waste of uninhabited solitude, which always has been, and must continue uninhabited forever."[16]

Yet less than a century later, another intrepid adventurer—Georgia O'Keeffe, destined to become a world-famous artist—would view the same high plains of the Texas Panhandle and eastern New Mexico quite differently. She reveled in the splendor of its sweeping vistas, its high clarity, and its "wonderful emptiness."[17]

Even before O'Keeffe, however, westering pioneers in the last quarter of the nineteenth century began to view those "inhospitable" plains through a different lens. In its pristine state, this wide, wild, and lonely land of subtle nuances was enigmatic. It had about it a mystical, even spiritual, quality that hinted of high adventure and thinly veiled promise. But the more perceptive might have also sensed a dark side to this prairie paradise, one that would test the mettle of the hardiest of dream-seekers, one that hinted of desolation, deprivation, great suffering, and, particularly in the case of pioneer women, months on end of isolation and soul-withering loneliness.[18] Still, to the deprived and the dream-seeker, there was that lure of high adventure, unfettered freedom, and the possibility of great wealth: a renewal of the American dream in a new land. Located at the southern reaches of America's Great Plains, it was known as the Staked Plains, or, in Spanish, *Llano Estacado*. The dreams and the challenges of the Llano Estacado would prove to be a powerful magnet to hardy pioneers such as those of the three families.

Following the Civil War, immigrants—mostly southerners—began pouring into the eastern portion of Texas, forcing the tribes westward. Nevertheless, until the mid-1870s the tribes fiercely defended their ancestral hunting grounds in the western half of

Texas. Noted historian Rupert Richardson later referred to it as "the Comanche Barrier" to the settlement of the western plains.[19]

That barrier, however, would soon be removed. By 1878 hide hunters had slaughtered nearly all the buffalo, thus destroying the plains tribes' commissary.[20] Even earlier, on September 28, 1874, the Fourth U.S. Cavalry led by Colonel Ranald Mackenzie in the decisive battle of the Red River War routed a large encampment of Comanches, Kiowas, and Cheyennes at the battle of Palo Duro Canyon.[21] Yet the Llano Estacado was still a primitive and lawless land with no settlements, no rail or transportation facilities, and no law enforcement or courts.

In the mid-1870s, a trading post named Tascosa appeared on the banks of the Canadian River, which serviced the mundane needs of a sprinkling of settlers within a two-hundred-mile radius. Soon it began servicing more exotic needs—namely, booze, cards, and whores. Plus, there was yet another powerful attraction: Tascosa was located in a land beyond the law, a fact that many frontiersmen found most appealing. One old-timer later reflected that almost everybody in the Panhandle in those days went under some "consumed" name.[22] Charles Goodnight pronounced Tascosa "the most lawless place on the continent."[23] And the tale is told that one Tascosan used to kill men just to see if his pistol was loaded.[24] The hell-raising and the music died in Tascosa in the late 1880s when the railroad pushed through the Panhandle; it bypassed Tascosa, dooming it to quickly become a ghost town.

The coming of the railroad may have been the demise of Tascosa, but it was the making of another town about twenty miles southeast of Tascosa. The pioneers named it Amarillo. There doesn't appear to be any particular reason why Amarillo was located where it exists today. It's not on the bank of any flowing river, or even a respectable creek. Not on any sea coast. Not in view of any mountain range. It's just a dot in the middle of an enormous pancake-flat, treeless sea of grass. Actually Amarillo's very existence as well as its location is primarily due to happenstance—it just happened to get in the way of a railroad. The Fort Worth and Denver City Railway laid tracks across the Panhandle in the 1880s. In 1887 it reached the spot where Amarillo is now located, and a town came to life. Sprouting a settlement in that general locality, however, did make sense. It was near the center of the Panhandle, plus it proved to be a commercial hub for an even larger area, reaching out for approximately two hundred miles in every direction, including parts of Oklahoma to the east and north, Kansas still farther north, New Mexico to the west, and the South Plains of Texas just below the Panhandle to the south. Furthermore, when extensive cattle-shipping facilities were constructed along the railroad, Amarillo became the cattle-marketing center for a huge area of lush, rich grasslands.[25]

Even before the coming of the railroad and the construction of the Amarillo cattle-shipping facilities, some intrepid individual cattleman recognized a great potential for the cattle industry on the Llano Estacado. Free grass, cheap labor, and minimal production costs added up to a beef bonanza for the bold and the daring. Soon, like news of a gold strike, the word spread far and wide, and it attracted deep-pocket investors not only from back east but also from England and Scotland. When they learned that millions of acres of Texas grasslands could be purchased from the state for a few pennies per acre, there was no holding them back. In the era between 1880 and 1885, these out-of-state capitalists bought empire-sized domains in Northwest Texas.[26]

The largest by far was the famous XIT Ranch, which consisted of more than three million acres of land that stretched for approximately two hundred miles, north to south, along the western edge of the Panhandle and South Plains and included parts of ten Texas counties. The story of the creation of the huge XIT Ranch is an interesting part of Texas history. In 1879 the Texas Legislature decided that the State of Texas needed and deserved a bigger and better state capitol building. But there were not nearly enough state funds available to build it. However, although Texas was cash poor, the state was land rich. (Texas had reserved ownership of all lands within its borders when it was annexed into the Union in 1845.) Therefore, the Texas Legislature decided to solve the problem by allotting lands to a private investor in order to finance the building of a new capitol. In 1880 bids were solicited—just in time, as it turned out, because in 1881 the old capitol building burned down. In 1882 the legislature awarded a Chicago consortium, "the Capitol Syndicate," a 3,050,000-acre land grant in consideration for the construction of a capitol building to be located in Austin. When the last stone was laid in place it was an impressive architectural work—a big, Texas-sized capitol built out of native red granite and towering 311 feet high, taller even than the U.S. Capitol in Washington, D.C.[27]

Colonel Boyce first viewed the three-million-acre XIT Ranch in 1885 when he trail-bossed a large herd of cattle from South Texas to the XIT range. The Capitol Syndicate had purchased the cattle from J. W. and D. H. Snyder. After the cattle were delivered, Colonel Boyce was hired as a cowboy for the XIT where, only two years later, in 1887, he was promoted to general manager, a position he held for eighteen years before retiring. During that time he lived at the ranch headquarters in the tiny village of Channing about fifty miles northwest of Amarillo.[28]

Prior to the time Colonel Boyce was named general manager of the XIT, the Capitol Syndicate had sustained losses due to lax management practices. The legion of wild cowboys they employed was ill-disciplined. Drinking, gambling, firing off pistols, and general hell-raising occupied much of their time and energy. Plus cattle rustlers found the sprawling XIT range ideal for their purposes: easy pickings. That soon changed with Boyce at the helm. Losses due to rustling dropped, and a new set of rules was imposed on XIT hands. Colonel Boyce imposed his strict Methodist rules of conduct on a most unlikely congregation. No drinking, no gambling, no carrying of six-shooters, and he insisted on strict religious observance of Sundays—rules theretofore unheard of on the ranges of the wild and woolly West. But Colonel Boyce made them stick. And, he tolerated no insubordination. As western historian J. Evetts Haley put it, "He was a dominant character, almost to the point of being domineering."[29]

In his seminal history of the XIT Ranch, Haley spins this anecdote that tells it all. Once, the foreman of the Spring Lake Division of the ranch sent word that he had fired a cowboy, but that hard case refused to leave and was making trouble. Boyce appeared at breakfast at that camp one morning shortly thereafter. He sat down with a six-shooter in his lap. When the unwelcome freeloader sat down for his coffee and biscuits, Boyce uttered a classic ultimatum that would have done John Wayne proud. He said, "This ranch is not big enough for both of us." Colonel Boyce then finished his breakfast, but the defiant troublemaker didn't.[30]

Just as Colonel Boyce refused to be intimidated by rough range rogues, neither could he be intimidated by bankers, lawyers, or judges. In 1901 while Boyce was still general manager of the XIT, some disgruntled minority shareholders of the Capitol Syndicate filed a lawsuit to place the ranch into a receivership. They obtained a court order granting the receivership and appointing W. H. Fuqua (who was president of the First National Bank of Amarillo) and J. V. Goode (who was superintendent of the Fort Worth and Denver City Railway) as receivers. Fuqua and Goode expected to reap quite

BOYCE FAMILY members in the parlor of their Channing, Texas, home, circa 1898. Left to right are Albert G. Boyce, Jr., Lynn Boyce, Mrs. Annie Boyce, Bessie Boyce, and Colonel Albert G. Boyce, Sr. *Photograph courtesy of the XIT Museum, Dalhart, Texas.*

Above: **COW COUNTRY ROYALTY.** Seated, left to right, are Charles Goodnight, Henry Stephens, and Colonel Albert G. Boyce. At far right is one of the owners of the XIT Ranch, John Farwell. Picture taken at the Spring Lake headquarters of the XIT Ranch. *Image from The XIT Ranch of Texas and the Early Days of the Llano Estacado, by J. Evetts Haley. Copyright 1952 by University of Oklahoma Press, Norman. Reprinted by permission of the publisher.*

Right: **MAP OF THE XIT RANCH.** The state of Texas granted three million acres of its public land to a Chicago consortium to rebuild the state capitol in Austin which burned down in 1881. The huge XIT Ranch sprawled for about two hundred miles, north to south, along the western edge of the Texas Panhandle and South Plains as depicted above. *Above map from The XIT Ranch of Texas and the Early Days of the Llano Estacado, by J. Evetts Haley. Copyright 1952 by University of Oklahoma Press, Norman. Reprinted by permission of the publisher.*

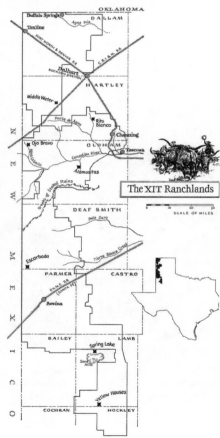

a windfall in lucrative receivers' fees. However, they had not done their homework. Neither Colonel Boyce nor the majority shareholders had been given the required notice of the application for receivership or an opportunity for a hearing on the matter. Nevertheless, Fuqua and Goode entered the XIT ranch, came to its headquarters in Channing, and demanded that Colonel Boyce surrender possession of the ranch to them on the strength of the court's receivership order. Colonel Boyce refused. Leaning his Winchester rifle against the door, he told the receivers that he did not propose to turn anything over to them and that he would resist force with force. Fuqua and Goode then—prudently—retreated. The receivership order was later voided, much to the chagrin of Fuqua and Goode, and they came away with a hole in their money sack.[31] As a result of this humiliation, Fuqua became embittered by Colonel Boyce, and he simmered patiently, waiting for an opportunity to exact his revenge. That opportunity would come more than a decade later in a context that neither of the principals could have imagined.

During his reign at the XIT, the prominence of Colonel Boyce steadily increased. He was a charter member, and later, the vice president of the prestigious Texas and Southwestern Cattle Raisers Association. Not only had his eminence increased, but also during the eighteen years he was the XIT general manager his net worth had multiplied. Upon his retirement from the XIT in 1905, he moved to Amarillo, where with Benjamin T. Ware, he helped organize the Amarillo National Bank and became one of its largest stockholders, and later president of the bank. This further exacerbated the ill will between Boyce and W. H. Fuqua, who was president of the competing First National Bank of Amarillo. Later, Colonel Boyce organized the Midway Bank and Trust Company in the north Panhandle town of Dalhart and was president of this institution until his death. In Amarillo, Colonel Boyce and his wife, Annie, maintained a palatial home in the silk-stocking part of town.[32]

Meanwhile, shortly before the turn of the nineteenth century, John Beal Sneed, Al Boyce, Jr., and Lena Snyder, children of the three pioneer Texas families, had attended Southwestern University together in Georgetown, Texas, twenty-eight miles north of Austin. While there, Beal proved himself to be the most intellectually gifted of the three. After Southwestern University, he attended and graduated from the University of Texas at Austin, then went on to earn a law degree. Al Boyce was by no means a dullard, but academia was not for him. In fact, he never got around to graduating from Southwestern. The open range suited him much better. Al was as open and straightforward as Beal was closed and devious. Lena also was not a dedicated scholar; she never finished her studies at Southwestern. Although she was no raving beauty, she possessed a compelling feminine mystique. According to some reports, both Al and Beal courted Lena during their college years,[33] but it was Beal who persuaded her to marry him and on October 17, 1900, they were wed in Georgetown. Beal was twenty-two years old at the time; Lena was twenty. Al Boyce, Jr., was then twenty-four.

Soon after they were married, John Beal and Lena moved to Hillsboro in central Texas where Beal practiced law briefly. Then he moved his office farther west to the town of Childress on the southeast cusp of the Texas Panhandle, and finally, in 1904, he and Lena moved farther west again: this time to the new and growing town of Amarillo.

The year before Colonel Boyce and his wife arrived in Amarillo, Beal and Lena Sneed had completed their move to that small frontier village. Ever alert for profitable opportunities, Beal sensed that the Texas Panhandle in 1904 was a lush fruit, ripe for the picking. And John Beal Sneed was never bashful in harvesting his share—and more—of the easy pickings. He also sensed that staying cooped up in some stuffy law office was not a fast track to the kind of big money that he craved. There were thousands of acres of cheap land to be bought and sold, and every day the trains were bringing in more settlers eager to buy farms, ranches, and commercial tracts in the new villages. Plus, Amarillo had become the hub of a booming cattle industry. It shouldn't have come as a surprise to anyone who knew him when John Beal Sneed decided to lock the doors to his law office and become the wheeler-dealer he was born to be.

Meanwhile, both Al Boyce, Jr., and John Beal's older brother, Joe T. Sneed, Jr., moved to the Panhandle. Al was hired by his father as the assistant general manager of the monstrous XIT outfit. In 1902, when the town of Dalhart was founded in the northern Panhandle, Joe Sneed, Jr., moved there and went into the banking business. He also began an aggressive land-trading enterprise, and then got into the cattle business with his brother John Beal, running the Tumbling A and the Pot Hook brand ranches.[34]

During the first decade of the new century—during those Texas Panhandle years—the bonds between these three cow-country royalty families grew even stronger. Al Boyce, Jr., and Joe T. Sneed, Jr., became particularly close friends, and even more so when Joe began courting Al's sister, Bessie Boyce. The courtship blossomed into an engagement, but the pending marriage was derailed by the untimely death of Bessie following a battle against a severe infection. It seemed that nothing could have threatened such secure relationships among the three families—relationships forged over the years by so many shared frontier experiences.

When Colonel Boyce retired as general manager of the XIT in 1904 and moved to Amarillo, Al and his brother Lynn pursued ranching interests on their own. They bought a ranch in Montana and later bought another one in the Pecos area of far West Texas.[35]

Amarillo, 1900: Saloons and Sunday Schools

The Amarillo to which John Beal Sneed and Lena moved in 1904 was a fledgling but thriving community—a city in the making. Less than two decades old, it had already earned the nickname "Queen City of the Texas Panhandle." Locationwise, it was the capital of the Panhandle—and more. Austin, the state's official capital, was a drive of almost five hundred miles from Amarillo. Compared to that, Amarillo was only a stone's throw from Oklahoma, New Mexico, Colorado, and Kansas, and it was closer to Denver, Albuquerque, Oklahoma City, and Wichita, Kansas, than to Austin. By 1899 Amarillo was already hosting the "Tri-State Fair," reaching out to denizens of Oklahoma and New Mexico. By 1890 Amarillo had emerged

as one of the world's busiest cattle-shipping points. After the arrival
of the Fort Worth and Denver City Railway in 1887, other railroads
came to the area. By 1903 construction of other railroads including the Southern Kansas, the Pecos Valley and Northern Texas, the
Santa Fe, and the Chicago, Rock Island and Gulf added to the ship-
ping facilities—and the population. Increasing production of wheat
and small grains also made Amarillo an elevator, milling, and feed-
manufacturing center during the early 1900s.[36]

The town's population began to increase, slowly at first but then
exponentially, from 482 in 1890 to 1,442 in 1900. When John Beal
and Lena arrived in 1904, the population was approximately 2,000,
but by 1910 it had grown to almost 10,000 (15,000 if one included
its "suburbs") and was picking up speed every year. Also by 1910,
Sneed had succeeded in establishing himself and Lena in a mansion in the elite part of Amarillo, only four blocks from the palatial
Boyce home.

Amarillo had also become a city of fascinating contrasts. In the
Bowery District, cards, booze, brothels, and brawls were the order
(or disorder) of the day—and night—and there congregated gamblers, hustlers, outlaws, prostitutes, ne'er-do-wells, and cowhands
fresh from months of isolation on the range spoiling for a rowdy
spree. At the other end of town, cattle barons, traders, lawyers,
bankers, and the affluent met in the fancy, upscale bar of the "high-
toned" Amarillo Hotel to swap tales, talk of markets, and cut deals.
No drunks, hookers, or rowdies allowed.[37]

The Grand Opera House, built in 1907, hosted live theater, public lectures, concerts, and other performances, including vaudeville
shows.[38] Meanwhile, churches, schools, hospitals, municipal build-
ings, and a courthouse sprang up out of the treeless plain where but
a few years earlier only Comanches, Kiowas, and buffaloes roamed.
It was also a city on the cusp of a new era when some of those "new-
fangled" inventions and conveniences of the Industrial Age were
becoming available, at least to the wealthy. Homes of the rich now
enjoyed the miracles of electricity and telephones, not to mention
indoor plumbing. Outdoor johns began to disappear. A few privileged souls even drove about town in one of those horseless carriages

DOWNTOWN AMARILLO, 1912. Note brick street with streetcar tracks on Polk Street.
Courtesy Amarillo Public Library.

that a self-taught engineer named Henry Ford produced. He called
them "Model T Fords." Most folks affectionately called them "Tin
Lizzies" or just "flivvers." But by whatever name, the homely contrap-
tion was destined to change America forever.[39] Meanwhile, streetcars
ran up and down unpaved Amarillo streets.[40]

A cultural dichotomy was glaringly evidenced by crowds that
overflowed Amarillo saloons on Saturday night and Amarillo
churches on Sunday morning. Preachers used up most of their
preaching time railing against the evils of booze. The populace was
sharply divided between the "wets" and the "drys," the latter group
tirelessly campaigning for prohibition. One observer of the day
wryly noted that the "drys" frequently put speakers on the podium
who most folks knew were imbibers. Some even showed up for their
orations slightly—or slightly more than slightly—intoxicated.[41]

Whether a "wet" or a "dry," most everybody in 1910 Amarillo
had southern roots, along with a deep-seated dedication to the
Old South's Victorian views on patriarchy, chivalry, gender, and
honor. At the same time, they felt a bone-deep disdain for the

liberal views of modern northerners who were leading the charge
against Victorianism.

In New York, that northern Sodom and Gomorrah on the
banks of the Hudson, all manner of outrageous doings were afoot.
Suffragettes were boldly marching up and down Fifth Avenue clam-
oring for the right to vote. Worse, a new kind of female was emerging: one who smoked cigarettes (sometimes even in public); one
who raced about the streets driving Tin Lizzies; one who bobbed
her hair, discarded pinched-in corsets and cumbersome petticoats,
and generally kicked up her heels—much to the consternation
of her elders. One Brooklyn priest, alarmed by these scandalous
notions of modern women, proclaimed: "We are living today in a
pandemonium of powder, a riot of rouge, and a moral anarchy
of dress," to which the noted Clark University psychologist Max
Baff added: "Every year some new fashion comes to remind us that
woman is still a savage."[42] To be fair about the matter however, it
should be noted that Baff was part of the "knowledge construction-
ist" movement promoting misogyny and the "emotional insanity"
of women.[43]

But other cries for cultural liberation were not to be hushed. In
the bohemian enclave of Greenwich Village, feminist Emma Gold-
man advocated free love and attacked the double standard that
prescribed chastity for women but not for men. Other bohemians
busily scribbled free verse, practiced free love, and championed a
host of odd notions like feminism, psychoanalysis, trade unionism,
and socialism. Intellectual authors such as Theodore Dreiser, Sher-
wood Anderson, and the cigar-smoking poetess Amy Lowell sought
to liberate the nation from "smug, saccharine conventionality."[44]

By 1910 the northern culture was emerging from a long reign of
Victorianism; but back in Amarillo—back in Texas, and for that matter, back in all the southern states—most, at least most of the Anglo
ruling class, were not having any truck with all that northern fool-
ishness, and they were determined to man the ramparts to ensure
that none of it invaded their homeland. During the second decade
of the twentieth century, Texas voters fought to establish greater
control of public and private morality. State laws and a myriad of

city ordinances across the state were passed in an effort to legislate morality: statutes that banned interracial marriage and interracial sex, prohibited amusement and business activity on Sundays, censored motion pictures and "indecent" publications, prohibited prostitution and gambling, and outlawed public "lewdness" and oral sex. Cities also passed legislation that rigidly segregated city recreational, transportation, and medical facilities.[45]

On June 23, 1914, the Reverend James K. Thomson in Muskogee, Oklahoma, delivered a sermon entitled "Whither Are We Drifting?" It was an old shopworn theme of generations of preachers, but still the question never seemed more pertinent to life in the United States as in the second decade of the century, a perplexing time for all Americans. The 1910–1920 decade would later be referred to as "The Age of the End of Innocence."[46]

Amarillo, 1910: John Beal, Lena . . . and Al

At this point John Beal and Lena were comfortably ensconced in their impressive mansion. They had two daughters, Lenora and Georgia Beal, ages eight and four, respectively. To outward appearances, all was well—Beal had the appearance of an upright citizen and a good provider for his family. By 1910 standards, Beal and Lena Sneed were living the good life: a "mansion" in the best neighborhood in Amarillo, fine furniture, a telephone, electricity, indoor plumbing, and even an automobile. True, Beal was away from home about two-thirds of the time tending to his business interests, but then such was not at all uncommon for wealthy wheeler-dealers with far-flung business interests, especially in a time when transportation facilities were limited.

In that first decade in Amarillo, no one accused Lena of any scandalous behavior, although it didn't escape notice that there was a certain "wildness" about her. Some neighbors later put it this way:

> Vivacious and likeable, she was a lot of fun, noted for the parties she gave for Amarillo ladies in broad daylight, with the shades drawn and candles blazing inside.[47]

Although those neighbors enjoyed her antics, one added this cautionary note:

> You did not want to lend her anything unless you were pre-
> pared to retrieve it. Somehow or other, she just never seemed
> to remember to return that ice cream maker or that extra set of
> dessert spoons.[48]

That amusing and mildly censorious remark may nevertheless provide an important insight into Lena's character. She was definitely a material girl; one with expensive tastes, and one who expected to have those tastes gratified. Annie Boyce would later reflect:

> She has always been used to having her own way in everything—
> her husband always granted everything she asked, whether it was a
> new piano, a Victrola or more diamonds. She was headstrong and
> only more determined to have her own way . . .[49]

These observations may well be the key to solving an early mystery in this unfolding drama. If both Beal Sneed and Al Boyce had courted Lena while they were still in school at Georgetown, then why would Lena choose to marry the humorless and rather physically unattractive Beal instead of handsome, fun-loving Al? Did that materialistic streak in her nature incline her to choose an ambitious lawyer over a freewheeling, unpredictable cowboy with an uncertain future? Did she assess Beal as a better—safer, at least—catch? Or perhaps Beal proposed and Al didn't; perhaps the rambunctious Al still had a sackful of wild oats he wanted to sow before he got marriage-serious about any girl. Speculations all. Perhaps, as some thought, there never was a serious romance between Al and Lena during those Georgetown years.

Even at this distant time, by studying family photographs, letters, and other documents, we are able to piece together surprisingly revealing, in-depth profiles of the three childhood friends after they reached maturity. A picture of Beal, Lena, and their two daughters taken about 1910 portrays Beal to be a dour, stocky, balding, no-nonsense authoritarian exuding the imperial air of a Victorian patriarch. His later actions would prove that he was the most cunning, determined, and manipulative of the three. An 1898 picture of the Boyce family relaxing in their living room at the XIT ranch headquarters catches Al fingering a banjo, his feet resting on a wolf pelt—a handsome young man about twenty-one years old with dark, sensuous eyes, and with a hint of brooding recklessness about him. Of the three, Al was by far the most open and least complicated personality—straightforward, yet somewhat naïve.

Then there was Lena—the wild card in the deck and perhaps an even more complex character than Beal. While Beal was the most domineering character, Lena was the most mystifying. Although pictures taken of Lena during that time disclose a woman slightly on the plain side of pretty, there is more than a suggestion of her intense, sensuous nature—a dark and powerful feminine mystique. One 1910 portrait of Lena captures that mystique. Her dark eyes, gazing directly into the lens of the camera, are at once frank yet secretive—boldly revealing that much is being concealed. And below that, there is a tantalizing hint of a smile that is somehow more Mona Lisa than Mona Lisa herself. Is there a subtle insinuation of hidden delights in it—a muted invitation that suggests delicious ecstasies . . . and dangers? Comparing those three pictures, it is obvious that the volatile sensuality projected by the portraits of both Al and Lena are much more compatible with one another than the sensuous image of Lena when juxtaposed against the cold, hard image of Beal Sneed.

Due to a drought in the Pecos, Texas, area in 1910, Al rounded up the herd he and his brother Lynn owned and drove them to Amarillo for shipment. His business matters taken care of, he lounged about the Boyce home with no immediate plans for the future. The Boyce mansion was located on Polk Street only four blocks from the palatial homestead on Tyler Street occupied by Beal and Lena Sneed.

Apparently, Al and Lena had not seen much—if anything—of each other since their college days in Georgetown more than a decade earlier. But with Beal gone for long stretches both Lena and Al had plenty of time to spare, so it was only natural that they should renew their acquaintanceship. Soon their visits became more frequent. And longer.

The inevitable happened in May 1911. At the time Al was thirty-four years old, Beal was thirty-two, and Lena was thirty-one. Once consummated, the love affair between Al and Lena burst into intense flame. In a letter that Lena wrote to Al about a year after their affair began, she opines:

> Can't you see now darling *why* I couldn't ever be happy with him [Beal]—I did try so hard to be a good wife to him and please him—but it was his iron will—contemptible dirty ways that he tries to hide that killed *all* the feeling over four years ago I ever had for him . . .[50]

Oblivious to reality—to the dreadful social consequences such a scandalous romance was bound to trigger in that rigid and puritanical Victorian society and to the dark, vindictive side of John Beal Sneed's nature—the starry-eyed lovers must have blissfully assumed that love would conquer all. But, of course, they were still young and they were very much in love. And . . . they were very wrong.

A Secret Too Big to Keep

"Let the Old Men Settle It"

FAMILIAR FOLKLORE has it that the husband is always the last to know. John Beal Sneed may not have been the last to discover his wife's affair, but he certainly wasn't the first. By the early fall of 1911, the intensity of the affair had become so heated that some family members and even some of the neighbors had become aware of it. Unlike Al Boyce and Lena Snyder Sneed, they all fully appreciated its gravity and how explosive that powder keg was in 1911 Texas society. But what to do?

Al's father, Colonel Albert G. Boyce, and the Colonel's wife were aware of the affair by early July 1911, and they were alarmed by its implications. They attempted to discourage Al from continuing the relationship and proposed to take Al in New Orleans to see a doctor whom they believed might cure Al of his infatuation. Al refused to go unless Lena gave her consent. She agreed, but before the end of the month Al returned—still uncured and still infatuated with Lena. On October 6, Al's brother Henry and Beal's brother, Joe, met in Dalhart hoping to head off an impending family disaster. After much discussion they in effect decided to "let the old men settle it," meaning Al's father, Colonel Boyce; Lena's father, Tom Snyder; and John Beal's father, J. T. Sneed, Sr., the patriarchs of the three prominent families. Accordingly, Joe wired a heads-up to his father.

In the meantime, Henry and Joe did, however, propose a trip to Hot Springs, Arkansas, for Al. The waters of the Hot Springs were touted to possess wondrously therapeutic powers, curing most anything from hiccups to hysteria, and they hoped that a good soaking would cure Al's passion. Al, however, didn't really want to be cured.

Another who discovered Lena's "misconduct" was her neighbor, Mrs. S. A. Morris. She later related that one day in mid-September 1911 Lena came to her home and asked to use the phone, a request that piqued Mrs. Morris's suspicions since Lena had a telephone in her own home. She described Lena as being nervous and suffering from "female troubles," the exact nature of which she did not explain, nor was she pressed to do so in that era of Victorian delicacy. Mrs. Morris denied Lena's telephone request.[1]

The affair was becoming more difficult to conceal as the lovers became increasingly reckless, and emboldened by their unbridled passion, they were heedless of the potential for disaster. Later evidence persuasively suggests that Lena's "female troubles" were due to a pregnancy of which Al was the author, and that Lena had a miscarriage, probably in September 1911. Much later, Lena, concerned that newspapers might uncover the story, wrote Al this: "It would kill me to have it all in the papers . . . All the facts about the miscarriage I had would come out—and that it was you . . . Beal knew all the time."[2]

The Sneed's family physician, Dr. R. L. McMeans, later testified that Lena had been unwell during the summer and fall of 1911. According to Dr. McMeans, Lena was suffering from both physical and emotional problems, although, again, he was not pressed to be specific. The doctor simply concluded that "she was nervous and rundown and had been given a tonic." Beal would later put his own spin on the matter; one that would be consistent with his strategy. He claimed that McMeans advised him that "if he didn't take Lena to the sea coast or some low place in a reasonable time that she might lose her mind."[3] Later, Beal said that at the time he heard McMeans's diagnosis he did not think Lena was insane.

Exactly when John Beal Sneed learned that his wife and their childhood friend, Al Boyce, Jr., had been having an affair is not

Tragedy of Sneed-Boyce Families to Be Reviewed at Trial Monday

John Beal Sneed and two children, Mrs. Sneed and Al Boyce.

PRINCIPALS IN THE LOVE TRIANGLE. John Beal Sneed pictured with daughters Lenora (left) and Georgia Beal Sneed. Pictured separately are Lena Snyder Sneed and Al Boyce, Jr. *Photographs from the November 10, 1912, edition of the* Fort Worth Star-Telegram.

clear—depends on who is telling the tale. Beal claimed that he first learned about it on October 13, 1911, when Lena confronted him, confessed, and asked for a divorce. Lena and Mrs. Boyce would later contend that John Beal knew about it earlier, and circumstantial evidence does suggest he probably became aware of it two months or so before that date. Lena's letter to Al stating that "Beal knew about [the affair and her miscarriage] all the time" suggests that Beal learned of the situation sometime during the summer of 1911 but, perhaps for the sake of his pride, chose to keep it a secret until that fall when Lena made that impossible by confronting him. By that time, the secret was simply too big to keep. Beal himself would testify that about two weeks before Lena's confession, he returned home one day unexpectedly and discovered Al holding Lena's hand while she rested in bed. Lena's explanation was that her fingernails were blue and that she was simply showing them to Al. Beal said that her nails were indeed "right purple or blue," so he accepted her story. He added that Lena had been sick for "a couple of weeks."[4] (It was later theorized that those "blue fingernails" were a symptom of Lena's pregnancy or the miscarriage.) After having ample opportunity to reflect on the tumultuous events of the night of October 13, Beal would later tell his own self-pitying story, but Lena's version of that dramatic confrontation was never recorded. In any event, the confrontation and confession touched off an immediate and violent eruption from John Beal Sneed. It also touched off a bizarre chain reaction that no one could possibly have predicted.

According to Beal, that October 13 confrontation was the first time he became aware of the affair. It is undisputed, however, that the other members of all three of the old-line Texas families—Sneed, Snyder, and Boyce—had already become aware of it. To handle the situation, Beal's father, Joe T. Sneed, Sr., traveled to Amarillo from his home in Georgetown; Lena's father, Tom Snyder, arrived shortly thereafter, and of course Colonel Boyce lived in Amarillo. A summit of the family patriarchs was thus convened. In 1911 Texas there still existed a strong dedication to the Old South's patriarchal concept of household decorum and order. In 1858, a South Carolina judge explained the commitment to the patriarchal concept of the household as follows:

> The obligation imposed on the husband to provide for their wants and protection, makes it necessary that he should exercise a power of control over all members of his household. [The law therefore], looking to the peace and happiness of the families and to the best interests of society, places the husband and father at the head of the household.[5]

In the society of the Old South, preservation of the family's good name was of paramount importance. A man's worth was judged not so much by what he was, but rather by what other people thought he was; an overweening concern for one's public image made appearances everything. Until well into the twentieth century in the South, including Texas, even uncontested divorces were considered a serious family scandal—so scandalous that divorcées in that culture often lied to census takers, claiming that they were widows. That's why the Beal-Lena-Al love triangle was a veritable bomb that, if and when it was allowed to explode, would be a major calamity. It is no exaggeration to say that in that society, a scandal of such magnitude was considered worse than an untimely death in the family. Even when such scandals were aired in courts, newspaper reports of the trial were heavily censored and downplayed, and community gossip, when matters sexual were discussed, was limited to whispered exchanges between close friends and then expressed only in the quaint and coded language of that prudish era. Within a short time even these guarded exchanges would usually be hushed up so that few members of later generations ever became aware of the scandal. Typically, subsequent community histories simply ignored the scandal and pretended that it never happened.

For upper-crust families, yet another Victorian notion came into play—the notion that a marital dispute was a matter of direct and vital concern to the family as a whole. The traditional view was that marriage was not so much a union of two individuals as it was a union of two families; it was considered less of a personal matter involving the private emotions, feelings, and desires of the two marital partners than an event that brought together and melded the two families, forging a permanent bond between them. Ergo, love, feelings, or sexual compatibility of individual family members had to be subordinated to the greater good: family unity, pride, and honor.[6] That being the case, in the matter of the family crisis at hand, it was taken for granted that a meeting of the three family patriarchs constituted the proper forum for resolution of the dilemma and that their joint verdict would be honored by all members of the families—including the star-crossed trio.

None of the three patriarchs underestimated the seriousness of the problem when they met that autumn in Amarillo. But arriving at a solution proved far more difficult than they ever imagined. There followed a week of chaos and turmoil and a series of furtive meetings between various members of the families and the patriarchs.

The three old pioneers had met and dealt with many crises on
the unforgiving frontier, ranging from Indian attacks to blizzards,
droughts, stampedes, cattle rustlers, and even war itself, but they
were buffaloed when it came to figuring out a strategy to deal with
this kind of crisis. Impending disasters of the heart and domestic
relations were simply beyond their coping expertise. At least this
one was. They could not agree on any viable plan to defuse that
ticking time bomb.

Coming up with a containment plan was one problem the elders
faced, but there was also another problem, one that none of them
anticipated. These three grizzled patriarchs of the plains were not
accustomed to having their views disputed by anyone, and certainly
not by anyone within their families. No objections to their orders
were tolerated. Yet in this matter, to their surprise, all three children were rebellious. Colonel Boyce and his wife did their best to
cool their son's ardor for Lena, but without success. Headstrong
Al wouldn't listen. Lena's father, Tom Snyder, turned on her, even
suggesting to Beal that he needed to give her a good whipping. But
that also failed to cool her passion for Al. She proved to be as stub-
born as her lover. John Beal Sneed was even more rebellious. Obedi-
ence was not in his character; he took orders from no one. Beal's
father gave him some advice that seemed quite sensible under the
circumstances. He told Beal to let Lena go, saying, "Your wife has
been false to you—a traitor to you, and there is not but one thing
in the world you can do. Throw her out and let her go."[7] But John
Beal Sneed wasn't about to let Lena off the hook that easily. She had
betrayed him, and worse, she had gone public with it. As he nursed
his wounded pride, an insatiable craving for revenge raged. A pound
of flesh had to be exacted. And so he began crafting a plan.

A Man with a Plan

Escape, Flight, and Pursuit

AT FIRST IT MUST HAVE SEEMED IMPOSSIBLE for John Beal Sneed to concoct any one plan that would accomplish all of his goals. Revenge had to be exacted—not only against Lena but also against Al. Both had publicly humiliated him. His battered hubris had to be assuaged; his honor in that Victorian society had to be restored. And he had to do all of that while publicly portraying himself in some heroic role. In 1911 Texas society he could kill Al, even waylay him from ambush and most likely get away with it—maybe even be applauded for it. After all, there was still a statute on the law books of Texas that justified the killing of a libertine provided the enraged husband caught him in bed with his wife.[1] But what about Lena? She had to be punished too. However, as any southern gentleman knew, killing a woman, even a cheating wife, was out of the question. There was just no way that slaying a woman could be portrayed as the act of a proud, courageous, manly southern hero. On the other hand, after it became public knowledge that Lena had committed adultery, he couldn't take her back—couldn't permit that soiled dove to return to the marital bed—without incurring public disdain and therefore disgracing himself.

Beal's father's advice certainly seemed to be the best possible solution to the dilemma: denounce Lena as a scarlet woman; kick her out; divorce her; take the kids and most, if not all, of the property. Good riddance to bad rubbish. Then deal with Al.

Still, that plan just wasn't good enough to suit John Beal Sneed. It didn't permit Beal to play the heroic role he craved. His pride and honor needed more nurturing than that, especially when bedeviled by that nagging, pride-deflating suspicion that the public might conclude that Lena had left him for a better man—especially when that other man was a tall, slender, handsome, personable young prince with a full head of hair while Beal was a heavyset, dour, balding toad.

Perhaps it was about that time that it occurred to the cunning, egotistical John Beal Sneed that any woman who would leave him for another man had to be out of her mind. Absolutely crazy. If so, then, as a loving husband and a devoted father, didn't he have a family duty to commit Lena to an insane asylum for her own good, and in the best interest of the children? That could certainly be made to appear as a noble and self-sacrificing thing to do. Much more chivalrous than simply throwing Lena out on the street. It would also achieve two other of his goals: it would punish Lena by depriving her of her lover and forcing her to return to Beal, and it would deprive Al of the woman he so desperately loved. Of course that was only step one in Beal's long-range plan for Al.

So far, so good. But there were a couple of loose ends still left a-dangling. Granted that Lena was crazy, but what, or who, drove her crazy? He couldn't have the public believe that *he* drove her crazy. And there was another problem: to most folks who knew Lena, she may have appeared a bit eccentric, but not crazy. How to explain that? Upon further reflection the agile brain of John Beal Sneed came up with a diagnosis of Lena's mental problems that neatly tied up both of those two loose ends. Under Beal's refined diagnosis of Lena's mental condition, she was sane most of the time. When she was "herself," she was a good, devoted wife and a loving mother. However, when she fell under the evil spell of that decadent libertine, Al Boyce, she became "possessed" and thus insane. Therefore, Al Boyce was the sole cause of Lena's insanity. Furthermore, since she was insane while under Al's spell, her decision to leave her good husband for this evil lecher was not a rational one. Finally, even if Lena was a "soiled dove," Beal could still take her back without dishonoring himself in the eyes of that Victorian culture since her debauchment was involuntary, perpetrated upon her while she was out of her right mind. In addition to all that, Beal could later explain that Lena had convinced him that she had not really been guilty of any "criminal intimacy" at all—just "a few kisses" by Al was the extent of it. However suspect that explanation was it was useful to Beal in keeping up his public image.

That then was the plan. It explained everything and tied up all the loose ends. It was an ingenious grand design that allowed Beal to wrap himself in the cloak of the martyred, self-sacrificing hero whose sole purpose in life was saving Lena from herself while valiantly protecting his home and children, all the while portraying that vile lecher, Al Boyce, as the sole villain in this melodrama. Good as it was from Beal's perspective, selling all that to the public would be a tall order indeed. He would need some independent experts to bolster his diagnosis of Lena's mental condition.

Meanwhile, the first step in the grand plan was to have Lena institutionalized. Which is why, a few days later, a very solemn group of travelers boarded a train in Amarillo bound for the Arlington Heights Sanitarium in Fort Worth. That most unhappy troop of campers included Beal, Lena, their two children, Beal's father, and Lena's sister, Eula Snyder Bowman. Upon arrival on October 27, 1911, Lena was committed without benefit of any official court order or other troublesome legal folderol. Ironically, October 27, 1911, was the eleventh wedding anniversary of John Beal Sneed and Lena Snyder Sneed. An involuntary commitment to a lunatic asylum at the insistence of her husband was hardly the anniversary gift Lena had hoped for. But it would be one she would never forget. Or forgive.

> Peter, Peter, pumpkin eater,
> Had a wife and couldn't keep her;
> He put her in a pumpkin shell
> And there he kept her very well.[2]

Or so John Beal Sneed thought.

In 1911 Fort Worth, a husband's unprofessional and unsupported diagnosis was all it took to incarcerate his wife in a mental institution. That is, if that husband was affluent and found a friendly asylum operated by such cooperative fellows as brothers Wilmer and Bruce Allison of Arlington Heights; otherwise the irate husband—then, as now—was required to comply with some bothersome legal requirements in order to cage a wayward spouse. Bothersome technicalities like obtaining a court-ordered commitment based on a jury's finding that the wife was more than simply annoying—she was indeed insane and was therefore likely to cause serious injury to herself or others. Then too the law provided that the intended inmate had a right to be present at the insanity trial and that she was entitled to assert her sanity and contest her proposed commitment. She was even entitled to have a lawyer to represent her. But John Beal Sneed was in no mood to put up with all that legal nonsense—especially when the helpful Allison brothers offered such a hassle-free alternative.[3]

John Beal Sneed was not the only prominent husband in 1911 Fort Worth who solved a messy domestic problem by resorting to such tactics. Rancher, oilman, and banker Burk Burnett, owner of the 300,000-acre Four Sixes Ranch in West Texas, was one of the most prominent, if not *the* most prominent, resident of Fort Worth—far more prominent than John Beal Sneed. By 1911 his marriage to Mary Couts Barradel Burnett had soured beyond repair. Burnett then faced the most unappealing prospect of a divorce that would undoubtedly prove socially embarrassing. Worse than that, however, a divorce might have cost Burk Burnett—a man known to be mighty tight with a penny—a very large chunk of his considerable fortune. Burnett adopted a strategy that sounds suspiciously like a plan to avoid such a financial catastrophe. He filed a petition in a Fort Worth court alleging that Mary was insane, suffering from a "hallucination" that Burk intended to kill her. It also does not seem far-fetched to speculate that, considering Burnett's tremendous wealth, prestige, and power in Fort Worth, he might not have experienced much difficulty in persuading a local judge to sympathize with his predicament and thus agree that Mary was insane. Whatever the case, the judge did in fact agree; Mary was found insane and institutionalized—a finding that later events would call into question.

To Burk Burnett's credit, however, instead of imprisoning Mary in a dreary state asylum, he arranged for the court to have her confined to a private home he purchased for her in Weatherford, Texas. And there the unwilling patient languished from 1911 until Burnett died in 1922. The day after he died, Mary escaped, hired a lawyer, and had herself declared legally sane. Then, since Burk Burnett had executed a new will leaving her nothing, she filed a successful will-contest suit in which she was awarded about half of Burk's $6 million estate—$6 million in 1922 being roughly equivalent to $72 million in 2006 dollars.[4]

Lena Snyder Sneed, however, as we shall soon discover, had no intention of obediently languishing in any loony bin for eleven years. Not even for one month.

At this stage of the drama, the ties that had bound those three pioneer families together began to fray. Within days, friends for years—friends who had weathered so many storms and hardships together—became enemies and split into two bitterly divided factions: the Boyce faction and the Sneed-Snyder faction. Lena's own father, Tom Snyder, turned against her as did her sisters, Eula Snyder Bowman and Susan Snyder Pace. Eula was married to Henry Bowman of Plano, Texas, who was described as being a "prominent mule trader." Susan was married to John Pace, a Clayton, New Mexico, attorney. Lena and the Boyce family originally thought that John and Susan Pace were aligned with them, but later events would dispel that belief. Of the Snyder family, only Lena's eldest sister, Pearl Snyder Perkins of Baton Rouge, Louisiana, stood firm in her support for Lena. Joe Sneed, Jr., was caught in the middle. He had been a good friend of the Boyce brothers and had been engaged to their only sister, Bessie Boyce, before her untimely death. Joe did his best to stay out of the fray.

That left Lena at the center of the maelstrom. She was Beal's captive, and she was dependent on him for support. She was also the mother of two daughters whom Beal held captive to ensure her cooperation. Yet her passion for Al smoldered, unabated. Their enforced separation only served to intensify their passion—and their determination to reunite.

Although John Beal Sneed was completely satisfied with his own diagnosis of Lena's insanity, he apparently was concerned that it might be subject to challenge somewhere down the road on account of his lack of psychiatric credentials. He engaged Dr. John S. Turner, formerly superintendent of the state asylum in Terrell, Texas, to examine Lena and render his diagnosis. During the last part of October, Dr. Turner saw Lena several times. At first, he refused to diagnose her as insane. That didn't suit Beal one whit. He sent the good doctor back for a second opinion. This time Dr. Turner improved his diagnosis—somewhat. He now said that he thought Lena might be insane. Still, not good enough. Beal sent him back for another examination—with instructions and, one wonders, what other incentives. This time Dr. Turner returned with a most peculiar diagnosis: Lena, he concluded, was suffering from "moral insanity," whatever that was. No matter. Whatever it was, it was sufficient unto the day for John Beal Sneed's purposes. Sufficient unto that day, perhaps, but it was a novel concept that would be explored and debated exhaustively as this drama continued to unfold.

Lena was thus confined to the Allisons' institution to remain there at the pleasure of her husband and Dr. Turner. Meanwhile, Beal and Lena's daughters, Lenora and Georgia, were sent to live with Lena's sister Eula and Eula's husband, Henry Bowman, in nearby Plano.

In later testimony, John Beal Sneed would claim that Dr. Turner had directed that Lena, for her own good, should be separated from both her husband and her children. (From this distance, one can hardly resist wondering if this was really Dr. Turner's directive. Or was it a part of Beal's plan to punish Lena, a lively people-person, for her betrayal? To isolate her from all others, including himself and her children, seemed like mighty strange therapy—especially for a "morally insane" patient who was supposedly sane when Al Boyce wasn't around.) Later, Beal would embellish the portrayal of himself as the self-sacrificing martyr by explaining how difficult it was for him not to visit Lena: "I would rather see her than anybody else in the world."[5]

On October 30—some two weeks after Lena was committed—Dr. Turner thought (again, according to Beal's account) that Lena's condition had improved sufficiently for Beal to visit her briefly. Beal reported that during that visit Lena seemed more affectionate toward him than she had been for the past several months.

Shortly thereafter, she wrote Beal two letters that appear to substantiate Beal's take on Lena's condition and attitude. On November 6, she wrote:

> My dearest Beal . . . I was so disappointed over not seeing the children I felt like I couldn't stand it. Please talk about me to them every day and don't let them forget me . . . Dr. Turner was over here yesterday but of course you know this. I don't like him at all . . . don't think I am mad or hurt with you for I am not, and I am trying so hard to believe you have done what is best for me but it is mighty hard at times . . . with lots of love and a million kisses for the babies. Your girl, Lena.[6]

Two days later Lena wrote this in a second letter:

> My dearest Beal . . . I was disappointed at not seeing you before you left for there were so many things that I wanted to know that nobody but you can tell me. You never said what the cattle brought, nor what cotton was worth . . . I know you have been so worried over the cattle and the cotton and I feel that I am to blame for it, and I am so sorry for it, and will try and be good to you and make up for it when I leave here . . . I am almost crazy to see the children . . . What did you do with the children's pony? . . . Please don't let [Dr. Turner] come any more. He don't know anything about me as he don't stay over 15 minutes, and I believe I would have seen you and the children if it hadn't been for him . . . If there is anything in my letter you miss it is because I want to tell you instead of writing. Lovingly, Lena.[7]

Love notes to Beal with endearments like "lovingly, Lena," and "your girl, Lena." Was she sincere? Or just "playing nice" to entice

Beal to get her out of lockup? The swirling subterranean currents of Lena's feminine mystique and deviousness ran much deeper than either John Beal or Al could have imagined. As both would soon discover.

Those terms of endearment to Beal were written on November 6 and November 8. However, just a few days earlier—about the time she was expressing her renewed "affection" for Beal—Lena fired off this desperate plea to Al Boyce, Jr.: "For God's sake, come and take me away."[8]

Al received Lena's plea on November 2, and true to his reckless, impulsive nature, he wasted no time in hastening to rescue the fair damsel in distress. He immediately liquidated his holdings, turned them into $60,000 in cash (a huge fortune in 1911 dollars), and caught the next train to Fort Worth. On November 8, the very day that Lena wrote her second letter to her husband promising to

THE LETHAL LOVE TRIANGLE. John Beal Sneed, Lena Snyder Sneed, and Al Boyce, Jr. from the September 22, 1912, edition of the *St. Louis Post-Dispatch*.

be good and "make it up" to him, Lena, with the connivance and cooperation of her asylum nurse, Nellie Flowers, slipped out of the confines of the Allisons' madhouse and rendezvoused with her lover in downtown Fort Worth. After a brief shopping spree financed by Al, they all went to the Frisco railroad station where Al and Lena caught the next train bound for St. Louis . . . but not before Al slipped Nellie Flowers a $500 tip in appreciation for her invaluable assistance, and, undoubtedly, to ensure her future silence. And so, Al and Lena eloped. Well, perhaps *eloped* is not quite the proper word for it. After all, Lena's inconvenient marriage to Beal did not allow the lovers to fulfill their deepest desire, a honeymoon as Mr. and Mrs. Al Boyce. Beal contended that the proper word was *kidnapped*. Al and Lena preferred the word *escaped*—an escape from John Beal Sneed.

They made it all the way to Winnipeg, Canada—far away from Texas and far away from Beal, and far away from Lena's father, and far away from the prudish, disapproving society of Amarillo and all those purse-lipped, tongue-clucking, gossiping puritanical dowagers. And far away from all unpleasantness. They exchanged rings: "Forever Lena" from her to him, and "Forever Al" from him to her. This was a fresh start in a new land, and in a much more tolerant society. There they would be safe. And, breathing the crisp, clean air of freedom in their Canadian paradise, they would live happily ever after. Love would conquer all.

Beyond any doubt their love, their passion for each other, was strong enough to withstand the ordinary slings and arrows that fate might hurl at them. But was it strong enough to withstand the fury of John Beal Sneed scorned? To suppose that Beal was livid with rage when news of Lena's escape—with Al Boyce—scorched his ears is hardly a matter of conjecture. Lena had played him for a fool; she had him believing she had repented, that she had regained her sanity and now truly loved him and wished to make amends, believing it when she wrote "Your girl, Lena." And all the while she was scheming to run off with that laughing libertine. To think that right now they were somewhere beyond his reach, beyond his control—probably laughing at him, mocking him, having fun, and

doing . . . the unthinkable! It was almost more than the proud
and pompous John Beal Sneed could stand. This just was not going
according to his carefully crafted plan. In addition, since she had
been institutionalized and beyond the reach of Al for almost three
weeks, it would now be more difficult for Beal to credibly contend
that Lena had run off with Al because she had fallen under Al's evil,
lascivious spell. Then, too, it would now be impossible for Beal to
maintain, for the public's consumption, the fiction that nothing had
really happened between Lena and Al except for "a few kisses." How
could he to take the defiled Lena back into his marital bed now
without publicly humiliating himself? John Beal Sneed immediately
recognized his peril: serious cracks had just fractured his artfully
designed fantasy structure and now threatened to collapse the whole
artifice, unmasking its architect for the pretender he really was.

One of the first things that Beal did after recovering his senses
was to march down to a Fort Worth gun shop and, under the name
of "John Smith," buy a .32-caliber Colt revolver. Then, in a rage, he
confronted the unfortunate asylum nurse, Nellie Flowers. When she
balked at revealing the details of the escape, Beal pulled his pistol
and threatened to shoot her on the spot, whereupon the terrified
nurse leaped out of the asylum window. Fortunately for Nellie it was
a ground floor window. Asylum doctors intervened to save Nellie,
but the determined Beal was not to be denied, and he finally succeeded in wheedling the whole story out of the poor nurse. Next,
Beal employed the Burns Detective Agency for a reported fee of
$20,000 to track down the lovers. Then he offered a $500 reward for
their apprehension. Finally, Beal filed an abduction charge against
Al with the Fort Worth district attorney, insisting that a warrant for
Al's arrest be issued.[9]

"Forever after" for Al and Lena lasted less than two months.
That was when Beal and his hired bloodhounds ran them to ground
in Winnipeg. If, during the two months following Lena's escape,
John Beal Sneed slept any, it wasn't much. In a frenzy of activity, he
scurried around, plotting, arguing, cajoling, demanding, and ordering folks about, hell-bent on regaining control of the situation and

control of everybody involved. John Beal Sneed's will be done! And heaven help any hapless mortal who got in his way.

On December 24, 1911, the Burns Detective Agency informed Beal of Lena and Al's whereabouts. Canadian authorities were notified, and two days later, on December 26, Al and Lena were arrested for illegal entry into Canada, having given Canadian officials false names. Canada could, therefore, deport Al and Lena, but it did not subject them to being extradited back to Fort Worth to face criminal charges. Al hired a Canadian lawyer, T. J. Murray, who posted bail and obtained their release. That was not nearly good enough for Beal. On December 28 he appeared before the Tarrant County grand jury in Fort Worth seeking to have the previous abduction charge against Al upgraded to an indictment. And not only that, Beal sought additional indictments against Al for rape and kidnapping. The basis of all the criminal charges was this: since Lena was insane she could not give Al effective consent to take her from the asylum or to transport her to Canada or to have sex with her, and therefore, the fact that she didn't resist or protest was immaterial. Still not satisfied, Beal wanted Canadian authorities to charge Al with the felony offense of grand larceny. The basis of the grand larceny charge was this: when Al was arrested in Canada on December 26 for illegal entry, he had in his pocket certain items of Lena's jewelry that she had taken with her. Again, since she was supposedly insane, she couldn't have effectively consented for Al to take possession of them. Hence, grand larceny.[10] Meanwhile, the Fort Worth felony charges of abduction, kidnapping, and rape were extraditable offenses. Beal's game plan was to get Lena deported for illegal entry and turned over to his custody so he could return her to the Arlington Heights asylum; he wanted Al extradited to Texas and delivered into the custody of Fort Worth lawmen where fitting "justice" could be administered. If Al lived that long.

On December 28, 1911, Lena, through her Canadian lawyer, released a statement to the press declaring that she and Al Boyce intended to live in Canada and would not return to Texas unless forced to do so.

The Tarrant County grand jury in Fort Worth returned the felony indictments two days later and wired warrants to Winnipeg. However, Beal Sneed didn't wait around for that. As soon as he got through testifying before the grand jury on December 28, he slipped the .32-caliber revolver into his pocket and caught the next train to Winnipeg, arriving there on December 30. Much to his chagrin he discovered that Al's attorney, T. J. Murray, had, once again, bonded Al out of jail. Beal fumed. The audacious temerity of anyone daring to frustrate his plan! Beal went around muttering threats against the uppity Canadian lawyer.

But that could wait. Beal immediately set about haranguing the Canadian officials to charge Al and Lena not only with illegal entry but also with being "undesirable citizens," thus making it an unbailable offense under Canadian law. Plus, he also persuaded the Canadians to charge Al with larceny under Canadian law for stealing Lena's jewelry.

Murray, Lena's astute Canadian lawyer, correctly anticipating that there would be legal battles either in Canada or Texas, or both, that would turn on Lena's sanity, hired two Canadian "alienists" (as psychiatrists were called in those days) to examine Lena and render an opinion. Both agreed that Lena was sane.[11]

When Beal arrived, Lena was being held in the Immigration Hall in Winnipeg, and Beal demanded an interview with her. The guilt and trauma that Beal's encounter caused the conflicted Lena is evident from a letter she managed to send Al immediately afterward. She wrote: "I feel now like we are lost and oh Albert, I blame no one but myself, and I will never spend another peaceful moment. I loved you too much darling. I lost sight of what was best for you."[12]

After Beal had one of the Burns Detective Agency men take a shot at breaking Lena's will, she added the following to her letter to Al:

> [T]he Burns man tried to persuade me to go back to Texas with
> him, said he would go all the way with me to any point I wanted to
> go + he used ever [sic] persuasive power in the world but of course

I didn't believe one word they said—They are tearing my heart out about the children, Beal brought a pr. of G. B.'s [Georgia Beal, their youngest daughter] shoes that he had in his grip + it almost killed me when I looked at them. He said you would hang as soon as you got to Texas—+ oh I can't think all he has said . . . I believe they are going to make trouble about the rings. Beal has tried every way on earth to make me tell where they are—He said he would shoot Murrays [*sic*] head off if he were in Texas + I am satisfied he will do some shooting here if everything goes against him . . . I believe if they ever take you back they would shut me up so I couldn't testify for you—Albert I know [illegible] a divine power to help me or I couldn't have stood all this.[13]

The *Manitoba Free Press* would later claim that Lena "bore testimony to [Beal's] selfishness, his preoccupation, his arrogance and his jealousy. Some of those who had to do with [him] in Winnipeg [have] it that he was a person of violent and malignant temper."[14] In an undated letter that Lena wrote to Al shortly thereafter she said, "Beal is nothing but a demon—plus, now he will be meaner to me than ever."[15]

January 2, 1912, was a busy day at the Winnipeg Immigration Hall. In the end, Beal won a partial victory in his battle with the Canadian officials, but he didn't get his way on all the issues. These were the decisions: Beal succeeded in getting the Canadians to deport Lena and release her into his custody. An immigration official escorted Beal, Lena, and two Burns detectives to the U.S. border and then released them. But the Canadians refused to extradite Al back to Texas to stand trial on the Fort Worth criminal charges.

The next day Beal, Lena, and the detectives arrived in Minneapolis where they were met by Tom Snyder and Henry Bowman. Beal instructed Snyder and Bowman to escort Lena back to Fort Worth and return her to the Arlington Heights sanitarium. Then he caught the next train back to Winnipeg, where he had some unfinished business to attend to—namely, Al Boyce. Still chafing at the Canadians' refusal to extradite Al, Beal now insisted that he be allowed to meet Al. But the Canadians were still obstinate. Lawyer Murray

wisely argued that no good would come of such a one-on-one meeting. Next, Beal insisted again that the Canadians deport Al back to
the United States. Again Murray pointed out that if Al was deported
it was unlikely he would get much past the U.S. border before Beal
shot him. The infuriated John Beal Sneed was once again thwarted
in his quest for "justice." Beal left Canada; a few days later the Canadians released Al from Immigration Hall detention on the condition that he leave Winnipeg and "disappear" somewhere into the
Canadian wilderness. At least until the dust settled.[16]

Meanwhile, Canadian authorities never bothered to pursue that
grand larceny charge against Al. While all these dramatic confrontations were going on at the Immigration Hall, the Winnipeg press
caught wind of the scandalous developments, and they jumped in
with both feet. The presence of those barbarous Texans questing for
justice, Wild West frontier style, was the source of great fascination
to the Winnipeg editors. The *Winnipeg Saturday* really lowered the
boom on Texans in general and John Beal Sneed in particular. The
editor first took Canadian officials to task for the "unwarranted per-
secution" of Lena in forcing her, "in desperation," to return to the
United States with an abusive husband. In a comment that underscored the vast difference between the way Canadian society and the
way Texas society viewed matters of gender and justice, the editor
lambasted everyone concerned with the debacle as follows:

> It is a fine thing, and, oh, what a manly thing!—for a mushy
> emotionalist to slop over in writing of the "injured husband"
> and "the erring wife"—but officials of the Canadian Govern-
> ment and officials of the Police Department in Winnipeg are not
> paid their salaries for the purpose of serving the ends of wife-
> chasing husbands who attempt to exercise a tyrannical authority
> by locking their wives up in lunatic asylums in the United States
> because those wives fail to love, honor and obey a male of the
> human species whose conduct, on his own admission, would make
> love impossible, honor a confession of depravity, and obedience
> an encouragement to brute force—Our whole legal machinery is
> improperly set to work to assist a high-handed husband from Texas

in gaining possession of his wife, who seems to have shown mighty good sense in running away from a person who treated her as if she had been a chattel somewhat difficult to control.[17]

John Beal Sneed's rebuttal to such "mushy" and "unmanly" northern nonsense would soon be spelled out in the courts of Texas, where men were men and wives knew to keep their place.

Meanwhile Beal Sneed began the long journey back to Texas seething in vengeance every mile of the way. That was the way 1912 began, and what a dramatic and a dreadful and a violent and an unbelievable year 1912 would prove to be!

It was also the year that the great ship *Titanic* went down.

The Gathering Storm

The Killings Begin

WHILE THE WINNIPEG PRESS was whetting the voyeuristic appetite of its readers with blow-by-blow accounts of John Beal Sneed's windmill-tilting tactics with the Canadian immigration officials, the Fort Worth press carried an entirely different kind of story— different, but one that was equally fascinating to its subscribers. Colonel Boyce and his wife had come to Fort Worth to testify before the grand jury on behalf of Al. While in town they were interviewed by a *Fort Worth Star-Telegram* reporter. The story he filed was not nearly as humorous as the Winnipeg musings, but it certainly was a lot more inflammatory. Colonel Boyce was quoted as saying this: "Nobody will believe that my son abducted Lena Sneed . . . She is as sane as anybody . . . I know that they sent Mrs. Sneed to the sanitarium to get her away from my son . . . She planned the whole thing, and I am going to see that my son's name is cleared of this false charge."[1]

But the quote attributed to Al's mother topped that. Mrs. Annie Boyce, an intelligent and articulate woman, had this to say:

> Albert was hypnotized by that woman. She hypnotized her husband, too, or he wouldn't have offered a big reward for her. She has ruined her husband and my son, and has broken my heart . . . Lena Sneed came to see me many times during the last year . . . She told me she loved my son and that she wanted to

be my daughter. She told me that she had asked her husband to let her get a divorce and that she would get a divorce somehow, and marry Albert. I told her it would be wrong . . . I argued with her and did everything I could, and I was so relieved when I heard they had sent her away . . . I told her what was her trouble, too much money, too much time to waste, and reading too many cheap novels. She was sane as anybody and planned the whole business herself. I am sorry for her in spite of the ruin she has brought upon us. We would rather have followed Albert to his grave than have him do what he has done—he was hypnotized.[2]

To twenty-first-century Americans, Annie Boyce's assertion that when the love affair between Al and Lena became public it caused a family scandal of such proportions that it had "ruined" both Al and Beal Sneed and that she and Colonel Boyce would rather have "followed Albert to his grave than have him do what he has done" seems hyperbolic at best. Hyperbolic to modern ears, yes, but not to 1912 Texans. Annie Boyce's comment spoke volumes about the prevailing cultural climate of that time and place.

In another statement to the press, Annie Boyce vowed that she and Colonel Boyce would "contest every step of the ground" in fighting any criminal prosecution of their son. She said: "We know our son did wrong, but we know that the charges against him are false, and we will not sit by and see him sent to the penitentiary."[3]

Al's parents voiced their extreme frustrations, their anxieties, and their anguish at becoming unwillingly embroiled in this catastrophic family scandal as well as their understandable concern for their son. It was also understandable for them to place most, if not all, of the blame on Lena. No doubt it was therapeutic for them to vent these pent-up emotions, and from their perspective, it was simply a matter of stating undisputable facts. However, when the Snyder and Sneed families read the Boyce interviews, they were infuriated. From their perspective the Boyce remarks were more than intemperate; they were outrageous. To the already enraged John Beal Sneed, of course, the Boyce remarks were not only inflammatory but also amounted to inexcusable meddling in his business—still more people interfering with his plan. However unintended, the Boyce interview escalated the war between the families and drove a wedge between the two factions that could never be bridged. In retrospect, it is clear that the *Star-Telegram* interview of Colonel Boyce and his wife was a turning point in the unfolding tragedy.

To add yet more fuel to Beal's fire, when he returned from Canada he had to quell a rebellion from within his own ranks. At Minneapolis, Beal had turned Lena over to Henry Bowman and Lena's father, Tom Snyder, with orders to take Lena back to the Arlington Heights asylum. Beal then returned to Canada to renew his attack on Al. But Tom Snyder, instead of taking his daughter back to Fort Worth and recommitting her, decided to take her to the home of Lena's sister, Susan Snyder Pace, wife of attorney John Pace in Clayton, New Mexico. (Tom Snyder and his wife were then living with the Paces. At that time Henry Bowman and Lena's other sister, Eula Snyder Bowman, were keeping Lena's daughters in their home in Plano, Texas.)

When Beal learned of Tom Snyder's insubordination, he wired Snyder to meet him. John Beal Sneed was in no mood to brook any disobedience. Accordingly, on January 11, 1912, Beal met with Snyder and promptly squelched that insurrection. Snyder quickly relented and agreed that his daughter ought to be locked up in the Arlington Heights asylum once again. Lena was not invited to participate in, or even attend, that executive session. However, the next day when she learned of her fate, Lena managed to slip away and wire this plea to Henry Boyce: "For God's sake protect me. Beal and Henry Bowman are here to put me in an asylum by force."[4] The next day that is exactly what Beal and Bowman did. On the train ride from Amarillo to the Fort Worth asylum, Beal yanked the "Forever Al" ring off Lena's finger and flung it out the window.[5]

However, this time Lena was not alone and helpless. This time Lena was receiving support, both financial and influential, from the Boyce family. Al had hired the Pinkerton Detective Agency to keep track of Lena and see where Beal would next imprison or hide her, thus resulting in a most interesting matchup: the Boyce-hired Pinkerton Agency versus the Sneed-hired Burns Agency. Also, while in Canada, Lena granted the Boyce family power of attorney to represent her interests, including the authority to employ lawyers on her behalf. Therefore, if Beal once again had Lena locked up in an insane asylum, the Boyce family could hire an attorney to file a habeas corpus proceeding and thus challenge the legality of her commitment on grounds that she was not insane. If the court found her sane, then, of course, the asylum would be ordered to discharge her. The same stone would also kill two other birds: first, having been declared sane, she would then be competent to testify in any court proceeding; and second, if she were sane, and if she would testify that she voluntarily consented to the escape with Al and to all sexual relations she had with him and that she voluntarily gave him possession of her jewelry, then it would effectively defeat the Texas state indictments alleging rape, abduction, and kidnapping as well as the Canadian charge of grand larceny in connection with the alleged theft of Lena's jewelry. To that end Colonel Boyce wished to reassure Lena of his support and thus ensure that Lena would testify favorably if and when any criminal cases against Al were brought to trial. Therefore he wrote a letter to Lena that was destined to become a vital, and much debated, piece of evidence in the subsequent murder trials. It would become known as the famous "stand hitched" letter. He wrote the letter to John Pace, whom the Boyce family mistakenly believed to be an ally. In the letter Colonel Boyce wrote:

> I hereby authorize you to say to Lena that I am with her. Since conditions have changed wonderfully since I last saw her that she now has my deepest sympathy, and she can count on me standing hitched to the end, provided she stands hitched.[6]

Lena and the Boyce family may have correctly assumed that John Pace and his wife Susan, Lena's sister, were on their side—at least initially. But, if so, that all changed when John Beal Sneed had a heart-to-heart chat with John Pace. Lena later wrote to Al that Beal had threatened John Pace; told him that if he supported Lena, he would "blow his _____ head off."[7] Somehow, in view of later developments, that account had a ring of truth to it.

In any event, the "stand hitched" letter was soon in the hands of Beal Sneed. By this time he knew that Lena had given power of attorney to the Boyce family, and John Pace had warned him of the likelihood that the Boyce faction, on Lena's behalf, would file a habeas corpus action if he recommitted Lena. Ignoring this information, headstrong Beal Sneed was determined to have his way, and he proceeded to have her incarcerated anyway.

In response, the Boyce family hired a Texas Panhandle law firm from Dalhart, Texas, which in turn employed Fort Worth counsel, state senator O. S. Lattimore, to represent Lena and contest her commitment. The Boyce family's Dalhart lawyer, Reese Tatum, in referring the case to Lattimore, wrote: "While there is no question that Mrs. Sneed is absolutely sane, and in fact a very smart woman, still they will perhaps use every means they can to have her adjudicated insane in order to make it hard on Boyce." Al's brother Henry added that he did not want "to see Lena shot full of dope and taken before a county judge and declared insane, and Al railroaded to the pen."[8]

On the same day that Beal once again had Lena committed against her will, Colonel Boyce was also in Fort Worth where he succeeded in persuading the head Tarrant County prosecutor, John Baskins, to dismiss all three state indictments against Al on grounds of "insufficient evidence." Once again somebody else had frustrated Beal's plan.

But the ever-resourceful John Beal Sneed had another ace up his sleeve and had done some legal maneuvering of his own. Perhaps anticipating that his attempt to convict Al Boyce on the state indictments returned by the Fort Worth grand jury would fail, he hired another lawyer. And not just a private lawyer either. Beal hired a federal prosecutor to prosecute Al. His name was Will Atwell. Atwell, it just so happened, was then the U.S. District Attorney for the Northern District of Texas, which included Fort Worth, Dallas, and all of North Texas! As it turned out, Beal Sneed and Atwell's friendship went back a long way. Both Sneed and Atwell graduated from Southwestern University at Georgetown, Texas, and Atwell was married to Lena's cousin.

Sneed hired Atwell to act as his private attorney in his battles against Al Boyce and the Boyce family, while at the same time encouraging Atwell, acting in his official capacity as a federal prosecutor, to obtain a federal indictment against Al Boyce. The federal criminal statute in question was the Mann Act, also known as the "White Slavery Act," which prohibited the transportation of females across state lines "for immoral purposes."[9] The gist of the allegation asserted that Al had transported Lena, a married woman, across a state line for the immoral purpose of having an adulterous relationship with her. From Beal's standpoint this was the ideal prosecutorial weapon, since the sanity or insanity as well as the consent or non-consent of the so-called victim were both immaterial. Beal now had on his payroll a prosecutor whom he could control. Will Atwell, brazenly, made no bones about his dual role. It was a blatant conflict of interest, even by 1912 standards. By today's standards, Atwell's egregiously unprofessional conduct would likely have earned him disbarment.

January 13, 1912, was the pivotal day in the unfolding tragic drama— the day that Beal recommitted Lena only to learn that the Boyce family would probably hire an attorney to challenge the commitment, the day that Beal learned about Colonel Boyce's "stand hitched" letter, and—even more galling—the day he learned that Colonel Boyce had talked the Tarrant County prosecutor into dismissing the state indictments against Al Boyce, Jr. All the while, Al Boyce was free and still beyond his reach in Canada. John Beal Sneed was furious. The very idea that anyone would have the audacity to challenge his righteous crusade!

Another incident undoubtedly fueled Beal's rage, and it would soon have great legal significance during a murder trial. Beal was informed that Colonel Boyce's old nemesis, W. H. Fuqua, then president of the First National Bank of Amarillo, had heard Colonel

Boyce make a most crude and insulting remark about Lena. Fuqua said that he had overheard an all-male conversation in an Amarillo drugstore during which someone had wondered aloud what it was about Lena that made one man willing to spend $20,000 to steal her and another man spend $20,000 to get her back. Boyce, being present, and being accustomed to blunt man-talk, voiced a very crude speculation on the matter. While today such remarks would, no doubt, be deemed crude, sexist, and offensive, in 1912 Texas, if the same were uttered to describe a man's wife, mother, sister, or daughter, it was an open invitation to violent redress. That same day, Henry Boyce read the inflammatory interview his father had given the *Fort Worth Star-Telegram*, and wired this wise advice to Colonel Boyce: "Don't talk so much."[10] Wise advice—but too late given.

That was the state of affairs on the fatal evening of January 13, 1912, when the paths of Beal Sneed and Colonel Boyce crossed in the Metropolitan Hotel in Fort Worth, the city's finest establishment. Colonel Boyce was sitting in the lobby talking to a friend, E. C. Throckmorton, a Fort Worth real estate dealer and the son of former Texas Governor J. W. Throckmorton, while waiting to catch the train back to Amarillo and give Annie Boyce the good news that the Fort Worth indictments against their son had been dropped. At that time Beal Sneed, Henry Bowman, and Will Atwell entered the lobby. Colonel Boyce noticed them and hailed Will Atwell, who came over to where he and Throckmorton were seated. He requested that Atwell allow him to present witnesses on behalf of Al Boyce when the federal grand jury considered the white slavery charge. Atwell would later testify that in an effort to head off a white slavery indictment, Colonel Boyce boasted that he could prove in half an hour "what kind of woman Mrs. Sneed was."[11]

Atwell, Bowman, and Sneed had intended to take their evening meal at the Metropolitan Hotel, but after encountering Colonel Boyce in the lobby they changed their plans and decided to eat at Joseph's Café nearby. Bowman and Sneed then left the hotel lobby while Atwell was talking with the Colonel. After Atwell's brief conversation with Colonel Boyce he departed the Metropolitan Hotel lobby and joined Sneed and Bowman at the café. During their evening meal, the trio undoubtedly rehashed Colonel Boyce's "stand hitched" letter to Lena, his crude remarks about her, and his boast about proving in half an hour "what kind of woman" she was—all that on the heels of the Colonel's success earlier that day in persuading the Tarrant County prosecutor to drop the state indictments against Al. Beal was also now informed by his lawyer—U.S. Attorney Atwell—that Colonel Boyce intended to oppose Beal and Atwell's attempt to indict Al in the federal courts. Undoubtedly they also discussed the probability—almost the certainty—that the Boyce family would exercise the power of attorney Lena had granted them to file a lawsuit on her behalf challenging the legality of Lena's confinement, and that if such a suit were filed, then Beal and the Allison family would have the burden of proving that Lena was insane. Beal Sneed was furious—not only at Al Boyce for running away with his wife and shaming him publicly, but also at Colonel Boyce and the rest of the Boyce clan for what he obviously considered was their unwarranted and outrageous interference in his personal affairs.

After their evening meal, Sneed, Bowman, and Atwell left Joseph's Café and walked back down the street past the Metropolitan Hotel. Colonel Boyce was still lounging in one of the comfortable lobby chairs chatting with his friend Throckmorton. Beal peeled off as they went past the Metropolitan and entered the lobby. (He would later claim that he entered the Metropolitan in order to go to the toilet although there was a toilet in the café he had just left. He would also claim that he thought Colonel Boyce had already departed en route to his home in Amarillo.)

Ed Throckmorton would later testify that only about forty minutes had elapsed from the time Bowman, Atwell, and Sneed left the lobby after their initial meeting until Beal Sneed reappeared. According to Throckmorton, Colonel Boyce exclaimed, "Oh, my God, there's Sneed now."[12] Then without warning, Beal Sneed drew his .32-caliber automatic pistol and opened fire on the unarmed old man. The first shot hit the Colonel while he was still seated. The Colonel leaped up, staggering, and attempted to flee. But John Beal Sneed kept firing. Five or six shots rang out sending other startled hotel guests in a panicky retreat, some diving for cover. Colonel

Boyce fell about six feet from his chair. Throckmorton would later testify that after the last shot, Beal Sneed snarled, "Now you're done with. You're out of it!" Throckmorton said he saw four bullet holes in Colonel Boyce's body, some of which he thought entered through his back. Then Beal bolted for the door and fled.[13]

An ambulance was called, but Colonel Boyce died en route to the hospital. He was seventy years old. Forever. John Beal Sneed was thirty-three. And counting.

S. M. Cherry, a salesman from Galveston, was in the lobby when Colonel Boyce was shot. He later testified that although he didn't witness the shooting, when he heard three gunshots he turned around and saw Beal Sneed exit the lobby. Cherry said that Sneed then walked back into the lobby and gazed around for a moment before leaving again. Cherry followed closely behind as Sneed walked down the street to the corner of Eighth and Main streets, stood there for a moment, then turned west on Eighth Street. Cherry continued to follow him while looking for a policeman. At the corner of Eighth and Houston streets, Cherry found an officer and told him that Sneed had just shot a man. At that point Beal Sneed began to run, but the officer soon overtook him and made the arrest.[14]

JOHN BEAL SNEED KILLS COLONEL BOYCE. A *Fort Worth Star-Telegram* artist illustrates how Sneed entered the lobby of the Metropolitan Hotel in downtown Fort Worth on January 13, 1912, and then fatally wounded the unarmed Colonel A. G. Boyce who was seated as depicted. Sneed then fled along the path indicated. *Sketch from the* Fort Worth Star-Telegram, *January 15, 1912.*

Left: **COLONEL ALBERT G. BOYCE, SR.**, general manager of the XIT Ranch, 1887–1905. *Photograph courtesy of the XIT Museum, Dalhart, Texas.*

Below: **FORT WORTH METROPOLITAN HOTEL.** John Beal Sneed shot and killed the unarmed Colonel Albert Boyce in the lobby of the Metropolitan Hotel on the evening of January 13, 1912. *Photograph courtesy of the University of Texas at Arlington Library Special Collections.*

After learning of John Beal Sneed's execution of Colonel Boyce, the *Manitoba Free Press* dateline January 15, 1912, excoriated the hot-blooded Texas barbarians in one blanket condemnation:

> [The Texans having an] apparent disregard for human life, and a
> low estimate of the heinousness of the crime of murder, feuds with
> accompanying deaths, appeared to have been a common feature
> of the life of the country, and the shooting of a man as a result of
> a quarrel seemed to be but little more serious than the shooting of
> a dumb animal.[15]

Al was still in Canada when he heard that Beal had killed his father. His Canadian attorney, T. J. Murray, learned about it the night of the shooting. He wired this telegram to the Canadian immigration officials with a copy to Al. It read, "Associated Press dispatch states Sneed shot and killed Albert's father tonight. Am assured report reliable. On no account allow Albert to return to Texas. This probably means opening feud. Answer. T. J. Murray."[16] Lawyer Murray was exactly on target when he anticipated that the killing of Colonel Boyce would likely trigger a bloodletting family feud. Immediately upon receipt of Murray's telegram, Al wrote this letter to Lena:

> I will go to Winnipeg tomorrow . . . I may return at once to
> Texas. I don't know. It will be my pleasure and duty to avenge him.
> Pa was the best of fathers and best and noblest of men and to think
> of his being killed in his old age by this kind of a brute is awful. I
> can't write more . . . I love you with all the strength I possess and
> will to my death.[17]

Lena did not learn about the murder until three days later when she was taken from the sanitarium in compliance with Will Atwell's subpoena to testify before the federal grand jury. Whatever her testimony was, the grand jury did not immediately return an indictment against Al, although, at the U.S. Attorney's behest, the grand jury continued the investigation of Al Boyce, Jr., on the white slavery accusation.

By this time, two armed and hostile groups formed in their respective Fort Worth hotels—the Sneed-Snyder camp in one, the

Boyce camp in the other—and that vortex of impending violence and drama was garnering international attention. Commenting on this gathering of bristling antagonists in Fort Worth, the *Manitoba Free Press*, perhaps exaggerating the situation somewhat, informed its readers that each camp was attracting a strong group of supporters of "rich and powerful west Texans. The two hotels resemble political conventions. Almost every minute, messages are brought in assuring support and promising financial aid. Hundreds of western cattlemen, capitalists, and bankers have taken sides."[18]

Indeed, the storm it was a-gathering.

~~~
        5
CHAPTER
~~~

To the Courts

From Guns to Gavels

AS THE STORY OF THE BLOODY Boyce-Sneed feud continued to unfold for more than two years—more melodramatic than any modern soap opera—lurid newspaper accounts of a scandalous romance, the stalking, the killings, and the sensational murder trials titillated readers all across America and Canada (where the press continued to take an unusually condescending and voyeuristic interest). Every twist of the tale seemed even more unbelievable than the last, and it not only shocked the nation but shook the pillars of West Texas society.

The courtroom dramas, riveting enough as they were in their own right, also served to bring into sharp focus the marked differences between the liberal values emerging in the northern states and the traditional Victorian morals, customs, and religious beliefs still so deeply imbedded in southern culture—all this at the dawning of the new century when these "Old South" values were first beginning to be seriously challenged.

~~~
           ∽‿‿∾
~~~

When they slammed shut the jailhouse door on John Beal Sneed for the killing of Colonel Boyce, the entire drama abruptly shifted from guns to gavels. Beal filed a habeas corpus petition to get out of jail. Lena filed a habeas corpus petition to get out of the asylum. The Fort Worth district attorney called a grand jury to get a murder indictment against Beal. The district judge set the wheels of justice in motion to try Beal for murder. Al Boyce, meanwhile, paced the sidelines in Canada, frustrated, embittered, forlorn, heartsick . . . and debating what to do next.

Lena's Sanity Hearing

First up to bat in the judicial ballpark on January 19, 1912, was Lena's habeas corpus hearing in which she challenged the right of the Arlington Heights Sanitarium to imprison her. The hearing was in the Sixty-Seventh District Court of Tarrant County, Judge Tom Simmons presiding. The sole issue to be determined was whether Lena was, or was not, insane—or more specifically, "morally insane," as John Beal Sneed and the sanitarium contended.

Dr. Wilmer Allison at the sanitarium concurred in the "morally insane" diagnosis originally made by Dr. John Turner at the behest of John Beal Sneed. Now Dr. Allison would be called on to defend it—and explain it. In anticipation of that onerous task, he hired high-powered legal talent to represent himself and the sanitarium: a former Texas attorney general and a former county judge. The Boyce family, by virtue of the power of attorney Lena had given them, employed state senator O. S. Lattimore to represent Lena; to bolster their team they added another state senator to the roster, W. A. Hanger of Fort Worth, putting two very expensive lawyers in Lena's corner.

Not to be outdone, John Beal Sneed hired the most ferocious and feared criminal defense lawyer in Fort Worth, W. P. "Wild Bill" McLean, a courtroom predator as brilliant and articulate as he was ruthless. McLean was a member of a dynasty of prominent and successful Fort Worth lawyers consisting of his father (Judge William Pinckney McLean), a brother (Jefferson Davis McLean), two sons (W. P., Jr., and John), and a grandson (W. P. III).[1] But "Wild Bill" McLean was the star litigator of the family. He first distinguished himself even before he received his law license. While a law student at the University of Texas, he became the captain and quarterback of the school's first football team. After graduation he served a short stint as a prosecutor, but soon found his true niche in the legal profession as a criminal defense lawyer. During the last thirty-five years of his legal career he successfully defended seventy-five clients charged with murder. The fiery, combative McLean earned his "Wild Bill" title by virtue of a booming voice, a forceful demeanor, and brash trial tactics in the courtroom.

Assisting "Wild Bill" in his effort to keep Lena locked away in Allison's asylum was his talented law partner, Walter Scott. To add even more beef to McLean's team, Beal Sneed summoned his own bought-and-paid-for public official, Will Atwell, U.S. District Attorney for the Northern District of Texas. Money, scruples, and ethics were beside the point—the point was to win. Whatever it took.

On the day the hearing began, McLean, Scott, and Atwell, upon behalf of John Beal Sneed, filed a motion contending that Lena "should not be turned loose in the world at this time." Will Atwell,

TARRANT COUNTY COURTHOUSE as it appeared in 1920s. Judge James Swayne presided over the Seventeenth District Court on the second floor of this courthouse when John Beal Sneed was tried there in 1912 for the murder of Colonel Albert G. Boyce. Postcard image. *Courtesy Fort Worth Public Library, Genealogy, Local History, and Archives Unit.*

FUTURE ALL-STAR DEFENSE LAWYER "WILD BILL" MCLEAN was quarterback of the first University of Texas football team in 1893. "Wild Bill" is seated, front row, second from left, holding the game ball. *Photograph courtesy of the University of Texas at Arlington Library Special Collections.*

probably hoping that Lena would be intimidated by the impending ordeal she faced, told the court that he believed "Mrs. Sneed wished to withdraw the [habeas corpus] application and 'go with her family.'"[2] He grossly underestimated Lena's indignation and resolve. She did not wish to withdraw her application, and she most definitely did not wish to "go with her family."

After Beal's lawyers put Dr. Allison on the stand and extracted the anticipated "morally insane" diagnosis, Senator Lattimore took him on cross-examination. From a spectator standpoint, the observers must have eagerly awaited an answer to the burning question of the day: What the heck is "moral insanity" anyway? The good doctor proved something less than forthcoming. "Disingenuous" and "forgetful" and "vague" more accurately described his performance. He seemed most adept at forgetting inconvenient facts. First off, however, he had to admit that Lena had been locked up in his institution on John Beal Sneed's diagnosis alone; there had been no prior court proceedings, no sanity hearing, and no judicial determination that she was insane. In fact, after she was incarcerated John Beal Sneed had to send Dr. John Turner back to examine Lena three times before he came up with the right answer—that is, an answer that suited Beal.

The January 19, 1912, edition of the *Fort Worth Star-Telegram* recounted a verbatim account of the cross-examination of Dr. Allison. It read, in part, as follows:

Q: You say you treated her—how did you treat her?

A: That is hard to say.

Q: Did you treat her this morning or yesterday?

A: I could hardly say without looking it up.

Q: What medicine did you give?

A: Calomel, for one thing, and a tonic.

Q: Isn't she your highest priced patient . . . paying $65 while the regular price is $35?

A: The rate varies according to the amount of attention a patient demands and the amount of care necessary . . .

Dr. Allison said that when Mrs. Sneed was brought to the sanitarium she protested violently and "screamed and hollered and fought." Afterward she "caused a great deal of trouble by often asking to talk to him, and by constantly wanting to do something or to go somewhere."

Q: Do you think she was of unsound mind?

A: I think she was in a condition of moral insanity . . .

Q: What do you mean?

A: That is hard to explain.

Q: I think so too, but you are an expert.

A: I mean a person that has lost their moral sense to a certain extent.

Q: Is calomel a remedy for moral insanity?

A: That was part of the treatment . . .

Dr. Allison then testified that in his opinion a lack of proper regard for the truth evidences moral insanity.

Q: Is every liar insane?

A: No.

Dr. Allison added that evidence of impairment of one's moral compass is detected "when a woman who has been reared under every proper surroundings becomes immoral." He also cited Lena's seemingly lack of remorse at running off with Al Boyce. "She seemed to regard the whole affair as an individual matter," he marveled. In those two brief answers, Dr. Allison succeeded in revealing much about the conventional Victorian views on class, gender, and family, which, even in the early twentieth century, still retained considerable potency.[3]

Dr. Allison finally concluded that "moral insanity affects the moral side of the brain." When asked if he regarded Lena's "mental faculties as unbalanced," he dodged again. Dr. Allison, the self-proclaimed mental health expert, replied, "I don't know."

Senator Lattimore's cross-examination of Allison was considerably less than exhaustive, and he let Allison off the hook with a few generalizations without pressing for many obvious follow-up questions—such as a more specific definition of "moral insanity," for openers. Exactly how does it differ from ordinary insanity? What are its symptoms, causes, usual duration? What, if any, harm is the patient likely to cause to others? To herself? How many previous cases of moral insanity, if any, had he diagnosed? Treated? What were the results? Case histories? Length of confinements? Therapy? Medicines? Also, what authorities on the subject had he studied? Is "moral insanity" a mental disease recognized by the medical profession? Since when? Any dissenting opinions? What other experts in the field, if any, had he consulted concerning Lena's case? The list goes on.

One thing is certain: had John Beal Sneed's pugnacious lawyer, "Wild Bill" McLean, been in charge of that cross-examination of Dr. Allison, the good doctor would have been on the hotseat for hours on end, if not days, composing a treatise on "moral insanity."

All of which demonstrates that politicians, however effective they may be on the campaign trail or in the legislative hall, are not necessarily great—or even good—trial lawyers.

Actually, there had been a few previous murder trials in which female killers had relied upon "moral insanity" (or something closely akin thereto) as a defense. On May 3, 1870, San Francisco's most respected lawyer, A. P. Crittenden, together with his wife and two children, was seated on a crowded ferryboat crossing San Francisco Bay. Suddenly a woman wearing a heavy black veil came out of a group of passengers, walked over to Crittenden, and exclaimed, "You have ruined me and my child." With that she drew a pistol and shot him in the heart. Then she dropped the pistol and walked away. When she was arrested a short time later she said, "Yes, I did it. I don't deny it, and I meant to kill him."

Laura D. Fair had been the mistress of Crittenden for seven years, during which time they carried on an open affair. Crittenden had repeatedly promised to divorce his wife and marry Laura. But each time, he reneged on his promise. Finally, when she witnessed the happy scene of her lover and his wife and family enjoying their cruise, she snapped.

A public outcry for Laura's noosed neck was promptly raised by an outraged community when it heard of the murder of its popular attorney. The district attorney made the sweeping assertion that it could be regarded as "the most important case in the annals of criminal jurisprudence of the United States." San Francisco and other area newspapers followed the trial, never missing any detail, and wailed like a Greek chorus in the background for swift and deadly vindication. One commentator would later describe it this way: "As Laura's trial for her life proceeded, it became a dramatic production of the first order, a morality play that put on public exhibition not only the moral values of the criminal but also the values of the community in which she lived, of the jurors, of the lawyers, and even of the judge."[4] The trial lasted twenty-six days. In the end, the jury found Laura Fair guilty. The judge sentenced her to be hanged. But she appealed and won a reversal of the conviction.

Upon retrial, the defense shifted tactics dramatically and played the "moral insanity" card, claiming that at the time she shot Crittenden her "reason was dethroned." According to the defense experts, there existed three types of insanity: total (permanent) intellectual insanity, partial (temporary) intellectual insanity, and "moral and partial insanity." The defense contended Laura was not guilty since at the time of the shooting she suffered from "partial moral insanity," brought on by "delayed menstruation." The jury agreed and acquitted Laura Fair.

Several other nineteenth-century female murder defendants played the same card with varying results. It became known as the "dysmenorrheal-temporary insanity" defense. Today, the terminology has changed from "dysmenorrheal" to premenstrual syndrome, or PMS.

The first female to rely on the premenstrual syndrome temporary "moral insanity" defense in a murder case was Mary Harris. She was tried in Washington, D.C., in May 1865 for shooting and killing Adoniram J. Burroughs, a clerk in the U.S. Treasury Department. Tearfully, she explained to the jury that Burroughs had promised to marry her, ruined her, and then married someone else. Mary was acquitted after her expert, Dr. Charles Nichols, superintendent of Washington's Government Hospital for the Insane, testified that Mary was "paroxysmally" morally insane from the "combination of being crossed in love and suffering from painful dysmenorrheal at the time of the shooting."[5]

Lawyers in some other nineteenth-century trials attempted to stretch the "moral insanity" diagnosis to cover cases in which that condition was supposedly caused by something quite different from premenstrual syndrome. In 1881 Charles Guiteau raised that defense (unsuccessfully) when he was tried for assassinating President James Garfield. One psychiatrist for the defense testified that Guiteau suffered from moral insanity, and another, testifying for the prosecution, concluded that he was just a "moral imbecile."[6] The scholar John Ellard later commented that it was about that time (late in the nineteenth century) that the distinction between moral insanity and wickedness was lost. Ellard went on to contend that moral insanity existed "only in the psychiatrist's imagination." He made this comment in rejoinder to a nineteenth-century expert who had written that moral insanity could be distinguished from ordinary garden-variety depravity because it was always preceded by "some diseased function of organs, more or less intimately connected with the brain and nerves." "Moral insanity," he concluded, was "so subtle that it could be detected only by a psychiatrist, but not a court or a jury."[7] Another noted scholar, however, went even further. Dr. John P. Gray, the superintendent of the Utica [New York] Lunatic Asylum who in 1865 criticized Mary Harris's psychiatric expert, in 1881 voiced the opinion that "moral insanity is indistinguishable from moral depravity"—this while testifying for the prosecution in the Charles Guiteau murder trial. It was he who pronounced Guiteau a moral imbecile.[8]

When Dr. Allison declared that Lena was suffering from "moral insanity," he was not pressed to give a precise and detailed opinion as to the cause of her condition. Indeed, to have attributed it to a menstrual cycle problem would not have suited John Beal Sneed at all. It wouldn't have been consistent with his diagnosis of the cause of Lena's "moral insanity." It was crucial to Beal's game plan that the whole thing be blamed solely on the evil influence of that libertine Al Boyce. In addition, blaming Lena's insanity on some menstrual problem would not have justified Dr. Allison in keeping Lena locked up indefinitely in a mental institution.

Before resting their case, Beal's lawyers called Lena's father, Tom Snyder, age seventy, to the stand to testify on behalf of Beal. Snyder identified himself as a real estate broker in Clayton, New Mexico, a stockholder in the State Bank of Commerce of that place, and a former trustee of Southwestern University in Georgetown where the Snyder, the Sneed, and the Boyce families had been neighbors and intimate friends for years. He testified as follows:

> I and my entire family will stand by Beal Sneed who has stood
> by my daughter in a manly way . . . I love him like a son and a

brother . . . As to our daughter, our hearts and our homes are all open to her. We feel that she has done no wrong, because she was not responsible for what she has done. It was upon my advice that her husband placed her in the sanitarium . . .[9]

After that, Lena's legal team called to the stand three physicians who had examined Lena. They all testified that they detected no evidence of insanity in Lena's behavior. Dr. R. O. Braswell put it bluntly: "She is not insane."

Meanwhile, Lena, described in the *Star-Telegram*, as being neatly attired in a tailored blue serge dress with a red ribbon trimming and also wearing a black seal fur hat and coat, remained "wonderfully composed" throughout the ordeal. She lost control only once, and that was when Dr. Allison testified that she did not love her children.

Finally, Lena was called to testify. She asked Judge Tom Simmons to allow her to tell how she had been treated at the sanitarium. He granted the request. The *Star-Telegram* reported this:

Then she told her story in a quiet, unhesitating way, answering every question without a moment's reflection . . . She declared that she was put in the sanitarium by force . . . "Dr. Allison and his brother and the matron grabbed me and I was taken away from my two children . . . My husband said to Dr. Allison, 'Here she is,' and they carried me and put apomorphis [a powerful crystalline emetic obtained from morphine] in my arm, right here (indicating), and that was the last thing I remember until I came to, upstairs, locked in the room" . . . She denied that she had any treatment for three weeks and had one bath. She complained she had no clothes to wear except for a nightgown and a "kimono."[10]

Up to this point in the sanity hearing, the *Star-Telegram* had printed a detailed account of the testimony of witnesses, yet when Allison's and Beal's attorneys began their cross-examination of Lena, the newspaper abruptly balked, presumably in deference to the chivalrous notion that any sexually explicit testimony was "not fit for the delicate ears of ladies" or the public.

The *Star-Telegram*'s censorship of Lena's testimony was partially explained by Lena a few days later when she wrote Al in Canada:

> Mr. Boyce had been dead three days before I knew anything about it—you know Beal had shut me up again at Arlington Heights— killed your dear father at the Metropolitan about one hour afterwards—this was on Sat. and I was summoned [*sic*] before the Grand Jury Tues. after [January 16, 1912] plus didn't know any-thing about it until I left the Grand Jury room—I had my trial for my sanity on Friday [January 19, 1912] plus was released from the Sanitarium—Darling it was horrible—they asked the vilest most horrible questions and I had to answer them. It was so horrible all of it was not allowed to be published in the newspapers . . .[11]

In his cross-examination of Dr. Allison, Lattimore forced him to admit that he had tried to persuade Lena to withdraw her appli-cation for a habeas corpus hearing, warning her that if she went through with it, it would be a "most humiliating experience" for her. (One wonders if Dr. Allison was more concerned with Lena or him-self having to go through a "most humiliating experience.")

At the conclusion of the hearing, Judge Simmons made his finding. He announced: "After hearing this testimony, I could not conclude there was a semblance of insanity developed here in this case, and I am clearly of the opinion that the applicant ought to be discharged, and I will discharge her."[12]

The Boyce family, meanwhile, urged Al to remain in Canada for three reasons: to forestall a feared bloodbath, to facilitate a convic-tion of Beal, and hopefully, to put an end to Al's relationship with Lena. In response, Al wrote Lena this:

> My desire and impulse was to return, but have received telegrams asking me to stay in Canada, and everyone here has told me my presence there would only aggravate the situation and weaken the prosecution. That I would be arrested upon crossing the line, would only mean more trouble.[13]

After Lena was released she made a short trip from Fort Worth to Plano where her sister Eula and Eula's husband, Henry Bowman, resided. The Bowman family had kept Lena's two daughters since her initial commitment to the sanitarium. After a tearful reunion with the two girls, Lena was informed that she could not remain in the Bowman home unless she would publicly admit that Beal was justified in what he had done. She refused, and called her sister Pearl Snyder Perkins, who lived in Lake Charles, Louisiana, for help. Pearl alone among Lena's family "stayed hitched" with Lena and supported her relationship with Al. Pearl then obtained funds from the Boyce family, traveled to Plano, rescued Lena, and took her back to Lake Charles.

Beal's Bond Hearing

Meanwhile, John Beal Sneed was imprisoned in the Tarrant County jail awaiting trial for killing Colonel Boyce. He had been denied bail, an imposition that he was not about to accept without a fight. He had McLean and Scott file his own habeas corpus action demanding bail.

Judge Tom Simmons of the Sixty-Seventh Judicial District Court heard the application. When he took the bench on January 23, 1912, tension was crackling as the Boyce, Sneed, and Snyder factions and their respective supporters crowded into the courtroom and glared across the aisle at one another. Wisely, Judge Simmons announced that no guns would be allowed in his courtroom, and he ordered anyone carrying a sidearm to disarm himself at once or go to jail. He called a ten-minute recess to allow anyone with a pistol to exit the courtroom and "stack arms" before returning. Then the hearing began.

Ordinarily, any person charged with a crime is entitled to bail set at a reasonable sum to ensure appearance at trial. However, in a capital murder case where the accused is charged with a deliberate and premeditated first-degree murder (a death penalty offense), and "the proof of which is evident," bail may be denied, as it initially was for Beal Sneed.

Beal's habeas corpus bond hearing was a dress rehearsal for the real thing. The state had the burden of proving that the killing was deliberate and premeditated and without any legal defense. The state's case seemed clear and unassailable. After all, Colonel Boyce was unarmed, had made no prior threats to Beal, and, at most, had simply tried to keep Beal from railroading his son to the penitentiary.

The only defense advanced by McLean and Scott at the bond hearing didn't suggest exoneration; it only aimed at mitigation of the offense—"manslaughter" rather than "not guilty" of premeditated murder. If manslaughter were a viable option for the jury, then Beal would be entitled to bail. The essence of the manslaughter offense in Texas is that the defendant killed his victim while in the throes of a "sudden passion arising from adequate cause." The defense team contended that there was a conspiracy by the entire Boyce family, headed up by Colonel Boyce, to alienate Lena from her husband and reunite her with Al Boyce. Heroic John Beal Sneed had just spent $25,000 tracking Lena down and bringing her home in an effort to restore her moral sanity, and now Colonel Boyce and his family were plotting to wrest her away from her husband again—thus causing Beal to fall into the throes of a "sudden passion" that was provoked by an "adequate cause."

Lena's father, Tom Snyder, weighed in for the defense. He said he had known the Boyce family for more than fifty years and had been an intimate friend and business associate of Colonel Boyce since 1858. Now, he continued, he felt that Colonel Boyce had betrayed that friendship and sacrificed the Sneed and Snyder families "and everybody else" to save his "drunken, cigarette-smoking fiend son." He concluded by exclaiming, "If I had a gun and Al Boyce was here, I would kill him!"[14]

In the process of proving its case, the state called Ed Throckmorton, Colonel Boyce's companion in the Metropolitan Hotel lobby at the time of the shooting. Throckmorton gave his eyewitness account of the fatal shooting of Colonel Boyce and the events leading up to it as recounted in the previous chapter. Throckmorton's testimony—particularly the part where he told of Beal Sneed standing over the dying Colonel Boyce and exclaiming, "Now you're done with. You're out of it!"—was crucial to the state's case because it tended to show premeditation on Sneed's part, and it tended to ward off any subsequent attempt by the defense to raise a self-defense issue.

In the end, the trial judge granted the defense motion for bond, his decision based not on the premise that Beal was innocent of the

killing of Colonel Boyce, but only that there was a viable manslaughter issue involved in the case. He set bond at $35,000—which Beal
Sneed made immediately. It is interesting at this point to pause and
note the support that John Beal Sneed commanded from affluent
Texans. The *Star-Telegram* reported that "Sneed's $35,000 bond was
immediately signed by his father, Joe Sneed, Sr., of Georgetown; his
father-in-law, T. S. Snyder of Clayton, New Mexico; his brothers, Joe
and Marvin Sneed of Dalhart; and by 100 prominent businessmen
from different parts of the state who had given Joe Sneed, Jr. power
of attorney to sign their names . . . to a bond in any sum."[15] That
one hundred prominent Texas citizens would volunteer to go on
Sneed's $35,000 bond (a sum equal to more than a half a million
dollars in today's money) is indicative of the intensity of feelings this
case generated and the depth of the rift it caused between the factions. In Amarillo, the town's social fabric was ripped down the middle, and it was not until decades later that anybody there would even
acknowledge that these events occurred—at least to an outsider.

The district judge, in granting the defense motion for bond,
made a curious remark from the bench:

> I have great sympathy for both sides in the case—they are all
> good people—but I can understand how Captain Snyder feels—
> how he can't conceive that his daughter lost her virtue before she
> lost her mind.[16]

That quote not only reflected the mores of the day but also was
an ominous harbinger of things to come in the courtroom battles.

In wrapping up the news story of Sneed's bail bond hearing, the
Star-Telegram noted that John Beal Sneed evidenced confidence in
a favorable decision from the start, and that he "sat composedly
smoking his pipe throughout the proceeding." Only Throckmorton's testimony seemed to provoke his ire.

The preliminaries were over. Now the curtain was about to rise on
a much anticipated drama, the trial of a killer who had assassinated
a Texas icon—a bedrock antebellum pioneer, a Civil War hero, an

early trail driver, the longtime and successful manager of the famous
XIT Ranch, a wealthy West Texas banker, a staunch Methodist, and
an esteemed citizen. Newspaper headlines across Texas and beyond
had keyed the audience to a fevered pitch.

The trial was to be held in Fort Worth—"Cowtown" as folks
called it. How fitting it was that Beal Sneed's murder trial would be
played out in Cowtown, fitting because all the principals involved—
Beal, Lena, Al, Colonel Boyce, as well as the three pioneer families
they represented—were all cow country royalty with intertwined
roots reaching far back into Texas history.

On the eve of the 1912 Sneed murder trial, Fort Worth was not
yet a city; it was still an overgrown, provincial country town of around
75,000, which had earned its well-deserved "Cowtown" handle. After
the Civil War when thousands of Texas cattle were trailed north
to railheads in Kansas, the little village on the banks of the Trinity
River was along the well-trodden path of the famous Chisholm Trail.
But by the mid-1880s, railroads had linked Fort Worth with the rest
of the nation, and it was no longer necessary to market Texas cattle
by making those long trail drives. Fort Worth soon became a major,
area-wide cattle-marketing center, and by 1912 the sprawling stock-
yards in the north part of town and the adjacent meat-packing facto-
ries were the city's largest industries.

Across town, another thriving industry had come to life and a
very lively one at that. They called it "Hell's Half Acre." That was
also a well-deserved handle. Many a thirsty, trail-weary cowboy shook
off the trail dust and looked for a little heaven down in Hell's Half
Acre—name your poison. Saloons, bordellos, and gambling joints
had no curfews or overly civilized rules of conduct.[17] But trail-weary
cowboys, railroad workers, and other unrepentant sinners were not
the only ones who enjoyed Hell's Half Acre. A sizeable cadre of civ-
ic-minded reformers as well as some noisy "hellfire-and-damnation"
Bible-thumpers, loved to loathe and denounce the Half Acre, but
with only limited success—at least until well into the twentieth century.[18] As one semi-repentant sinner was once prayed: "Lord make
us good . . . but not right now."[19]

"The Greatest Legal Battle Ever"

The 1912 Fort Worth Murder Trial of John Beal Sneed

WHAT A TANTALIZING TREAT was in store for trial spectators poised on the edge of their seats breathlessly waiting to witness what had been billed as "The Greatest Legal Battle Ever Fought in Texas Courts"[1] featuring those larger-than-life characters they had heard and read so much about—John Beal Sneed, Lena Snyder Sneed, and Al Boyce—who would disgorge all those juicy, intimate details of the scandalous romance and the killing of a Texas pioneer icon. As fascinating as that promised to be, yet another riveting story would unfold as the trial progressed—one that only the more seasoned courtroom railbirds were likely to have anticipated. How could any trial lawyer, no matter how skillful, experienced, or imaginative, devise and execute a viable trial strategy that would stand any chance of keeping John Beal Sneed's neck out of a noose? Public sentiment in Fort Worth was tilted in favor of the prosecution: the defendant had killed an unarmed old man—a prominent and respected pioneer—whose only crime was an attempt to protect his son from unjust prosecution. The state's case seemed to have "slam-dunk" written all over it. One thing was certain: to have any chance of success, the defendant would have to enlist the services of a courtroom wizard. Or wizards. Plus, perhaps, the assistance of some questionable characters to carry out clandestine extralegal assignments.

John Beal Sneed, himself an able and savvy lawyer, spared no expense in hiring the toughest, most combative, and most expensive battery of trial lawyers in Texas. Team captain was W. P. "Wild Bill" McLean. Early on in the Sneed trial one newspaper reporter who observed McLean in action commented that McLean not only talked the loudest of any other lawyer in the courtroom but "by far and away, the most," adding that he was better at "getting in a word edgewise than any woman." The reporter concluded the description this way:

> He does not stop a mile ahead of the mere spoken word. He is the
> human illustrator of the trial. He talks with his hands and feet, with
> his shoulders and an upward toss of his head . . . Pugnaciousness
> is a pitifully inadequate word for this stocky, square-jawed lawyer.[2]

Not far behind McLean, talentwise, were his two law partners—his father, Judge McLean, and the theatrical Walter Scott. Rounding out the team was perhaps the most famous orator in the state of Texas, Cone Johnson, who had recently made an unsuccessful run for the Texas governorship, and who was then campaigning (unsuccessfully as it turned out) for a seat in the U.S. Senate.

The lead prosecutor, in name at least, was Tarrant County Attorney John Baskin. However, not satisfied by Baskin alone, the Boyce family reinforced the prosecution by hiring well-known attorneys to assist Baskin. To shore up the prosecution team they employed a well-respected Fort Worth lawyer and politician, state senator W. A. "Bill" Hanger. A small man, Hanger was, in contrast to the boisterous McLean, described by the same court observer as being reserved and contemplative. The Boyce family also hired two other attorneys, Jordan Y. Cummings and Harry Hendricks (the latter being a law partner of Al's brother, Will Boyce of Dalhart). It was a formidable team of litigators indeed.

Prosecution was in the Seventeenth Judicial District Court of Tarrant County, Texas, in Fort Worth, presided over by a stern and incorruptible judge—J. W. Swayne.[3] Judge Swayne was known as a tough "law and order" judge. With public opinion against them, and with the prosecution holding what appeared to be a lay-down hand, the last thing John Beal Sneed's defense team needed was a straitlaced law-and-order judge wielding the gavel. McLean filed a petition seeking to oust Judge Swayne and have another judge appointed. Swayne overruled it.

Judge Swayne's lengthy and venerable legal career, both on and off the bench, proved that he was not a man easily intimidated. Although small of stature and never in the best of health, he held fast to his principles when duty called. He believed in equal justice for all under the law—rich or poor, black or white. He hesitated not a blink to take on Klansmen, gamblers, illegal liquor dealers, brothel keepers, or the establishment in his crusades against crime and injustice. Before ascending to the bench, he once, in 1892, defended a black man, Jim Burris, a "sporting man," who killed a white police officer. Swayne believed the officer was a bully and a racist who had provoked the fatal incident, so he defended Burris. Although a white Fort Worth jury convicted Burris and sentenced him to hang, Swayne appealed the case to the Texas Court of Criminal Appeals but lost again. Still not giving up, he eventually persuaded Texas Governor James Culberson to commute Burris's sentence to life in prison. Still not satisfied, seven years later he persuaded then Texas Governor Joseph Sayers to grant Burris a full pardon.[4]

After the change-of-venue petition was denied, Beal's attorneys filed another pretrial motion, this one seeking a continuance. Judge Swayne denied this motion as well. Jury selection began January 31, 1912—less than three weeks after John Beal Sneed had shot Colonel Boyce dead.

As formidable as was Beal Sneed's legal defense team, there were hints, even before the actual trial began, that Sneed undertook to ensure success by stacking the deck in his favor through some highly unorthodox machinations not taught in any reputable law school. On examination of the jury panel, one prospective juror (a

"WILD BILL" MCLEAN, the pugnacious and overpowering defense attorney whom John Beal Sneed hired to represent him as lead attorney in Sneed's murder trials. *Photograph taken from the February 6, 1912, edition of the* Fort Worth Star-Telegram.

WILLIAM PINCKNEY MCLEAN, SR., father of "Wild Bill" McLean, was a Texas statesman who assisted his son as co-counsel in defending John Beal Sneed in his Fort Worth murder trials. *Photograph courtesy of University of Texas at Arlington Library Special Collections.*

Right: **JAMES W. SWAYNE.** Known as "the straight-arrow" judge, he presided over both of John Beal Sneed's Fort Worth murder trials for the killing of Colonel A. G. Boyce. This picture was taken in about 1891 or 1892 when Swayne was a state senator representing the Thirtieth Legislative District in the Texas Senate which included Tarrant County. This is the formal portrait of Swayne which is displayed on the wall of the State Senate Chamber in Austin, Texas. *Photograph taken by Monte Neal in author's collection.*

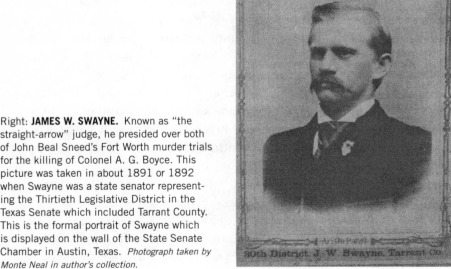

30th District. J. W. Swayne. Tarrant Co.

U.S. DISTRICT ATORNEY WILLIAM H. ATWELL (pictured on the right) was employed by John Beal Sneed to act as his private attorney during his difficulties with his wife and the Boyce family. The dual and conflicting roles seemed not to have bothered Atwell in the least. Fort Worth Star-Telegram *photograph courtesy of the University of Texas at Arlington Library Special Collections.*

Left: **HENRY BOWMAN**, "prominent mule trader" from Plano, Texas, was John Beal Sneed's brother-in-law and active supporter. *Sketch from the February 1, 1912, edition of the* Fort Worth Star-Telegram.

bartender) testified that another prospective juror had approached him about his possible service as a juror in the case, and casually remarked that "there could be $1,000 to $1,500 in it" for him.[5] The bartender also testified he had later seen the same man talking with a man whom he identified as John Snyder of Amarillo. Both venire-men were excused, but there was insufficient evidence for a prosecution. That, however, would not be the last that would be heard about suspicions of bribery.

Even more suspicious was the sudden and mysterious death on the eve of the trial of the state's most important witness—Ed Throckmorton. Witnesses related that Throckmorton had been seen drinking heavily with two strangers on Saturday evening, January 26, 1912. The next morning he was discovered in his hotel room having convulsions. Throckmorton lapsed into unconsciousness and died a few days later. Just before he died he regained consciousness briefly and recognized his wife and son who were at his bedside. His last words, addressed to his wife, were: "Anna, I have been doped."[6] He did not name the suspects. Prior to his death, Throckmorton had been in good health. County Attorney John Baskin suspected Throckmorton had been given "knockout drops," and he ordered an autopsy and called a grand jury to investigate the death. Lawmen launched a search to identify and apprehend the two mysterious strangers who were the drinking companions of Throckmorton, but they were never found or identified.

Then another strange thing happened. Throckmorton's body was taken to a funeral parlor in his hometown of McKinney, but before an autopsy could be performed, the undertaker embalmed the body, making a meaningful autopsy impossible. Cause of death was eventually marked down as "acute alcoholism." Ed Throck-morton's eyewitness testimony to the assassination of Colonel Boyce was of critical importance to the prosecution, and his sudden departure from the scene seemed simply too convenient to be dismissed as a mere coincidence, especially when it had been reported that Throckmorton's account of the killing given at Sneed's bail bond hearing several days earlier had enraged Sneed. In the end, although nothing implicating Sneed or his henchmen in Throckmorton's death could be proven, the whole episode emitted a distinct aroma of foul play.

Even with Throckmorton's absence, prospects for winning an acquittal for John Beal Sneed seemed unlikely at best. Aside from the legal problems, the defense faced public opinion tilted against Sneed and in favor of his elderly and unarmed victim who was a well-known and respected pioneer. Two days after the trial began, Lena wrote Al Boyce this: "Judge Swayne and public opinion is against Beal."[7]

The state's case appeared to be overwhelming and straightforward. Although the defense might possibly be able to persuade a jury that the killing was not a cold-blooded murder, but instead a killing committed by a very distraught Beal Sneed while in the grip of a "sudden passion arising from an adequate cause," still, that would only have reduced the conviction from murder to the lesser offense of manslaughter—two to five years in prison. But to the proud and arrogant John Beal Sneed, the specter of anything less than total victory (even one hour in prison) was unthinkable—totally unacceptable. Yet what possible strategy could the defense come up with to avoid a conviction—even with "Wild Bill" McLean, Walter Scott, and Cone Johnson at the helm?

True, there were two archaic, antebellum-era Texas penal statutes still on the books that provided relief to husbands determined to avenge dishonor to themselves and their wives. One such statute had been passed by the Texas Legislature in 1856 and was destined to remain in force until finally repealed in 1973. It provided free shooting rights for a husband to dispatch his wife's lover provided he caught the pair *in flagrante delicto*. Article 562 of the Texas Penal Code spelled it out this way: "A homicide is justifiable when committed by the husband upon the person of anyone taken in adultery with the wife; provided the killing takes place before the parties to the act of adultery have separated."[8] Obviously the express language of that old law would offer no relief to Beal Sneed in his upcoming trial. The statute did, however, underscore the point that in Texas a man's life was not held as dear as a man's honor, and lent credence to the *Manitoba Free Press*'s contention that Texans generally had a low regard for the value of human life. Astute trial lawyers are always keenly attuned to cultural mores of their society, and McLean and company could be counted on to pitch their jury presentation accordingly.

Yet another archaic statute might have afforded some benefit to defendant Sneed. Also enacted in 1856, it was one of the strangest pieces of legislation ever to festoon the pages of the Texas Penal Code. Commonly referred to as the "insulting words or conduct" law, this manslaughter statute was also still on the books in 1912. Since repealed, Article 597 granted hunting rights not only to outraged husbands but also to the entire family of the wronged woman, and the sanctioned retaliation was not limited to cases of adultery. Mere "insulting words or conduct" directed toward any "female relative" were deemed sufficient provocation to permit any member of her clan to vindicate the family honor by unlimbering "Old Betsy" and dispatching the scoundrel. Furthermore, unlike Article 562 where revenge had to be exacted "before the parties separated," there was no designated time limit for exacting revenge under Article 597. Revenge could be exacted years later, provided the shooter shot the suspected reprobate the first time the defendant encountered his target after learning of the outrage. Texas courts cut the revenge-seeker even more slack by their liberal interpretation of the law. It placed no duty on the outraged relative to investigate the truth of the allegation that the intended target really was guilty of authoring those "insulting words or conduct." It was sufficient for the shooter to have previously heard about the supposed insult (from whatever source) and *believed* it. But there was one big problem with that statute insofar as John Beal Sneed was concerned. As broad, sweeping, and defendant-friendly as it otherwise was, it did not furnish a "get-out-of-jail-free" ticket for the killer of an "insulting" libertine. Like the previously discussed "sudden passion arising from an adequate cause" statute, the 1856 law only served to reduce the criminal offense from murder to manslaughter. But John Beal Sneed and his attorneys had no intention of settling for anything less than total victory, as in "not guilty."

Of immediate concern to the defense was the matter of Lena's alleged moral insanity. How was McLean to deal with that delicate, and potentially disastrous, issue? Defense attorneys in the two 1870s murder trials in San Francisco of Laura D. Fair had adroitly played the moral insanity card to win her acquittal on September 30, 1872. But, here in Fort Worth, it was John Beal Sneed on trial for murder, not Lena. Could McLean, Scott, and Johnson somehow concoct a defensive strategy based on Lena's alleged moral insanity?

Before the lengthy trial finally concluded, the defense would have much to say about Lena's moral insanity.

Another strategic decision the defense had to make was whether or not to put Lena on the stand. Under the Texas Rules of Evidence, confidential communications between a husband and wife are privileged. Also, Lena had the privilege to refuse to be called as a witness for the state. Even if she chose to voluntarily appear as a state's witness, Sneed's attorneys could prevent her from revealing all confidential conversations between herself and Beal Sneed, her husband. But there was much additional and critical testimony Lena could give—confidential communication with Beal aside—which would be devastating to the defense: testimony that she loved Al very much, that Al had not kidnapped, abducted, or raped her, and that she had willingly gone with him to Canada, that she wanted to marry him. Most importantly, she could testify that neither Colonel Boyce nor Annie Boyce had ever encouraged her romance with Al and most definitely were not attempting to reunite them at the time Beal shot the Colonel. Her lucid performance on the witness stand would debunk the defense contention that she was insane.

As a practical matter, however, due to the existing emotionally tumultuous state of affairs, the prosecution dared not call her even if Lena agreed to be a state's witness. To have done so would have been akin to rolling a loose cannon on the deck and lighting the fuse—no telling which direction she might fire. On the other hand, there was nothing to prevent the defense from calling Lena as a witness, but would they dare to take the same risk? Could she be trusted to give testimony adverse to her lover and favorable to Sneed, and how would she hold up under cross-examination? Especially if questioned about her feelings toward Al Boyce, Jr.? She just might sink the mighty battleship *Defense* with one well-aimed torpedo. Then,

too, only two weeks previously at Lena's sanity hearing, Sneed's lawyers had contended that Lena was insane and "shouldn't be turned
loose on the world." How could they now account for Lena's sudden
and dramatic mental and moral recovery? The McLean team was
also well aware that Lena was smart and articulate, and even if she
could be persuaded to testify favorably for her husband, wouldn't
her rational and intelligent demeanor tend to undermine John Beal
Sneed's portrayal of Lena as the poor, wounded bird he had been
forced to sacrifice everything for on the altar of a heroic effort to
save her from herself?

Resolution of all those strategy problems was difficult enough
for the defense team, but underlying all that was a major legal
hurdle that had to be surmounted if nothing less than an acquittal
was acceptable—namely the penal laws of the State of Texas. Even
without Throckmorton, the state could prove beyond any doubt
that John Beal Sneed had intentionally killed the unarmed Colonel
Boyce. So, what legal justification was available? Not mistaken identity. Not alibi. Not self-defense. Temporary (intellectual) insanity?
Possible perhaps, but not likely. In the end, there seemed to be no
loophole under, around, or through the written statutes of the State
of Texas large enough for John Beal Sneed to wriggle his way to
comeuppance escape. The operative word in that last sentence is
written. If the defense couldn't rely on the official written laws, then
how about the unwritten laws?

Resorting to the unwritten law (often referred to as "the higher
law") had become common in the nineteenth century in Victorian
America—even in the North—sanctioning self-help justice when the
deceased victim had somehow besmirched the honor of the defendant.[9] The first American trial of note during which "the higher law"
was relied on by a husband to justify the killing of his wife's lover was
the 1859 murder trial of Daniel Sickles. Sickles would later distin-
guish himself as a Union war hero during the battle of Gettysburg.
However, in 1859 he was a congressman from New York City residing in a mansion in Washington, D.C. He learned that his young
wife, Teresa, had been having an affair with U.S. District Attorney
Philip Barton Key, the son of Francis Scott Key, who composed "The

Star-Spangled Banner." Upon learning of the affair, Sickles began keeping a lookout from his front window. One day he observed Key signaling Teresa to meet him for still another tryst, whereupon Sickles grabbed his pistol, raced out the front door, and shot Key dead on a public street near Lafayette Park and the White House. Sickles hired an immensely talented team of lawyers who proceeded to articulate, for the first time in American legal history, a definitive statement of "the higher law" as it applied to wife-seducing libertines. The court allowed it; the jury bought it; and Sickles was acquitted.[10]

One commentator on the Sickles case noted that it did more than any other case to formulate the basic tenets of the unwritten law. Divine law and historical tradition, it was contended, constituted a major part of the foundation for the unwritten law, and avengers of sexual dishonor were only agents of God acting as "divine functionaries applying natural principles which could not be altered by human law."[11]

The Sickles trial advanced another tenet as well. This one held that women were physically and morally weak and, therefore, in need of the constant and vigilant protection of their menfolk. One defense attorney in the Sickles trial, borrowing a line from Shakespeare's *Hamlet*, declared, "Frailty, thy name is woman," then went on to inform the jury that because a woman could not "resist herself and others," God had placed her "under the protection of man." Moreover, there was only one way for a cuckolded husband to redeem his honor: private vengeance. Deadly private vengeance. When informed that Teresa Sickles's adultery was public knowledge, one of his advisors told the distraught husband that "there is but one course left for you as a man of honor."[12]

Although the unwritten law was the basis for defense arguments in such cases as the Sickles trial in all the states until late in the nineteenth century, thereafter it was advocated primarily in the Old South as a part of its "Code of Honor." But the southern states did not have a monopoly on its advocacy. Until well after the turn of the century, lawyers in Texas and other western states continued to invoke *lex non scripta* (the unwritten law). The heavy migration of southerners to Texas and the western states both before and after the Civil War doubtless accounted for this cultural export. The South's Code of Honor owed much to England's Victorian stereotypes of male dominance in the family, strict differentiation of gender roles, separate standards of morality for males and females, a firm belief that females had no sexual desires, and a prudish reluctance to speak of sex—all that coupled with images of chivalrous, gallant knights in shining armor protecting refined and defenseless ladies who seemed inclined to faint upon the slightest of provocations. The unwritten law was constructed on, and nourished by, such stereotypes and beliefs.

In the presence of juries, defense attorneys carefully avoided speaking the words "the unwritten law," typically referring to it euphemistically by some code phrase such as "protecting the home." But jurors of that day knew well what "protecting the home" really meant; realized that the defense attorney was appealing to them to ignore the Texas statutory law, as well as the court's instructions, and thus exonerate his client on the basis of "the higher law."

All that said, and true enough, the question remained, would McLean and company be able to sell the unwritten law to a 1912 Texas jury? The strength of the unwritten law appears to have peaked in the late nineteenth century and thereafter was on the wane. By 1912 it had lost its potency in the North and was beginning to be challenged even in the South and the West. A discerning reader of the *Fort Worth Star-Telegram* might well have picked up a revealing clue as to the remaining vitality of the unwritten law in Texas by noticing a seemingly unrelated article that appeared near the time of the Sneed murder trial. On the surface, it seemed to be nothing more than a routine news report of a meeting of the Fort Worth chapter of the Women's Christian Temperance Union. The short report inadvertently revealed much about the public's Victorian attitude on the sexual mores of the time—including the mind-set that a trial lawyer might expect from a Fort Worth jury. With no bothersome folderol or prelude, the members voted, without dissent, to "denounce freakish dances" such as the turkey trot, the tango, and "other terpsichorean innovations."[13] While they were in a denouncing mood, they went on to denounce "modern dress and the lack

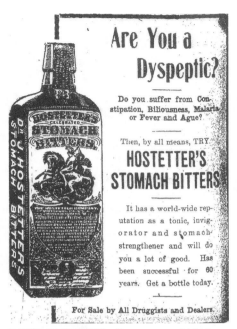

FLAVOR OF THE TIMES. Newspapers of 1912 were crowded with patent medicine miracle cures including Hostetter's Stomach Bitters, Dr. Shoop's Rheumatic Tablets, Dr. Thurman's Lone Star Catarrah Cure, plus a variety of hemorrhoid salves. Also hernia trusses, ladies "Dip Hip" corsets, 29 cents, and Dr. F. O. "Painless" Carter bragged that he charged only 50 cents per tooth for extractions. *1912 advertisements in the* Fort Worth Star-Telegram.

W. C. T. U. Members Denounce Freakish Dances and Dress

The turkey trot, tango and other terpsichorean innovations, modern dress and the lack of proper home training for both sexes were condemned by members of the Woman's Christian Temperance Union of Fort Worth Friday afternoon.

A mothers' meeting of members was held at the home of Mrs. H. M. Price, 415 W. Leuda street. "Shall We Have a Single Standard of Morals for Both Sexes?"

Mrs. John A. Rice, 412 West Terrell avenue, led. She told of a visit she made recently to governor Colquitt.

The conclusion reached by the meeting was that the single standard could be attained by lowering the standard now recognized for women or by raising the standard of men's morals. The latter alternative was decided proper.

Papers were read by Mrs. Lou Prickett and Mrs. W. R. McBill.

At the conclusion the meeting was turned into a social affair and refreshments were served. Miss Nellie Daniels of Dallas assisted the hostess.

FLAVOR OF THE TIMES. Women's Christian Temperance Union of Fort Worth denounces freakish dances and modern dress, debates the proper moral standards for men and women. Fort Worth Star-Telegram, *July 26, 1913.*

Dallas Country Club to Fight Freak Dances
By Associated Press

DALLAS. Nov. 26— The house committee of the Dallas Country Club has started a campaign against the bunny hug, grizzly bear, turkey trot, eagle rock. Boston dip and other dances known by their peculiar style and variation from the old time dances. The committee is taking a vote of the club's membership to support its stand that these dances are deemed contrary to the best interests of the club.

FLAVOR OF THE TIMES. The November 26, 1918, edition of the *Fort Worth Star-Telegram* reports on the Dallas Country Club's crusade against "freak" dances.

Times Will Megaphone Returns
Dempsey-Gibbons Fight July 4

Returns from the Dempsey-Gibbons fight and preliminary bouts at Shelby, Montana, July 4th will be megaphoned from the Times building Wednesday afternoon.

The preliminaries are scheduled to start at 1 p. m.- and the main bout is expected to start at 4. The Times will receive the report from the Associated Press leased wire, blow by blow, and as it is ticked off the report will be megaphoned. Jimmy Maxwell, oil editor of the Times, and the best little megaphoner that ever came out of Joplin, Mo., will handle the cone.

Immediately at the conclusion of the main bout an extra will be issued giving the report of the fight in detail.

FLAVOR OF THE TIMES. The July 3, 1923, edition of the *Wichita Falls Times* told its readers that a blow-by-blow account of the Dempsey-Gibbons heavyweight championship bout would be "megaphoned" to sports fans from the Times building the next evening by Jimmy Maxwell "the best little magaphoner that ever came out of Joplin, Mo."

of home training for both sexes." That out of the way, the ladies got down to a serious debate, the formal issue being framed as follows: "Shall We Have a Single Standard of Morals for Both Sexes?" After a spirited discussion, the members resolved that issue in the affirmative. However, that resolution only gave rise to an even more vexatious issue, framed thusly: "Should the Single Standard of Morals for Both Sexes Be Attained by Lowering the Standard Now Recognized for Women or By Raising the Standard of Men's Morals?" It is hardly worth mentioning the result of that vote. Or that it was unanimous. While the debate reflected the distaff view on those burning issues of the day, still women were not allowed to serve on juries. Would male jurors be as straitlaced, as rigid, and as censorious?

Even if male jurors were inclined to give serious consideration to the unwritten law, that still did not get the Sneed defense team home free in this trial. In previous cases, such as the Daniel Sickles murder trial, the unwritten law had been successfully argued to justify a husband slaying his wife's seducer. It had even been stretched to exonerate others in the husband's family who killed the wife-despoiling lecher and stretched even further to free female killers who exterminated false-hearted seducers who reneged on precoital promises to marry them. But, such was not the case here. It was not the wife's lover—the adulterator of the husband's marital bed—who had been slain. It was the lover's unarmed father, Colonel Boyce, who had been shot dead and who had done nothing to encourage the illicit affair. Would the McLean team dare try to stretch the unwritten law defense to reach that unexplored frontier? And, if so, how?

One thing was clear: the defense had to put somebody other than John Beal Sneed on trial; had to focus the jury's attention on some other wicked villain. There was Al Boyce, of course, and he would make a handy villain and an easy target. But Al Boyce alone wouldn't do, even if the defense could persuade the jury that "he needed a damned good killin'." He wasn't the one who got executed; Colonel Boyce was the target. The jackpot question remained: regardless of whether the defense invoked the written law or the unwritten law, how could the McLean team portray Colonel Boyce as such a dastardly villain that he deserved what he got? Could even courtroom magicians such as McLean, Scott, and Johnson pull that rabbit out of a hat?

The written law or the unwritten law? The answer was not long in coming. Questions the defense lawyers propounded to prospective jurors in the jury selection process left no doubt. McLean asked every man this question: "Do you believe in the protection of the home against the world?" Cone Johnson, for the defense, took it one step further in his jury selection questions: "In the protection of the home should a man be allowed to use weapons?"

The next jury question from Johnson echoed a distinctly Victorian view of male honor that harked back to the aftermath of the 1859 Daniel Sickles murder trial. After Sickles was acquitted for killing his wife's lover, he took his wife back—an act that brought shame and condemnation down on him by contemporary Victorians. Such notions of male honor prompted Cone Johnson to ask: "If a man discovered that his wife had done wrong, but he took her back, would that excite in you as a juror a prejudice against him?" That jury-selection question highlighted a dilemma the defense team would have to surmount: if a jury was seated that would heed the tenets of the unwritten law, wouldn't that same Victorian mind-set cause jurors to condemn Beal Sneed for taking Lena back after she had committed adultery—for allowing a debauched wife to return to the marital bed?

While McLean and Johnson were indoctrinating the jury panel on the implied acceptability of the unwritten law, lead prosecutor W. A. Hanger, instead of strenuously objecting to this blatantly out-of-bounds tactic, benignly sat on his hands and kept his mouth shut. Perhaps Hanger's complacency during the defense team's effort to divert the jury's attention from the written to the unwritten law was due to the prosecution's overconfidence in what it believed to be a lay-down winning hand. In any event, Hanger was content to mildly inquire of prospective jurors if they "believed in the enforcement of the law." And he let it go at that. By so doing he committed a cardinal sin in any trial lawyer's bible: he allowed the defense to reframe the central issue even before the trial began. The defense had just taken the first step in refocusing the jurors' assigned duty from rendering a dispassionate, evidence-supported verdict under the duly enacted laws of the State of Texas in favor of a more emotionally seductive duty of bravely standing up for their heritage as true sons of Texas and rendering a verdict under the unwritten laws of the Victorian Code of Honor of the Old South and the western frontier. Hanger and the prosecution also let the defense get away with committing another cardinal sin: not only must a courtroom gladiator refuse to allow the opponent to reframe the issue, but he must also refuse to permit that opponent to redefine the meaning of the terms of the issue, or, as veteran barristers often put it: "Let me define the meaning of the terms in any debate, and I'll win every argument." So, "Are you going to condone the cowardly assassination of an old, unarmed man?" became "Doesn't a man have the divine right to protect his home and family by whatever means he deems necessary?" Hence, while the prosecution slept, "protecting the home" became the euphemistic shibboleth that the defense preached during the rest of the trial. Moreover, McLean's team had just succeeded in seizing the initiative, thereby putting the somnolent prosecution on the defense.

Another telltale indication of where the defense was headed became apparent by reading the next day's *Star-Telegram* article. The reporter noted that the defense preferred jurors who were married men and who had been born in the South. That was confirmed when jury selection was complete. It was composed of twelve white men, ages twenty-three to forty-four—all except one married. And every last one of them was a son of the South.

One amusing incident occurred during the prolonged jury selection process. Because of the sensational nature of the case and the dramatic play given it by the *Fort Worth Star-Telegram*, it required the summoning of an additional panel of veniremen. The jurors first selected were sequestered, which didn't permit any contact with the outside world. In an effort to relieve their boredom, a deck of cards was sent to the jury room. But a complaint soon came back: two of the jurors were Methodists and their religious beliefs were such that they shunned the playing of cards, even if no money were involved. This problem was soon solved by sending up a set of dominoes. That placated and entertained the Methodists.

Then the trial began. As is often observed, every person has a story. True enough, but in every criminal trial there are at least two stories—competing stories. Eventually the jury must answer which of the two stories—prosecution or defense—it believes to be more credible (unless, of course, there is a hung jury). Beginning journalism students are taught that every news story should answer six basic questions, the five *W*s and one *H*—who, what, when, where, why, and how? A trial lawyer has to answer those basic questions in telling his or her version of the story to the jury. In the John Beal Sneed murder trial, five of those six questions had already been answered: John Beal Sneed, age thirty-three, intentionally shot to death unarmed Colonel Albert Boyce, age seventy, with a .32-caliber Colt revolver shortly after 8:00 p.m. on January 13, 1912, in the lobby of the Metropolitan Hotel in Fort Worth, Tarrant County, Texas. That left only one of the six basic questions unanswered: why? Thus it would appear, at least at first glance, that the case had been greatly simplified. But it would prove to be anything but a simple case. Not with Bill McLean and his client, John Beal Sneed, at the helm of the defense.

The "why" that lay at the heart of the case involved a question of motives—motives of all the central characters. What was it that caused them to do what they did? Veteran trial observers were left to speculate on fascinating questions of competing trial strategies that were about to be revealed. How would the prosecution portray the motives of those central characters? How would the defense portray those motives? What was Al Boyce's motive for having the affair with Lena? Love? Sex? Or both? And if sex, was it a normal sexual attraction or licentious depravity? And what about Lena? What was her motive, or motives? Love? Sex? Or both? And if sex, was she bad or bewitched? Morally insane? Was Lena, as occasional furtive whispers speculated, a nymphomaniac? Or was the high-spirited, adventuresome Lena simply bored with the often absent Beal and the blandness of marital sex with him, thus succumbing to the temptation of tasting that delicious forbidden fruit? Did devious Al dangle the forbidden fruit in front of her? Or was it Lena who dangled that taboo apple before the naïve cowboy? Who did the dangling? Or was it mutual attraction? Could it have possibly been that Al and Lena simply fell deeply in love and lust with each other?

What was John Beal Sneed's motive in his determined pursuit and recapture of Lena? Selfless love? Concern for an emotionally crippled Lena and an attempt to rehabilitate her? Preservation of the family? A self-sacrificing dedication to his children? Or was it an aggravated case of wounded vanity resulting in a fierce resolve to exact vengeance? What was John Beal Sneed's motive for killing Colonel Boyce? Was it Colonel Boyce's interference with Beal's efforts to save Lena from herself? Or was Beal's goal to prevent Colonel Boyce from helping his son steal Lena? Had Beal heard some "insulting words" Colonel Boyce said about Lena and become infuriated at him? Or was it pure vindictiveness on Beal's part stemming from Colonel Boyce's perceived interference with Beal's inviolable plan to restore his honor and thus massage his battered pride? And what about Colonel Boyce? What was his motive, or motives? To help Al steal Lena away from Beal and bring her into the Boyce family, as Beal maintained? Or was he simply attempting to prevent a vindictive Beal Sneed from sending his son to the penitentiary? Or combinations of those motives and possibly others?

Of those four principal characters, only one of them would speak for himself or herself during the upcoming trial. Obviously it would not be Colonel Boyce. Would Al testify? Would Lena? Would John Beal Sneed? As a defendant in the criminal case, he could choose to testify or choose to remain silent and have the judge instruct the jury that the defendant's refusal to testify should not be counted against him—thereby avoiding the risk of many embarrassing and potentially incriminating questions on cross-examination.

The state's case was simple and direct, and it didn't take long to present. Several men who had been inside the lobby of the Metropolitan Hotel when Sneed shot Colonel Boyce testified. Their testimony was basically consistent, and they identified John Beal Sneed as the gunman; testified that he had fired several shots at the unarmed Colonel Boyce, all but the first one while the victim was trying to run away from Sneed. None, however, except Throckmorton were close enough to hear any verbal exchanges between Sneed and Colonel Boyce—if indeed any had occurred. The prosecution did suffer a major defeat when Judge Swayne refused to allow the state to read the bail-bond hearing sworn testimony of Ed Throckmorton to the jury. Inexplicably the judge sustained McLean's hearsay objection, so the jury never got to hear Throckmorton testify that after Sneed shot Boyce, he stood over the dying man and snarled, "Now you're done for. You're out of it"—words that clearly evidenced both premeditation and motive. And cold-blooded vengeance.

Then the state rested.

At the outset, McLean told the jury that the defense would prove that Colonel Boyce not only encouraged his son Al to run

away with Lena Sneed but thereafter conspired with other Boyce
family members to keep Lena's whereabouts concealed. Furthermore, McLean claimed that at the time of the killing, Boyce was
engaged in an effort to reunite Al and Lena, and that's what John
Beal Sneed believed when he shot Boyce. Notice was thus given
that the motivations of both John Beal Sneed and Colonel Boyce
would be placed in issue. More than that, it would be the crux of
the defense.

But what about Lena? The defense issued a subpoena for Lena
to appear as a witness. She was in Fort Worth at the time and available, yet McLean told the press that he did not know whether the
defense would put her on the stand.

The suspense was put to an end a few days later when Lena's
father, Tom Snyder, took the stand for the defense. After Snyder
vocalized the same furious rant against Colonel Boyce and his
"drunken cigarette-smoking fiend son," Senator Hanger began
cross-examining him about bruises Snyder had observed on Lena's
arms and shoulders while he was escorting her back from Canada,
apparently aimed at proving that Beal had physically abused her in
his efforts to force her to return to Texas with him. McLean objected
to this question, whereupon Senator Hanger retorted that this evidence would be brought out anyway when the defense put Lena on
the stand. At that point McLean announced that the defense would
not call Lena as a witness, adding this self-serving sidebar remark in
the jury's presence:

> There is not a man connected with the defense who does not
> believe this woman to be insane, and her testimony would be
> worthless in any court.[14]

Although Judge Swayne instructed the jury to disregard
McLean's shameless "unsworn testimony," it was a waste of his
breath. As veteran trial lawyers are apt to put it: the judge's after-
the-fact instruction was about as effective as tossing a skunk into
the jury box and then ordering the jurors to ignore the stink. Consequently an excuse for the failure to call Lena was implanted in
the jury's mind.

Had Hanger been alert and quick-witted enough, he could have turned McLean's out-of-bounds sidebar remark against him and defused it with a sidebar rejoinder of his own, such as:

> If all the defense lawyers really believe that Mrs. Sneed is insane, then isn't it strange that less than a week ago they had a subpoena issued in this court for her to appear as their witness in this trial? Could it be that the real reason the defense is not going to put her on the stand and let you hear her testimony is that Mrs. Sneed refuses to testify the way they want her to?

The real reason why the defense decided not to call Lena as a witness was a question that would be answered definitively . . . but it was an answer that the jury would never hear. On February 7, 1912, the same day that McLean made the assertion to the court and jury that Lena was a worthless witness because she was insane, Lena wrote a letter to Al in Canada saying:

> Oh my boy you will never know or understand the pleadings, plus persuasion I have withstood. Beal's lawyers—everyone has offered every inducement to try to make me testify for him. They pleaded for the sake of the children—plus oh, Albert it was awful. They said I could clear him if I would just testify that your father had influenced me plus knew where we were, plus that I didn't realize what I had done. I told them I knew nothing to tell plus if I did I wouldn't tell it. That I wouldn't tell a lie to save him—plus that if I was going to tell a lie to save him I wouldn't lie on the dead—plus when they saw it was useless you see what McLean has had to say about no court believing my testimony on account of me being insane.[15]

Despite the browbeating, Lena refused to cooperate and follow the perjury-laden script written by McLean, Johnson, Scott, and Sneed, leaving the defense team with only one alternative scenario for jury consumption: Lena was still "morally insane."

But what about Al? Would the prosecution dare call Al as a witness? Aside from the risk of precipitating a Wild West shootout between Al and Beal on the steps of the Fort Worth Courthouse, it was a close question. Al could have, if believed, refuted much of the

testimony the state anticipated Beal Sneed would offer—testimony
to the effect that Beal and Lena had a "happy home" and that Lena
was deeply in love with her husband prior to the affair; that Al had
seduced Lena by somehow causing her to become "morally insane."
Even more important, Al could have refuted the defense's contention that Colonel Boyce had somehow encouraged or approved of
his affair with Lena or had conspired to reunite them after Lena's
return from Canada.

On the other hand, the prosecution certainly anticipated that if
Al were put on the stand he would be subjected to devastating cross-
examination by Bill McLean in explaining his seduction of Lena,
the betrayal of his lifelong friend, Beal Sneed, and his callous indif-
ference to the grief the elopement caused to the children and other
members of all three families. Had this case been tried in twenty-
first-century America, most likely the jury would have adopted the
anti-Beal sentiment that the Winnipeg newspapers voiced. The jury
probably would have concluded that it was simply a case of a sane
woman who got tired of her steel-willed, cold, and unromantic husband and fell in love with another man who was much more romantic and compatible. Modern jurors likely would have viewed it as the
unfortunate and painful breakup of a marriage under circumstances
that provided Beal with sufficient grounds for a divorce action, but
certainly not justification for his premeditated murder of the par-
amour's unarmed father. Yet jurors in 1912 Texas, nourished from
birth in notions of Victorian patriarchy, took a decidedly different
viewpoint. That being the case, it was probably a wise decision to
leave Al in Canada.

The prosecution had two other very good reasons for keeping Al out of the courtroom. First, while the state wanted to keep
the jury focused on trying John Beal Sneed for the premeditated
murder of an elderly defenseless man, the defense was aggressively
dedicated to refocusing the jury's attention on trying anybody and
everybody else for various and sundry crimes—and Al Boyce would
have given the defense a very visible and vulnerable target. Second,
with U.S. District Attorney Atwell bought and paid for by Sneed, if
Al had come to Fort Worth, Atwell, no doubt, would have had him

arrested and jailed under the white slavery law before he could have mounted the witness stand.

Even with Al unavailable as a visual target, it was clear that McLean and company would lambaste him from the opening bell. How could the prosecution respond? How would the state explain its failure to call him as a witness? Would the prosecution seek to excuse Al's conduct? If so, how? In that Victorian milieu, it would be more than risky for the prosecution to attempt to whitewash Al Boyce. The best that the state could do was to take the position that Lena was sane and then lay at least some of the blame for the affair on her. As a result, the prosecution was forced to construct its case without the benefit of the testimony of Al, Colonel Boyce, and Ed Throckmorton. Or Lena.

The absence of Ed Throckmorton as a live witness prevented him from quoting Beal Sneed's last words to Colonel Boyce: "Now you're done for. You're out of it!" But that wasn't all. Throckmorton's absence also presented the defense with another rare bonanza of testimonial opportunity: perjury. And McLean and company hesitated not a moment to seize the advantage. With both Throckmorton and Boyce "out of it," the defense was free to concoct its own defense-friendly version of the fatal drama—what Colonel Boyce did or did not say or do, what Ed Throckmorton did or did not say or do, what Beal Sneed did or did not say or do, as well as assigning to Beal Sneed whatever sympathetic motive for killing the Colonel the defense might invent—and do all that without fear of contradiction or refutation. Sneed's team was also free to sponsor whatever other alleged eyewitnesses they could enlist, even those whose credibility was highly suspect, and some who were not even present at the time.

One such witness of suspect veracity was called by the defense to prove that Colonel Boyce had insulted Beal just prior to being shot. E. D. Powers claimed to have been in the hotel lobby at the time, and he testified that when Beal entered the lobby he heard Colonel Boyce exclaim, "Here comes the _____ now!" (The epithet

Colonel Boyce allegedly uttered was omitted by the *Star-Telegram* reporter in deference to the tender sensibilities of its readers.) The prosecution questioned the reliability of Powers's claim, and further doubt was cast on his veracity when the night after Powers testified, he got into a fistfight with a friend of the Boyce clan.

In rebuttal to the testimony of Powers, the prosecution called John W. Covey, a druggist who knew Colonel Boyce and who had ridden in the ambulance that carried the dying man to the hospital. Covey testified that he asked Colonel Boyce who shot him, and he replied, "Beal Sneed." Then Covey asked him if he and Sneed had had any words before shots were fired, to which Boyce replied, "Not a word."

It was at that point in the trial that the defense introduced through Lena's brother-in-law, the Clayton, New Mexico, attorney John Pace, the "stand hitched" letter that would become the focal point of much debate during the rest of the trial. As noted earlier, it had been written by Colonel Boyce to Pace under the misapprehension that Pace and his wife, Susan (Lena's sister), were aligned with Lena, and that, accordingly, Pace would pass it on to Lena but keep the message confidential. Instead, Pace delivered it to Beal Sneed. The letter was dated January 8, 1912. Lena had just returned from Canada, and only five days later, Beal again confined her to the Arlington Heights Sanitarium. That same day, Beal killed Colonel Boyce.

The defense team contended that the "stand hitched" letter evidenced a conspiracy on Colonel Boyce's part from the very beginning to encourage the romance between Al and Lena as well as a conspiracy to reunite the lovers and, in the process, destroy Beal Sneed's marriage and wreck his home. Despite the fact that this defense-friendly interpretation placed on Colonel Boyce's "stand hitched" letter seemed strained at best, ridiculous at worst, nevertheless, McLean made it a centerpiece of Beal's defense.

Meanwhile, the drama played to overflowing courtroom audiences, most of whom were women. To its credit, the *Fort Worth Star-Telegram*, in a leap forward for 1912 West Texas journalism, sent a female reporter, Kitty Barry, to cover the story from a woman's perspective.

Her job was not to report the straight news story about the trial as was the assignment of her male colleagues, but to write human-interest stories. Kitty Barry's comments, which ran as sidebars to the main stories, provided insightful observations about the character and personality of the principals as well as the dramatic human relationships and the interactions of the parties, all of which proved to be at least as interesting as the daily account of the official doings of those who were pulling the levers of the legal apparatus. Interesting and insightful as her reports were, there was about her interpretations a rather curious naiveté when she described the interests and motives of her own gender. Perhaps, in those pre-radio, pre-TV days, when the enormous female appetite for soap operas was as yet undiscovered, Kitty Barry's seeming puzzlement as to the women's reactions could be better understood. In remarks that may reveal more about Kitty Barry than the female spectators she described, Barry marveled that the females seemed to be very interested in the romantic and "personal" aspects of the unfolding courtroom drama and yet bored by the intellectual and legal issues presented. Barry, early in the trial, reported as follows:

> Curiosity seems to be the chief motive that brings women to the Sneed trial. They have not the excuse this early in the trial of enjoying the eloquence and intellectual display of the argument. The women present . . . do not belong to that rapidly growing class of American women who are proudly interested in all the phases of existence common to humanity. They do not appear to be women who come there for instruction in the inside working of the judiciary, because the expressions for the most part on their faces are frankly curious and not studiously analytical. This facial expression of curiosity intensifies when the evidence tends in any way toward involving personal issues and personal characteristics of the defendant. The fundamental feminine view is essentially personal. Only the woman student of books or of people and conditions can in any appreciable degree ally her attitude with the impersonal. The women at the Sneed trial do not seem to be able to do this in a successful degree, and only the personality of the trial strikes the fire of their attention. During the routine of the examinations they

are looking at the toes of their shoes or fumbling with their dress accessories or whispering very quietly to each other or calmly staring at people who sit in the enclosure in front of them.[16]

Barry further remarked on the "deterring effect" that the "proximity" of large numbers of female spectators had on all witnesses in this trial, particularly when a witness was called on to repeat profanity or to describe sexual activity and other delicate personal matters. She also reported the instances when Judge Swayne, anticipating specific, sexually charged testimony, cleared the courtroom of females.

One afternoon when Judge Swayne anticipated that sexually explicit testimony "unfit for the ears of women" would be elicited the following morning, he informed the spectators that women would be excluded from the courtroom. That order turned out to be about as effective as throwing chunks of bloody raw meat into a pond and then forbidding the sharks to attack. A dozen or more women ignored the order and showed up bright and early, determined not to miss a word of it. The deputy sheriff repeated Judge Swayne's warning, but the determined females refused to be deterred. They barged in anyway. Ultimately Judge Swayne had to call in more deputies in order to get rid of them.

The testimony "unfit for female ears" turned out to be some of those statutorily addressed "insulting words" referring to a "female relative." Namely, what Colonel Boyce allegedly said about Lena. It was at this point in the trial that McLean unveiled a clever hybrid strategy, blending the written law and the unwritten law. While his ultimate goal was a "not guilty" verdict based on the unwritten law, he now relied on the written law as a steppingstone to get there. The "insulting words" statute afforded McLean a legal basis to introduce testimony about any insulting words that Colonel Boyce was alleged to have said about Lena. Otherwise such offensive remarks would not have been admissible, and the prosecution could have kept them out of evidence with irrelevancy objections. True, the "insulting words" statute was not an exonerating statute—it simply reduced the killing from murder to manslaughter—but it permitted McLean to put Colonel Boyce on trial before the jury while, at the same time, adding emotional ballast to the defense's "honor code" appeal.

The witness who was to pass along Colonel Boyce's uncouth remarks about Lena to the jury undoubtedly relished his role. He was none other than Colonel Boyce's bitter enemy from years past who had long awaited such an opportunity: W. H. Fuqua, president of the First National Bank in Amarillo, and the man whom Colonel Boyce had personally—and successfully—confronted when Fuqua attempted to take over the XIT ranch as its receiver.

Fuqua was then permitted to tell the jury the same "insulting words" story he had previously related to Beal Sneed. Although Fuqua recited the exact words he claimed the Colonel used in the Amarillo drugstore in December 1911, none of the Fort Worth or Dallas papers reported the quote, explaining to readers that the language was simply "unprintable."

Fuqua had landed a telling blow on his old nemesis, but he wasn't done yet. The defense next proposed to introduce a maudlin letter crammed full of self-pity that Beal had written to Fuqua on November 23, 1911, while Beal and his detectives were in pursuit of Lena and Al. The prosecution vigorously objected to the letter as being nothing more than a "self-serving declaration" as well as hearsay and contended that if Beal wanted to burden the jury with such sentimental tripe, he should take the stand himself and subject his testimony to proper objections on direct examination and then defend it on cross-examination. Judge Swayne appeared to be on the verge of sustaining the state's objection when crafty McLean took a different tack. He conceded that allowing Fuqua to read what somebody else wrote (Beal Sneed in this case) was undeniably hearsay; however, McLean claimed, he was offering the letter into evidence under an exception to the hearsay rule that permitted him to show Beal's state of mind. This, McLean continued, was relevant because later in the trial he was going to introduce testimony proving that Sneed was temporarily insane when he pulled the trigger. With that rather dubious assurance Judge Swayne finally, and unwisely, relented and allowed it. Even more surprising, the obsequious prosecution withdrew its objection at the last moment and agreed to let Fuqua read Beal's letter to the jury:

> I want to thank you from the bottom of my heart for what you have done for me. I have thought and thought and tried to think and I don't see why God wants me to suffer and suffer and yet live . . . You know I love the little children and would gladly give my life for them. But she loved them more than I, and I will always know that had she been herself she would have stood to be burned and tortured to death before she would have heaped this ignominy and disgrace on their little lives . . . [S]he would sympathize with me and help me as no one else could, instead of killing me by degrees . . . I am sure it will be only a matter of time until she will be the most miserable of human beings and probably become more insane. Or should she recover her mind by some act of Providence she would be just as miserable and probably destroy herself . . . You may think this is a crazy letter, and it may be, but at the same time I feel that you will come nearer understanding the motive which prompted it than anyone else, and that is the reason I have written.[17]

With friend Fuqua's assistance, counselor McLean's cunning connivance, and the combined gullibility of Judge Swayne and prosecutor Hanger, John Beal Sneed was allowed to soar to yet unexplored depths of self-promotion and self-pity. McLean never got around to honoring his representation to Judge Swayne that he would eventually present substantive evidence that Sneed was temporarily insane when he pulled the trigger. In retrospect, it became clear that McLean's assertion that Beal's letter to Fuqua was being offered as a prelude to a temporary insanity defense for Sneed was only a smokescreen to obscure the real purpose—two other purposes in fact. First, it was a clever device to allow a third-party witness (Fuqua) to strum the jurors' heartstrings for that self-sacrificing martyr John Beal Sneed, and do so without interruption or bothersome cross-examination that the author of those words (Sneed) would have been subjected to had he taken the stand and read his letter. More importantly, however, it allowed a third-party

W. H. FUQUA, president of the First National Bank of Amarillo, was a close friend of John Beal Sneed and a bitter enemy of Colonel Albert G. Boyce, Sr. *Photograph courtesy of the Panhandle-Plains Historical Museum, Canyon, Texas.*

witness to lay the groundwork, not only for Beal Sneed's alleged temporary insanity, but also for Lena's alleged moral insanity. Thus, through Fuqua, Sneed was able to present to the jury his own unsubstantiated, inexpert, self-serving diagnosis of Lena's moral insanity. By now it had become apparent that Lena's moral insanity was to be the keystone of McLean's defensive strategy.

U.S. Attorney W. H. Atwell was a key defense witness.[18] He testified that shortly after Lena and Al disappeared, Beal employed him to locate them, apprehend them, and prosecute Al, her "abductor." Atwell began his duties by exercising his authority as a federal prosecutor to order a "watch" put on all U.S. mail exchanged by Boyce family members. Although he denied it on the stand, it turned out that either he or postal inspectors under his authority did more than just note names and addresses on the envelopes—they opened the letters and read the contents. Colonel Boyce had noticed that his letters were being opened and complained to the postmaster. The Amarillo postmaster, W. H. Ingerton, would later testify that the Boyce letters were opened by "someone in Dallas." That, unsurprisingly, was the location of U.S. Attorney Atwell's office. However, no prosecution of this patently illegal act was ever pursued—which came as no surprise because nobody expected Atwell to prosecute himself. The next day's edition of the *Dallas Dispatch* newspaper featured a scorching editorial demanding a congressional investigation of this fundamental violation of a citizen's rights by the federal government, but nothing ever came of it.

The next thing that federal prosecutor Atwell did was to appear before the state grand jury in Fort Worth in aid of state prosecutors who, as already noted, succeeded in getting Al Boyce indicted for abduction, rape, and kidnapping.

Realizing that these charges could be defeated if Lena were found to be sane and testified that Al had not abducted, raped, or kidnapped her, or stolen her jewelry, Atwell admitted that he then set the wheels of the federal judiciary in motion to have a federal indictment returned against Al Boyce charging him with violation of the federal white slavery statute prohibiting the transportation of a female across a state line "for immoral purposes." The distinct advantage of this prosecution was that it was immaterial whether Lena was or was not crazy or whether she did or did not consent to Al transporting her across state lines "for immoral purposes," or whether she did or did not consent to having sexual relations with him.

Atwell then gave his account of the evening of January 13, 1912, when Colonel Boyce was killed in the lobby of the Metropolitan Hotel. It was the same day that Colonel Boyce had succeeded in persuading state prosecutors to dismiss the state indictments against Al. According to Atwell's version of events, when he, Beal Sneed, and Henry Bowman came through the lobby, they observed Colonel Boyce and Throckmorton sitting and visiting. Colonel Boyce called Atwell aside and said he wanted to discuss the white slavery indictment Atwell was seeking. Atwell said that Colonel Boyce contended that he "could prove in half an hour what kind of woman Mrs. Sneed was." Atwell declined to discuss the case but said he told Boyce he would give him an opportunity to appear before the federal grand jury. Although Atwell was then under employment by Beal Sneed as his private attorney, he assured Colonel Boyce that his actions with respect to the white slavery prosecution of Al "would have to be determined" by his "own official heart."[19] On that less-than-reassuring note he took leave of Colonel Boyce.

Later, during the evening meal at nearby Joseph's Café, Beal, Atwell, and Bowman discussed the Sneed case, although exactly what was said would be the subject of considerable speculation. Atwell said that they discussed the likelihood that the Boyce family would hire attorneys to file a habeas corpus proceeding seeking to have Lena declared sane and thereby released from the asylum where Sneed had recommitted her earlier that day. One of the important issues that would be addressed during the trial was whether, during that evening meal, either Atwell or Bowman repeated to Beal any of those insulting words about Lena that Colonel Boyce was alleged to have said. (It will be recalled that to come within the scope of the "insulting words" statute the defendant was required to kill the insulter the first time he encountered him after hearing about the insulting words.) After the meal, they departed. As they passed the Metropolitan Hotel, Atwell testified that Beal went inside, saying he needed to go to the toilet. That was when he entered the lobby and killed Boyce.

On cross-examination, Senator Hanger, predictably, attacked Atwell for his blatant conflict of interest. He began by asking Atwell to describe each action he had taken in the Sneed case, then followed that by asking whether each of those acts was performed in his role as a federal prosecutor or in his role as Beal Sneed's private attorney. Atwell proved to be an exceedingly slippery fellow to pin down, and Senator Hanger proved he was no "Wild Bill" McLean in forcing a reluctant witness to give a direct answer to an embarrassing question. In the end, he let Atwell slide by, loftily pontificating, "My two duties were entirely harmonious and moved along together."[20]

Then, too, Atwell suffered numerous memory lapses when Senator Hanger seemed to be on the verge of making an important point.

Atwell added two other defense-friendly tidbits to his testimony. During their evening meal, he said that they discussed Colonel Boyce's "stand hitched" letter. He also added that he told Sneed about the brief conversation he had just had with Colonel Boyce in the hotel lobby. Atwell contended that Ed Throckmorton had butted into the conversation and asserted, "Hell, they [Lena and Al] will be back together in thirty days." Atwell claimed that Colonel Boyce then said, "Well, they will but let's not discuss that now."[21] That particular exchange among Atwell, Throckmorton, and Colonel Boyce has a distinctly contrived ring to it; sounds very much like an after-the-fact fabrication that was tailored to neatly fit McLean's contention that Colonel Boyce supported the affair from the beginning, or at least approved of Al and Lena getting back together—especially since neither Colonel Boyce nor Ed Throckmorton were available to challenge the assertion.

Hanger continued his cross-examination by calling Atwell's attention to a news article that appeared the day after the killing. It was written by the *Dallas Times-Herald* city editor, E. R. Hambrick. In the article Hambrick reported to his readers that he had interviewed Atwell immediately after the shooting, and he quoted Atwell as saying that the reason Sneed killed Colonel Boyce was that he was angry about Colonel Boyce's success in getting the state indictments against Al dismissed earlier that day. Such an assertion was definitely at odds with the explanation Beal's defense team was now trying to sell to the jury. Obviously, when Atwell gave that interview to the newsman, he hadn't yet been schooled on the defense team's official story line. It just wouldn't do for the jury to believe that a member of the defense team had admitted that revenge was Beal's motive. Atwell was therefore caught in a very tight place during Hanger's cross-examination. He had to do some hasty backpedaling. Unsurprisingly, he flatly denied that he had made such a statement during the Hambrick interview. But he went a bit too far by adding that Hambrick, whom he described as "an honorable man," if asked, would verify the fact that Atwell had not made the statement.

But he was wrong about that. The state later called Hambrick to the stand, and Hambrick proceeded to verify under oath that Atwell had indeed made that statement.

Next the defense called Henry Bowman, Beal Sneed's own Sancho Panza, the "prominent mule trader" from Plano who was married to Lena's sister Eula. The highlight of Bowman's testimony was a heart-rending description of the dreary 1911 Christmas at the Bowman home after Lena and Al had eloped but before their whereabouts were discovered. Bowman described tearful scenes during which Lena's two daughters clung to Beal while crying for their mother.

Bowman also testified that after Lena was released from the asylum, she wanted to come to the Bowman home to visit her children but that he had advised against it. He reminded her that Plano was a small town and that her children were enrolled in school there. Bowman warned Lena that if she came, her children would be embarrassed by questions other school children would ask about her. On cross-examination, Bowman admitted that he had never heard Colonel Boyce threaten to kill Sneed. When Hanger asked if he had ever heard Sneed threaten Al Boyce, Jr., Bowman responded, "I heard him say a number of times that he would kill Al Boyce anywhere, anytime he found him—or would get killed."

Finally, the whole trial refocused on the issue of the motives. It was Lena's motives—whether driven by sanity or insanity—that lay at the heart of the case. Both the prosecution and the defense took turns painting a picture of Lena to suit their competing versions not only of her motives but also of the resulting motives and actions of the other three principals.

It was now evident that John Beal Sneed was going to testify. It was also clear that his entire defense hinged on his ability to convince the jury that Lena was "morally insane" and had been driven so by Al Boyce. That, in turn, required a recall of Beal's moral insanity expert, Dr. John S. Turner, to lay the groundwork for Beal Sneed's story. As expected, Dr. Turner's opinion hadn't changed:

Lena was still insane. Upon cross-examination Senator Hanger asked Dr. Turner whether he still contended that Lena was "morally insane." In reply, Dr. Turner offered this startling clarification: "Moral insanity is only one element. I mean she is morally, physically, and mentally insane."[22]

What sweeping vistas of cross-examination explorations that gift to the prosecution offered; what low-hanging plums ripe for the picking dangled from that plum tree! A skillful cross-examination could have underscored the fact that Dr. Turner had previously testified that Lena had suffered only from moral insanity, but her condition must have taken a terrible turn for the worse. She was not only morally insane, now she was mentally and physically insane as well. Hanger should have nailed him right then and there, demanding that Turner explain the differences. The symptoms of each? The causes? The treatments? The prognosis for each? Authorities relied on? And on and on. Hanger, however, continued to slumber in peace while that train pulled out of the station. He did ask Dr. Turner what his view would be if he were put in an asylum against his will. Turner rather lamely contended that he would think his relatives "had taken the charitable view of the matter, even if pellagra patients and maniacs were about." On redirect questioning, Cone Johnson rode to Dr. Turner's rescue by attempting to establish that moral insanity was a recognized form of insanity. On recross, Hanger at last got around to asking Dr. Turner if he knew of any authorities that authenticated "moral insanity," but the doctor gave only vague and evasive answers, and Hanger finally let it drop. The foundation for Beal's dramatic appearance on the witness stand was thus laid by Dr. Turner.

At last John Beal Sneed took center stage. It was obvious that he had learned his lines well, and it took little prompting from his dramatic coach, "Wild Bill" McLean, to give a performance worthy of a Shakespearean tragedy. It was also of enormous assistance to his cause that he could testify to almost anything he chose without fear of contradiction by Colonel Boyce, Ed Throckmorton, Al Boyce, or Lena.

The McLean-Johnson-Scott-Sneed team had an ace in the hole that it played with great dramatic effect. Sneed brought his two young daughters to the court and seated them with the defense team just a few feet from the jury. Nobody in that day saw anything inappropriate about subjecting young children to such a traumatizing ordeal. Clearly, standards of sensitivity had not yet evolved much past the Dark Ages. It was, after all, a time when public hangings attracted large crowds, and parents often brought their children along, considering the spectacle good family entertainment. And so, with the stage properly set, his lines down pat, the curtain went up, and the show began.

Highlights of John Beal Sneed's testimony were as follows: First he described the fateful night, October 13, 1911, when Lena told him of her affair with Al Boyce and demanded a divorce, revealing that she and Al planned to flee to South America with one or both of the children. After that revelation, Beal testified that they went into the bedroom and talked. The *Star-Telegram* article reported Beal's account of the dramatic confrontation:

> "I appealed to her"—as he reached this part of the narrative Sneed's lips twitched beyond his control, his eyes were wet and he spoke with difficulty, being obliged to pause momentarily to control himself before going on. "In such broken sentences, I told her of our home. I told her of our children, of our struggles—finally, I realized that my wife was serious." Again his eyes filled. "She told me she never had loved me; she would give up the children if she couldn't take them; that she didn't want anything but to go and live with this man the rest of her life."[23]

Finally, Beal continued, after spending sleepless hours that night talking, crying, and trying to get Lena to give him some reason for her infatuation with Al, he pulled his pistol. "I was so desperate, or wrought up, or was not myself, I do not know what . . . I started to kill her. She grabbed hold of me, and trying to get her loose from me so I could kill her and then myself, she screamed several times, and the elder little girl ran into the room, and caught hold of the pistol and I put it up."

True to form, as McLean and Beal must have expected, Senator Hanger sat quietly on the sideline and observed while McLean tossed Beal softballs, then got out of the way. Beal was left free to soliloquize and rhapsodize about the traumatic ordeal he had survived through his heroic struggles, meanwhile volunteering all sorts of inadmissible testimony. In a trial, interrogation of witnesses is supposed to be conducted by a question-and-answer technique— the questions asked are supposed to be specific and the answers supposed to be responsive and confined to the scope of the question. But Hanger raised no objections—thus letting his adversaries get away with testimonial murder.

Beal next told the jury about the conversation he'd had with his father after the elder Sneed found out about the scandal; told how his father had advised him to "wash his hands of Lena and let her go," warning that it was something he had to do because "people won't respect you if you don't." For the jury's benefit, Beal put a most altruistic spin on his motivation for rejecting his father's advice—one that had nothing to do with getting even with Lena or Al, and had nothing at all to do with salving his bruised ego. Beal explained it this way to the jury: he rejected his father's advice because he believed that Lena was "mentally unbalanced" (caused by Al Boyce) and therefore not responsible for her infidelity, and that he felt he owed it to her and the children to try to restore her sanity. Then (offering more hearsay), Beal revealed that his father told him that Colonel Boyce and his wife had known of the affair for some time but had done nothing to stop it and that the Boyce family "had done wrong to let it go on as they did."

When McLean asked Beal what kind of a home he built for Lena, Beal modestly explained: "I tried to fix it like my wife wanted it—I put in about $10,000 [roughly $230,000 in 2009 dollars]. I furnished it the best I could. My wife liked nice things, and it always gave me a pleasure to give them to her." Beal then went on to embellish his account of his happy home that had been despoiled by that hard-drinking Al Boyce whose family supported him in his lechery, and of the terrible suffering this caused both himself and the children.

Adding yet more hearsay to his tale of woe, Beal testified that while Lena was in Arlington Heights, Dr. Turner advised him that it would be better if he didn't visit her. Beal shared with the jury his anguish at having to commit Lena to a sanitarium in order to rehabilitate her and then being forbidden by Dr. Turner to visit her there. "I would rather see her than anybody else in the world," Beal claimed he told Dr. Turner, "but my wishes and desires are not to be considered at all—I can walk on my heart for the rest of my life if it is for her good."

That Beal's testimony was scoring points not only with the jury and the spectators but also with the press is evidenced by this quote from the next day's *Fort Worth Star-Telegram*:

> The defendant is making a great witness, his lawyers say, and the same sentiment is expressed by those who heard him. No juror has had to tell him to speak louder, for his enunciation is clear, although at times his voice broke as he told of his wife and her infatuation for "that man." The jurors . . . and every spectator craned his [*sic*] neck in expectancy in order to miss no word of the tragedy from the lips of the central figure.[24]

After Lena eloped with Al, Beal had a conversation with his friend W. H. Fuqua back in Amarillo, and it was then that Fuqua quoted Colonel Boyce's crude remarks about Lena. Beal testified that Fuqua told him (more hearsay) that Colonel Boyce had "said things about my wife that he wouldn't have said about a prostitute."[25]

The next topic of Beal's testimony focused on the bleak Christmas of 1911 at the Bowman home when his oldest daughter begged to see her mother. He told Lenora that her mother had "lost her mind and run away." The *Star-Telegram* attributed this quote to Sneed:

> On Christmas day, Lenora put her arms around my neck, and all the toys I gave her couldn't satisfy her. She said that everybody had a mother but her, and begged me to bring her mother back. I told her I didn't know where her mother was, but I would try.[26]

Beal also testified that when he went to Canada to retrieve Lena, he took one of their daughter Georgia's baby shoes with him. When he gave it to Lena, it "wrung her heart" and she tied it around her neck and wore it, then took it off and "crushed it and cried over it" in his presence. Both of Beal's young daughters were conspicuously present in front of the jury while he was relating these soul-wrenching episodes.

In view of what we know from letters, documents, and other sources that were not introduced into evidence during the trial (as well as subsequent conduct of the parties), John Beal Sneed's next jury story sounds, suspiciously enough, much more like John Beal Sneed and "Wild Bill" McLean than it does Lena. Beal claimed that when he met Lena in Winnipeg, she made a confession to him; she said that with the connivance and support of Al, Henry Boyce, and Colonel Boyce, she had planned to sneak back to Plano and steal her daughters away from the Bowman home and take them back to Canada to live with her and Al. (Blatant hearsay—thrusting gut deep into the state's case.) Had Hanger been cast in the same mold as "Wild Bill" McLean, he would undoubtedly have roared an objection, probably adding a McLean-like sidebar comment to his hearsay objection such as: "If Lena was sane enough to be believed such a short time ago, then how come she is not sane enough at this time for the defense to put her on the stand and let her tell us all about this childnapping scheme? Can we not hear it straight from the mare's mouth?"

Beal next testified about the letters of support that Henry Boyce and Colonel Boyce had written to Lena after her return from Canada but prior to the time Beal recommitted her to Arlington Heights, including Colonel Boyce's "stand hitched" letter, which the defense argued proved that Colonel Boyce was conspiring to reunite Lena and Al. That Beal Sneed's performance completely captivated Kitty Barry can be gauged in her almost reverential sidebar account appearing in the next day's *Star-Telegram*:

> He spoke with a monotonously even tone, with a low but perfectly audible pitch, and the resonance peculiar to a strong masculine voice. Only the closest attention could detect changes in the tone-placing, but the effort of emotional control . . . produced subtle differences.

His voice never broke when he told how certain friends and relatives had tried to persuade him to abandon the idea of getting his wife back and how he had refused to listen to the persuasion. The words came with a labored effort, however, as if each one had been slightly jerked before it left his lips. When he answered the question as to how he treated his wife by saying that all his life he had given her the best he could, and that whatever he was or had was due to her, he made it a simple statement of fact, and without the least suggestion of boasting or self-vindication.

. . . Mr. Sneed had the sympathetic attention of the jurymen from the moment he began speaking until the judge adjourned the session.[27]

Kitty Barry reported that many men in the courtroom took out their handkerchiefs, wiped their eyes, and "looked downward with flushed faces" when Beal recounted the desolate 1911 Christmas with his children at the Bowman home while Al and Lena were gaily cavorting about in parts unknown. The reporter added that while Beal related the 1911 Christmas episode to the jury, his two daughters were "sobbing their little eyes out."

In a telling (although, no doubt, unwitting) comment on the effectiveness of the Sneed-McLean defense performance as contrasted with the ineffectiveness of the somnolent prosecution team, the credulous Barry made this observation:

There were no noticeable interruptions in Mr. Sneed's testimony. The [prosecutors] sat about quietly and gave their most minute attention to the things he was saying. Mr. McLean, who manifested considerable feelings at times, put his queries in the most considerate way possible, doing nothing more than gently directing the course of the evidence.[28]

Barry noted that throughout this emotional narrative, all the desultory prosecution team did was to scribble a few notes. The public relations battle as well as the battle for jury sympathy had just taken a hard right in the direction of the defense.

In McLean's final questions to Sneed before cutting him loose for
cross-examination, he asked Sneed if he had any intention of shooting Colonel Boyce when he returned to the hotel lobby that night.
Predictably, Sneed denied having any such intention. Beal testified
that when he reentered the lobby he heard somebody make a "vile"
remark. The vile remark was the same epithet that E. D. Powers, the
defense-sponsored witness of suspect veracity, had previously claimed
to have heard. It was a remark that nobody else in the lobby seemed
to have heard, including Ed Throckmorton who had testified in the
earlier bond hearing that no words were spoken before Beal started
shooting. It was also contrary to Colonel Boyce's dying declaration:
no words had been spoken by anybody before and during Beal's
rampage. In any event, relying on the silence of Throckmorton and
Boyce plus the dubious testimony of Powers to lay the groundwork
and bolster his own credibility, Beal Sneed repeated the alleged vile
remark attributed to Colonel Boyce. Although he repeated it verbatim
in open court, the *Star-Telegram* account deleted the offensive words,
characterizing it as a "vile" remark, and reported it as follows:

> I heard somebody say: "There comes the _____." I looked to
> the left and saw Boyce and Throckmorton rising from their chairs.
> I pulled my pistol and commenced firing as fast as I could.[29]

While the unwritten law (which included "protecting the
home") remained Beal Sneed's primary defense, he made at least a
cursory stab at raising a legal justification for killing Colonel Boyce:
self-defense. Contradicting an earlier explanation, he now claimed
that after hearing the Colonel's "vile" remark, he turned and saw
both Boyce and Throckmorton rising from their seats, and therefore "supposed they were going to attack" and so opened fire.

McLean apparently still wasn't satisfied with Sneed's "motive"
explanation, so he gave him another shot at it. This time Beal did much
better. In a response—one that had to have been well rehearsed—
Beal "brokenly," as noted in the *Star-Telegram* account, replied:

> I thought like a flash of how he had helped that man take my wife
> away, of what I had gone through to bring her back, and how now,

he was wanting to get her away from me again and send her back
to the life of shame from which I had rescued her. I went—I went
all to pieces and commenced shooting.[30]

McLean would argue that this part of Beal's testimony redeemed
McLean's previous representation to Judge Swayne that later in the
trial he would offer evidence that would raise the issue of temporary
insanity. Judge Swayne, however, didn't agree that this testimony rose
to the level of temporary insanity and so refused, in his jury instructions, to submit "temporary insanity" as a possible justification.

With that, McLean cut Sneed loose and turned him over to
Hanger for cross-examination. Without doubt, the cross-examination
of the wily John Beal Sneed would have been a formidable task for
even the most skilled trial lawyer. Still, Hanger's attempt was almost
a textbook example of how not to cross-examine an important, hostile witness. The questions, which were often vague and open-ended,
simply invited Beal to avoid giving direct answers and allowed him
to give rambling, self-serving explanations. For example, Hanger
asked Sneed if he hadn't told Al's and Lena's Canadian attorney, T.
J. Murray, that if he (Sneed) had Murray in Texas he would "blow the
top of his head off." (Murray had angered Sneed by, among other
things, insisting on talking with his client, Lena, outside of Sneed's
presence.) Instead of forcing Sneed to give a responsive "yes" or
"no" answer, Hanger allowed him to evade the question. Not only
that, he let Sneed deliver a self-serving speech. Sneed answered, "I
will explain it. They told me up there [Canada] that there was no
law against a man living with another man's wife; that they had not
the same high standards of morals . . . I knew if a man got into
trouble up there the way they regarded home and honor, it would
be different from anywhere in the South."[31] Hanger let it go at
that—and drifted off down another path. The newspaper reporter
covering the trial that day made an observation that not only underscored Hanger's inept questioning but also clearly showed that
Beal Sneed and McLean had already converted the press to their
side. The public relations battle had been won. In commenting on
Hanger's cross-examination, the reporter said: "The much abused

newspaper men, who have followed the trial, had themselves been put to the limit to keep track of the questions started—dropped, half connected and jumbled around."[32]

The closest Hanger came to scoring was when he asked Beal if he hadn't employed U.S. Attorney Will Atwell, "because of his influence with the federal mail inspectors," in intercepting the Boyces' mail. Beal replied that he "wanted all the help he could give me," then lamely hastened to add, "I wouldn't say that I was influenced by any influence he might have because of his office."[33] Hanger then dropped the subject.

John Beal Sneed was the final witness for the defense.

Protecting a Home
or Protecting a Killer?

The Conclusion of the 1912
John Beal Sneed Murder Trial

IN SPORTS CONTESTS, there comes a time during most games when the momentum shifts to one of the teams. At that point it is crucial for the other team to reinvigorate, to shift strategies, to seize the initiative and stop that momentum before the game turns into a rout. So it is with most hotly contested jury trials. That crucial point in the Sneed murder trial came when McLean concluded his direct examination of John Beal Sneed. Beal's virtuoso performance, enhanced by the tearful accompaniment of his two daughters, had been carefully orchestrated; it hit all the right notes at the right time to captivate the hearts and minds of the rural and unsophisticated jurors imbued with Victorian values. When McLean ended his direct examination and announced, "No further questions," momentum was clearly with the defense. It was now or never for the prosecution.

It was also precisely at that point that an excellent opportunity was presented to the prosecution to turn the tide by attacking the Achilles' heel of the defense: Lena's alleged moral insanity. Beal's carefully scripted portrayal of himself as the heroic, self-sacrificing martyr depended on convincing the jury that Lena had been—and

still was—morally insane. Failing that, the entire defense structure
was likely to collapse.

Had Senator Hanger been a perceptive and skilled cross-examiner he would have put some very embarrassing—and deflating—
questions to Beal, queries that called for a "yes" or "no," and then
forced Beal to give direct, responsive answers. And when Beal
started his usual evasions and explanations, he would have immediately interrupted him and repeated the question. If Beal again
attempted to dodge the question, he would have interrupted again,
and this time requested Judge Swayne to instruct the witness to give
direct and responsive answers, and limit his answers to the scope of
the question. There is nothing quite like a witness who continues to
evade answering simple, direct questions that causes that witness to
lose credibility before a jury.

By asking simple yes-or-no questions, Hanger could have forced
Beal to make a number of damaging admissions, casting much
doubt about Lena's alleged moral insanity. Questions that would
force Beal to admit the following: that there had been no judicial
determination that Lena was insane when Beal originally had her
committed to the asylum; that there had been no judicial determination that she was insane when he had her recommitted; that when
Lena finally forced a sanity trial, the presiding judge, District Judge
Tom Simmons, heard Lena herself testify as well as three doctors
who all testified that she was sane; that the defense expert, Dr. John
Turner, also testified at that hearing and told Judge Simmons that
he believed Lena was insane, but that Judge Simmons didn't believe
him; that the judge then found Lena sane and ordered her released
from the asylum; that Judge Simmons made the determination that
Lena was sane on January 19, 1912, less than a month ago; that Beal
and his attorneys must have believed that Lena was sane five days ago
when they subpoenaed her to testify in this case, but Mr. McLean
now tells this court that the defense isn't going to call Lena as a witness because everybody on the defense team now believes that she is
insane; therefore please tell us on which of those past five days after
the defense issued the subpoena did Lena lose her sanity. Finally, he
might have ended with this question: Isn't it a fact, Mr. Sneed, that

the real reason your defense team decided not to call Mrs. Sneed to testify in this trial and let the jury hear what she has to say is that she refused to testify the way you wanted her to?

After Senator Hanger finished this cross-examination of Beal, Hanger should have immediately called as the state's first rebuttal witnesses Dr. R. O. Braswell and the other two doctors who testified for Lena at the sanity hearing. All three experts could have again certified Lena's sanity. (The state did eventually call Dr. Braswell to testify, but he was the last witness in the entire trial—much too late to have enough jury impact.) Then Hanger should have called District Judge Tom Simmons and let him tell the jury that he presided over Lena's sanity hearing, heard her testify, and concluded that Lena was sane. Judge Simmons would most likely have made a dynamite witness for the prosecution. Hanger should have called on the judge to repeat the statement he made at the conclusion of the sanity hearing:

> After hearing this testimony, I could not conclude that there was a semblance of insanity developed here in this case.

Finally, Hanger should have called the district clerk who, at McLean's request, had issued a subpoena for Lena to appear in this trial as a defense witness, and he should have required the district clerk to produce her official subpoena register to evidence that fact in black and white.

But Hanger and the prosecution failed to identify and attack the Achilles' heel of the defense by demonstrating that Lena was not morally, mentally, or physically insane, and that Beal, McLean, and the rest of the defense team had fabricated this scam to hoodwink the jury. During the remainder of the trial, and especially during final arguments, the prosecution could have used this potent ammunition to hammer home the message that Lena did not elope with Al Boyce because she was insane; she eloped with Al for a very rational reason—she wanted to escape from a tyrannical husband who falsely accused her of insanity and then had her locked up to keep her from being with the man she loved.

The prosecution did have some lesser weapons in its arsenal to fire during the state's rebuttal. These were directed primarily to prove that Colonel Boyce had done nothing initially to encourage Al Boyce's love affair with Lena nor had he done anything after Beal brought Lena back from Canada to encourage a rekindling of the affair. The state introduced a letter written by Colonel Boyce just eight days before his death. It was addressed to a friend in Chicago who apparently was close to President William Howard Taft. Concerned for Al's safety, Colonel Boyce urged U.S. federal intervention to pressure Canadian authorities not to deport Al. In the letter he expressed bitterness toward U.S. Attorney Will Atwell for his "active part in the affair" and toward Lena: "She is no more insane than I am; she is mean as the devil and smart as a whip. After [Beal] placed her [in the sanitarium] she wrote Albert . . . to come and get her away . . . hence this elopement is the consequence." He went on to state that he and Mrs. Boyce wanted Al liberated but kept in Canada where he would be safe and beyond reach of either Beal or Lena. Canadian authorities could be assured, the Colonel added, that Al would "make them a good citizen." He added this plaintive note: "This affair has wholly unnerved Mrs. Boyce, and she has become in a bad condition, and absolutely refuses to be comforted."[1]

STATE SENATOR WILLIAM A. HANGER was one of the special prosecutors hired by the Boyce family to prosecute John Beal Sneed for killing Colonel Albert G. Boyce. *Photograph courtesy of Texas A&M University Press.*

Al's brother, Henry Boyce, also took the stand. He emphatically denied that either he or Colonel Boyce had any part in any conspiracy to encourage or aid Al in either beginning or continuing his affair with Lena. On the contrary, he pointed out that his father had expressed his hope that Al would stay in Canada, "regain his senses," and end the romance.

An example of the defense's grandstanding tactics in adding inadmissible and inflammatory sidebar remarks to its objections occurred when the state offered a hearsay statement purported to have been made by Al Boyce. Cone Johnson objected that the question called for a hearsay answer, adding that there existed no rules of evidence to permit "secondhand testimony of this man who had debauched the defendant's wife, and who is still alive with two good legs, and who is way up in Canada."[2] Although Senator Hanger was to blame for frequently failing to make objections to such inadmissible comments, Judge Swayne was clearly at fault for allowing McLean and Johnson to repeatedly get away with those outrageous sidebar outbursts.

CONE JOHNSON, unsuccessful Texas gubernatorial candidate in 1912, but a spellbinding orator and highly effective trial lawyer whom John Beal Sneed employed to represent him in his two Fort Worth murder trials. *Photograph courtesy of Texas A&M University Press.*

Finally it came time for the testimony of Annie Boyce, Colonel Boyce's widow, and *Fort Worth Star-Telegram* reporter Kitty Barry was much impressed.

> She belongs to the pioneer type of American womanhood who could stand by the side of the fighters and load muskets while she saw her loved ones being shot down around her. No more magnificent evidence of the courage of the freeborn American woman had ever been given in their state.[3]

A packed courtroom watched as the slight figure took the witness stand, and, sitting very erect, began her story. A widow's veil completely concealed her hair and hung down about her head and shoulders. She was dressed very simply in black with not a single accessory relieving the dull mourning color. She gave her testimony directly to the jury in clear, emphatic tones, and her words could be easily heard in the farthest corner of the courtroom. She enforced her dramatic statements with gestures made by a closed black fan held in her right hand. When Judge Swayne expressed his concern by telling Mrs. Boyce that she might be kept on the witness stand for a long time and offered to call recesses to relieve her stress, she politely refused his offer. "This is the last thing I can do for Mr. Boyce—I am willing to stay here all day," she told the jury. Continuing, she said that she and Colonel Boyce feared that the affair could only lead to disaster and they did everything they could think of to break up the romance between Lena and Al. Of her son Al she said: "There was never a better boy . . . He took less correction than any of the other children; he was considerate of others and slow to get angry or censure anyone, but when his mind was set, he could not be changed." She had, she related, remonstrated with Al, telling him this: "This is not New York City. This is not the Four Hundred Society. I do not think Beal Sneed would like this. This is imprudent!" But to no effect, she said. "This woman had influenced him, and he wouldn't obey me or Mr. Boyce . . . I felt like taking Lena across my knees and beating her."[4]

Annie Boyce further testified that shortly after Lena told Beal she was in love with Al and wanted a divorce, she (Annie) observed that Lena was "terribly bruised." Mrs. Boyce also verified that the Boyces' mail had been opened prior to delivery after Al and Lena eloped.

But the most important testimony the state wanted to elicit from Annie Boyce was blocked by McLean's hearsay objections. Unlike Senator Hanger, who sat placidly with nary an objection while John Beal Sneed piled hearsay on top of hearsay, "Wild Bill" McLean was not about to cut the prosecution any slack. When the prosecution attempted to relate several key conversations between Annie Boyce and Lena that had occurred before Beal discovered the affair, McLean interrupted: "Hearsay, your honor!" The judge finally ended up ruling that Mrs. Boyce could recount what she said to Lena, but not what Lena said to her in reply. "I don't see why I can't tell the whole story," she complained to Judge Swayne. This incomplete and one-sided conversation testimony was frustrating to the prosecution but better than nothing.

She was allowed to tell the jury this much: that the Colonel and Mrs. Boyce first discovered the affair on July 22, 1911. Afterward she had several conversations with Lena, warning her about her bad judgment and the risks she and Al were taking. "Oh, Lena, I didn't think it would ever come to this. I knew you were imprudent, but I never thought of such a thing as this. What would Beal think of this? What about your children?"[5]

But Mrs. Boyce was not allowed to tell the jury what Lena said to her—which most likely would have included important details of the alleged abuse, coldness, arrogance, and other shortcomings of Beal on the one hand, and of her love and devotion for Al on the other, as well as his love and devotion for her. The jury never heard any of that crucial testimony, which let stand unchallenged Beal's very different portrayal of the affair, of Lena, of Lena's mental state, of their marriage, and of his own character and motives. Under rules of evidence forbidding hearsay evidence it was a correct ruling, but what about all the inadmissible evidence the court allowed the defense to introduce? That fiasco for the prosecution has to be laid at Hanger's doorstep—the judge can only rule on the admissibility of evidence when the other side objects!

In one of Kitty Barry's sidebar stories she had described Bill McLean as "pugnacious"—and then some. Typically his fiery, scornful demeanor was never showcased better than during his cross-examination of a key adverse witness. But his overly aggressive cross-examination of Annie Boyce backfired on him. Mrs. Boyce had testified that she did not know that Lena was to be "put where there are insane people." Then she added that if Lena "had been the least bit insane when this thing first started . . . she would be a raving maniac by now," and that if she had known Beal was going to have her committed she would have objected. Pit bull "Wild Bill" McLean wasn't satisfied to let it go at that. "But she was insane, wasn't she?" McLean sneered. Mrs. Boyce snapped, "No, she was not. She was nervous; Al was nervous; everybody was nervous; there ought to have been more people nervous." Still not letting it alone, McLean asked why she was so concerned that Lena might be sent to a sanitarium.

> **Annie Boyce:** I wouldn't have put a child of mine in a place where there were crazy people.
>
> **McLean:** You wouldn't have put Albert there?
>
> **Annie Boyce:** No sir.
>
> **McLean:** Don't you think a man running over and disgracing his mother and father and stealing another man's wife and killing that man's little children—don't you think such a man is a fit subject for the asylum or penitentiary?[6]

Lynn Boyce, the youngest son of Mrs. Boyce, characterized in the *Star-Telegram* as a "big westerner," was sitting in the courtroom whittling with a long-bladed, pearl-handled knife. When McLean demanded that his mother answer that outrageous non-question, Lynn suddenly threw down his knife and sprang at McLean. The lead paragraph in the next day's *Star-Telegram* read: "Lynn Boyce, youngest of the brothers, furnished the first demonstration of the tense feeling which has lain like a smoldering volcano beneath the surface through the Sneed trial, when he sprang with concentrated fury toward Attorney W. P. McLean, Jr. [who was] cross-examining his mother."

Lynn Boyce was restrained by supporters who kept him from attacking McLean. Judge Swayne then fined him $100 for contempt of court. McLean didn't thereafter press Annie Boyce for an answer. Perhaps he realized that browbeating a widow in front of the jury was a counterproductive trial tactic. *Star-Telegram* reporter Kitty Barry observed that McLean often "delivered up a wrathful glower" directed toward adverse witnesses and prosecutors. In any event, McLean's so-called question to Annie Boyce amounted to a classic McLean ploy of making an inflammatory (and inadmissible) jury argument and then attempting to thinly disguise it as a question or an objection.

This inflammatory question illustrates yet another trial tactic that McLean and Johnson employed to great effect. Every good trial attorney has to be a good storyteller, telling his or her story through the mouths of the witnesses called to the stand. In this trial, the key storytelling witness for the defense was John Beal Sneed; the key storytelling witness for the prosecution was Annie Boyce. Both had very important and emotionally persuasive testimony to give. For a storyteller to be most effective, the teller needs to gain the audience's attention at the outset and then hold that attention without interruptions or distractions as the tale unwinds and the listeners become more and more engrossed in the story line. Beal Sneed was allowed to tell his story (inadmissible parts and all) without interruption by Hanger. Thus the jury was drawn into his tale with undivided attention as it unfolded and, as a result, experienced the full emotional impact of his story. As a result, Sneed hit a home run with the jury. But when Annie Boyce attempted to tell her story, her testimony was interrupted almost every other sentence by either McLean or Johnson leaping up and barking objections to which they usually attached sarcastic sidebar remarks. Because of valid objections, the jury never got to hear some vital parts of her testimony. In addition, a number of defense objections were frivolous and raised for the obvious purpose of simply disrupting Annie Boyce's story line and dissipating its emotional impact—which they also succeeded in doing.

The grand finale of "the greatest legal battle ever fought in Texas courts" was about to begin. The day dawned cold and dreary. Winter rain fell. But it didn't dampen the enthusiasm of the crowd that showed up two hours before the courtroom doors were scheduled to open. All of Fort Worth that could get inside did so, shoving and pushing. Even women with babies in their arms. Small children too.

In a horse-and-buggy time before the advent of mass media— before the movies, before television, before radio even—it was not only a great legal battle, it was the greatest crowd-drawing attraction ever dangled before the public in those parts. No political rally, no hallelujah-shoutin' revival, no three-ring circus, no patent medicine show, no Wild West rodeo ever equaled this extravaganza. Perhaps not even a hanging.

One enthusiast interviewed by a *Star-Telegram* reporter while standing in line braving the rain, cheerfully volunteered, "I haven't seen such a crowd as this since a hanging down in Hillsboro." He recalled that the hanging took place on just such a drizzly day and that the rain was falling as the black cap was drawn over the head of the soon-to-be-deceased while he shivered on the open-air scaffold. But the cold rain didn't dampen the crowd's spirits. Then or now. A holiday spirit electrified the multitude.

In that entertainment-starved era, old-fashioned, melodramatic stem-winding orators were a great draw—the more florid, flamboyant, maudlin, tear-jerking, and long-winded the better. Bombast trumped reason, logic, and law every time. Quotes from the Bible and classical authors were always well received. The throng of spectators could be assured beyond any doubt that they were in for a rhetorical feast when final jury arguments began in the Sneed murder trial. The roster of spellbinders waiting in the wings was impressive. Judge Swayne allotted the state and the defense a total of ten hours each to harangue the jury. Hence there were enough verbal fireworks and bombast in store to satiate the appetite of even the most ravenous melodrama addicts.

When the courtroom doors finally opened, the hordes rushed in jousting each other for seats. The north gallery of the courtroom was reserved for women. Once those doors were opened, women raced in, actually falling over each other in their rush to get seats in the front row. Some even carried stools so they could sit in the aisles or stand on them behind the last row of seats. When the courtroom was packed to capacity, the deputies closed the doors. One woman openly wept when the deputy told her that no more people could enter.[7]

A *Star-Telegram* reporter captured the atmosphere of the women's section as follows:

> The north gallery presented more the scene of some brilliant social function than a grim murder trial. It had been reserved entirely for women and handsomely gowned misses and matrons leaned from it as over a ballroom balcony, here and there a diamond flashing against a white arm standing out on a background of costly fur.[8]

Nearly all who did gain entrance carried lunches, each realizing that if she vacated her seat, it would immediately be occupied.

At last, the arguments began. Jordan Cummings for the state opened with a dramatic flourish. He portrayed Colonel Boyce in the last minute of his life: hit by John Beal Sneed's fatal fusillade, Cummings staggered in pretended agony across the courtroom, until finally, grasping the jury box rail, he fell to the floor with a mighty groan.

The underlying legal issue to be debated was soon defined, and defined very clearly. It was as clear-cut a debate between the written law and the unwritten law as could have been conceived by even the most imaginative novelist. The underlying philosophies of each were spelled out succinctly and dramatically. Compare Jordan Cummings for the prosecution with Cone Johnson and Bill McLean for the defense. Jordan Cummings:

> Regard for human life is the highest and the ultimate test of a country's civilization. In a barbaric nation, among savages, life is held cheaply, but in civilized countries safeguards have been thrown about human life, reducing justification for killing to the narrowest limits.[9]

Cone Johnson:

> Human life is not the highest consideration of our laws, being less regarded by the law than domestic relations.[10]

Again one has to wonder . . . where, oh where, was Bill Hanger when Johnson and McLean were clearly misstating the homicide laws of the State of Texas? While Hanger sat silently and failed to make valid objections when he should have during the final jury arguments of McLean and Johnson, the defense peppered the prosecution lawyers' closing arguments with constant objections, most of which were frivolous and made for the sole purpose of destroying the speaker's flow and momentum as well as the speaker's and the listeners' concentration—and as a result the effectiveness of his argument. Even worse, the defense team continued its outrageous tactic of adding abusive and insolent rebuttal comments to their objections. And Judge Swayne continued to let the defense get away with tacking those outrageous sidebar comments into their objections.

Each side then argued its version of the "facts" and the competing motives it assigned to the principal characters. The prosecution maintained that Colonel Boyce was guilty of nothing more than attempting to secure the dismissal of false charges against his son. The defense, of course, begged to differ. According to the defense, Colonel Boyce was the Meddlesome Mattie who had encouraged Al and Lena's affair from the beginning and at the time of his death was attempting to reunite Al and Lena. The prosecution further scored the defense for failing to call even one witness who, prior to the fatal encounter, had ever heard Colonel Boyce utter any threat to harm or kill Sneed.

The defense could not say enough about Al Boyce, and none of it was complimentary. He was the villain of the century—the devil incarnate. The defense much preferred to focus its verbal firepower on the sins of that vile, wife-stealing libertine Al Boyce than to berate the slain victim of this murder trial. If the defense struggled to credibly paint Colonel Boyce as a villain, the prosecution had the even-more-daunting task of finding anything good to say about Al that would not offend the jury. The best the prosecution could do was this rather lame attempt to shift part of the blame for the affair onto Lena's shoulders. Harry Hendricks argued this:

A great deal has been said in this case in denunciation of Al Boyce. It is natural . . . that we should condemn him with more or less bitterness, but you can't say, because the curtain is drawn over that part of it, just what share of the blame should be borne by a married woman who participated in the wrong with him.

You have heard about his ranch on the Pecos, and of his ranch life in Montana, and you know what limited experience he must have had with women. And you have heard Dr. Braswell testify that this woman was brilliant, gifted with reasoning powers beyond the average woman.[11]

Hendricks concluded by saying that while it might be natural for the jurors to condemn Al, nevertheless, "the iniquity of the son should not be visited upon the father."

So much for Al. At least, insofar as the prosecution was concerned. But McLean could find no excuse for Al, no mitigating circumstance at all. He expressed the horror he would feel as a father if any son of his had brought such shame on his family.

Then there was Lena. It all came back to Lena. Her state of mind and her motives lay at the heart of the case. The prosecution maintained Lena was sane, "a brilliant woman of acute intellect, smart, and rational"—sane all right, though morally lax.[12] The state made much sport of the defense's difficulties in grappling with that elusive "moral insanity" diagnosis. But the defense had to stoutly defend that insanity analysis, whatever its brand or flavor, since it was essential to John Beal Sneed's portrayal of himself as the honor-preserving, self-sacrificing hero. Neither the prosecution nor the defense dared posit a third alternative: a sane Lena simply fell out of love with grim, iron-willed John Beal Sneed and fell in love with carefree, loving Al. That scenario fit neither side's theory of the case: the defense couldn't afford to portray Lena as sane; the prosecution couldn't afford to portray wife-stealing Al as heroic. Or even as a human being who cared more for Lena than his own security, social standing, or financial well-being.

How strange it was that Lena's sanity, or insanity, was the key issue in the trial, yet the jury never got to see or hear her although, during the entire trial, she sat in a hotel room hardly a stone's throw from the courthouse. A prosecution jab at the defense must have smarted when Jordan Cummings called attention to the fact that McLean could have put Lena on the stand and let the jury decide for themselves whether or not she was insane. But wily Bill McLean cleverly deflected the prosecution thrust—even while deftly dodging the issue and even though his reply conflicted with his previous trial comment asserting that the defense was not calling Lena as a witness because Lena was insane. Now, shifting gears, he explained that Lena had not been called to the stand because John Beal Sneed wouldn't hear of it. The caring husband wouldn't allow his wife to be humiliated by forcing her to confess her sins in public. McLean let the jury in on this bit of confidential client-attorney communication that had not been previously revealed. He confided this to the jurors:

> Why [John Beal Sneed], whether his wife is sane or not, would not put her on the stand and have her tell this courtroom full of people the story of her downfall for all the world or to save his neck. God bless him!"[13]

Self-sacrificing hero to the end.

T. S. Henderson, another lawyer on the defense team, chimed in and predicted that if the jury convicted Sneed and sent him to prison, the people of the State of Texas would rise up in indignation and erect a towering monument to him upon which would be inscribed: "Beal Sneed—Hero."

Senator Hanger didn't share such an exalted view of Sneed. He ridiculed Sneed's portrayal as a "God-like man, and a brother of Christ" and denounced him as a murderer. And he ridiculed the defense efforts to accuse Colonel Boyce of encouraging or aiding or abetting the affair between Al and Lena. Why, he wondered, would the Colonel and Annie Boyce want their son to bring "the vilest of common women" into their family? At another point in the jury arguments, the prosecution referred to Lena as a "prostitute." At the next recess, Lena's father, Tom Snyder, enraged by that remark, trailed the offending lawyer out of the courtroom, braced him, demanded an apology, and demanded that he publicly take back what he said. Although the lawyer managed to pacify Tom Snyder, somewhat at least, still the mental image of old Tom Snyder stalking out of the courtroom and collaring the lawyer on the courthouse steps, all in defense of his daughter's tarnished honor and reputation, seems—at least from a modern perspective—both amusing and pathetic: better she be loony than loose.

About this time, the judicial proceedings were interrupted by a stifled scream from the spectator section when one woman stabbed another in the rear with a hairpin, driving her from her seat, which the attacker promptly seized for herself. Judge Swayne then assigned a deputy to patrol the women's section and prevent any further disruptions of judicial decorum. Judge Swayne reckoned that would put a stop to any further spectator disruptions. But he was wrong. In fact, Judge Swayne came close to getting shot in his own courtroom that day. Crazy Mary Rea was waiting in the wings.

Over the past three years or so, Crazy Mary, a classic paranoid, had spent most of her waking hours haunting the halls of the Tarrant County courthouse filing frivolous lawsuits. With increasing venom she had conducted an ongoing vendetta against Judge Swayne ever since he had presided over a messy, hotly contested, and very public divorce suit Mary's husband, Fort Worth police officer John T. Rea, filed against her in 1910. During the 1912 John Beal Sneed trial, Crazy Mary was in attendance every day, glaring at Judge Swayne. When one of the bailiffs warned Judge Swayne that Crazy Mary might be armed and dangerous, the judge ordered her barred from the courtroom. Mary sat in the hall outside the courtroom and steamed. After the Sneed trial was adjourned for the day on February 19, 1912, Judge Swayne ordered the officers to bring her into the courtroom for a confrontation. And that was when the brawl began. She fought frantically—kicking and screaming and scratching—while the officers dragged her down the aisle. Breaking free, she proceeded to berate Judge Swayne. "Enough! Enough!" he finally cried, and found her in contempt of court and ordered the deputies to haul her off to jail for a two-day penance. That is when they found the pistol in Mary's purse.[14]

In the final jury arguments, racism—open and unabashed—was voiced by both sides. During the trial the defense team had called an African American as a witness. He was a porter on the train that Al and Lena boarded when they eloped, and he verified that they had slept in the same berth. The state had already admitted this, and during his argument Senator Hanger scolded the defense for unnecessarily calling "a yellow nigger" to the stand.[15]

Cone Johnson, in his argument for the defense, went outside the trial record with criticism of Al Boyce for "kidnapping" Lena and taking the deluded "innocent lamb" to Canada, a foreign land that Johnson said he once visited. He confided to the jury that in that ungodly foreign place, he had observed a white woman living with a black man.[16]

By this time in the marathon jury arguments, each side had staked out its legal position, rehashing and interpreting the acts and motives of the principals in a manner that suited its position. Now that all the underbrush had been whacked away, it was show-time. The scene became more theater than courtroom; the participants, more melodramatic hambones than legal scholars. They were down to the rhetorical goodies that all the edge-seated fans had salivated to hear—ready to soar with the master spellbinders to the thundering oratorical peaks of Mount Olympus. And the fans would not be disappointed.

Not all of it was maudlin melodrama, however. Bill McLean drew the only real laugh from the crowd when he suddenly interrupted his glowing account of Beal Sneed's life, character, career, and his happy home (before Al) and what an ideal husband he had been with this observation: "My God, women have a hard enough time getting good husbands these days. Do you want to put this one in the penitentiary?" *Star-Telegram* sidebar reporter Kitty Barry commented that the women led the laughter.

Cone Johnson fully lived up to his billing as a premier orator during his five-hour exhortation, condemnation, and denunciation. Discussing, and relying upon, the "insulting words to a female relative" statute, Johnson reminded jurors that under that Texas law "no lapse of time could be considered," so long as the insulter was killed "at first opportunity." He elaborated:

> Southern chivalry and Southern lawmakers say there is one insult which carries no limitation of time, that blow which strikes deepest into the heart, an insult to women relatives; they have said that no lapse of time is too long to carry the barb in one's heart provided the injured person kills at the first opportunity.[17]

But had Beal Sneed really killed Colonel Boyce "at the first opportunity" after allegedly hearing about some "insulting words" that the Colonel said of Lena? It will be recalled that Sneed shot the Colonel the second time he saw him the night of the killing. The first time was the encounter in the hotel lobby before Sneed, Bowman, and Atwell exited the lobby to take their evening meal at Joseph's Café. It was after the meal that Sneed returned to the hotel lobby and shot the Colonel. But Cone Johnson neatly sidestepped this pitfall by explaining that it was during the evening meal that Bowman had informed Sneed of some insulting words that Colonel Boyce made about Lena. The banker Fuqua supposedly overheard these remarks and later related them to Bowman. Therefore, according to Cone Johnson, the killing did happen during Sneed's first encounter with the Colonel after hearing about these insulting words.

Therefore, Johnson continued, under that Texas law, Sneed was legally "justified" in killing the Colonel. But Johnson conveniently forgot to tell the jury about the last part of that Texas law. The rage incited in the killer upon hearing some such "insulting words" did not "justify" killing the speaker; it only reduced the offense from first-degree murder to manslaughter. The shooter would still be guilty of a felony under that law. However, as so many nineteenth-century defense lawyers had done in the past, Cone Johnson got away with "reworking" that statute before the jury so that it magically morphed into an exonerating law instead of a mitigating law. But the question that must be asked is, where was the somnolent Hanger when Cone Johnson misstated the law by contending that the statute legally "justified" the slaying of Colonel Boyce?

Now that he had personally amended man-made law to suit his purpose, Cone Johnson was ready to ascend the celestial ladder to that "higher law," which he obviously found more to his liking. For openers, he compared John Beal Sneed to Jesus Christ:

Beal Sneed is the only man I have ever heard of since the days of Christ that has stood by his wife under all circumstances. There was a time under the old Israelitish [*sic*] law when it was a life for a life, and a tooth for a tooth, and when it read that if a woman did

wrong she was to be stoned to death. But the time came when one
stood on the banks of Galilee, and when they brought a woman
who had done wrong before Him, wrote in the sand, "Neither do I
condemn thee—go and sin no more."[18]

This biblical excursion by Johnson bestowed a splendid opportunity for a biblical rejoinder by the prosecution. Since the biblical
woman who had "done wrong" was forgiven (even when she apparently didn't have a "morally insane" excuse), then why was Al Boyce,
her co-sinner, not also entitled to divine forgiveness? And what about
old Colonel Boyce, whose wrong, at worst, seemed, in comparison, to
have been a biblical misdemeanor? Was he still stuck in that Old Testament justice—that "old Israelitish" eye-for-an-eye and life-for-a-life
business—and thus beyond redemption or forgiveness—even when
he didn't cause the loss of a life? Or even put anybody's eye out? Did
God order his humble Jesus Christ look-alike servant, John Beal Sneed,
on a holy mission of vengeance: slay Colonel Boyce, that despicable,
unredeemable, sin-stained villain? However . . . dozing off again, the
prosecution lawyers failed to pick up the fumble and run with it.

Cone Johnson then ridiculed the state's contention that John
Beal Sneed had locked Lena up in an asylum surrounded by pellagra
victims just to keep her away from Al and further ridiculed the notion
that Al had taken Lena from the sanitarium at her request. He said:

Oh, Al, better a thousand times that you had left her to the touch
of the pellagra death, than to have laid upon her the touch of your
lecherous hands.[19]

T. S. Henderson, for the defense, speculated that Lena was "evi-
dently unconscious" when Al's "bribed nurse," Nellie Flowers, "brought
her down and turned her over, a defenseless lamb, to these wolves."

It was easy enough for Johnson and the defense to incense the
jurors by invoking their firmly embedded Victorian beliefs by railing at that lecherous reprobate, Al Boyce. Still, that left the difficult problem of how to convince a jury that the slaughter of old,
unarmed Colonel Boyce was somehow necessary to "protect the
home." To that end Johnson spoke at length about the sacred

right—and duty—of a man to protect his home, to protect his wife from debauchery. He said:

> Captain Boyce was planning to take away the wife of Beal Sneed again, even by law, when he was killed. He was going to put her back in the embrace of Al Boyce and Beal Sneed killed him for that. He thought it was the only way.[20]

Regarding Colonel Boyce's letter urging Canadian authorities not to deport Al, Cone Johnson had this to say:

> Captain Boyce had written that Al Boyce was a good citizen, but the woman was as "mean as the devil." The miserable, contemptible doctrine that a man who debauches a woman . . . [and more especially, one who is] another man's wife, will make a good citizen, but the woman is as mean as the devil and must be cast out, is what is undermining American civilization and spreading the poison.

T. S. Henderson seconded that opinion, adding that such "contemptible doctrines" were "corrupting the very foundations of government." He concluded that the only place Al Boyce would make a good citizen would be "in the regions of the damned," then, tacking on this graphic eye-opener to his denunciation of Al, he declared, "go into the houses of lechery and there the cry of innocence will stay the hard hearts."[21]

Johnson then returned to his favorite source: the Bible. To hear him tell it, Beal Sneed, the righteous, obeyed all of God's commands while the dastardly Al Boyce broke nearly every biblical injunction in the book. As to Beal Sneed:

> Sneed obeyed the highest law, when he forsook his father and mother, and stood by his wife through evil report . . . He has violated no law and is not a fit subject of the penitentiary system.[22]

Continuing his Bible-based condemnation of Al Boyce, Johnson needed to cite that passage, reading "Thou shalt not covet thy neighbor's wife." Yet Johnson must have recognized that by so doing, he was setting a trap for himself. How could he rail against Al for violating the biblical injunction against committing adultery without inviting the prosecution to respond by calling attention to Beal Sneed's violation of that companion injunction, "Thou shalt not kill"? However, Johnson was up to the task. He cleverly—if illogically—sidestepped the trap as follows:

> The source of all this tragedy began with the violation of God Almighty's written law—"Thou shalt not covet thy neighbor's wife." That law is found in the same category as the law that says, "Thou shalt not kill." . . . [Al Boyce], you have violated God's commandment, "Thou shalt not covet thy neighbor's wife," and you have brought death into your family.[23]

Johnson's voice choked with emotion and his eyes brimmed with tears when he reached the climax of his appeal. Pointing to the two Sneed daughters who were clinging to their father, Johnson, in hushed, melodramatic tones, concluded:

> Did you notice those two little children, gentlemen? They are parties to this case. You can't render a verdict that won't reach them. Send this man to the penitentiary and Beal Sneed is robbed of all right to control those little children. This other crowd here already, through Al Boyce, destroyed these little children's mother and now they are asking this jury to make a felon of their father . . . We have had sorrow enough. There's the home of Beal Sneed at Amarillo gone forever. Its inhabitants scattered; the father here standing trial for his life . . . *The Boyces ought to be satisfied. The Sneeds ought to feel that there's been enough calamity.* Beal Sneed will go somewhere with his children and begin life over again, as he said he would do at first.[24]

The italicized portion of Cone Johnson's argument is both puzzling and ironic. "The Boyces ought to be satisfied." One wonders why any of the surviving Boyce family ought to have felt satisfied. "The Sneeds ought to feel that there's been enough calamity." Perhaps they ought to have felt so, but in view of the bloodshed yet to come, that comment was to prove sadly ironic.

Not all the melodrama emanated from the defense side of the aisle. Bill Hanger challenged the defense's notion that Beal Sneed was entitled to sympathy. The Boyces were the only ones entitled to sympathy, he contended, and that on account of Sneed's "handi-work." What about next Christmas in the Boyce home? Senator Hanger told the jury this:

> The defense has painted you one Christmas picture. I ask you to look at the picture of next Christmas in another home. No more the footsteps of that old father will be heard in his house—this defendant has put them to rest forever. No more will his voice be heard in admonition, in cheerful word, in sage advice—this defendant has stilled that voice forever.[25]

Hanger once again reminded the jurors that the defense failed to call any witness who had ever heard Colonel Boyce make any threat to attack or kill John Beal Sneed and that the evidence demonstrated that the entire Boyce family had tried to end the affair and separate Al and Lena. The senator concluded by saying that only by a guilty verdict would the law be vindicated and the defendant properly punished. As logical as it was and as sound as it was from a legal standpoint, still the question remained: would Hanger's argument be sufficient to overcome the combined emotional firepower of Johnson and McLean?

Cone Johnson was a spellbinding orator, but even he was no match for Bill McLean when it got down to the bottom of the ninth inning. "Wild Bill" McLean was a world-class closer, and he was about to prove it. McLean began by reviewing the evidence supporting the defense story line. By the time he finished the summary, the *Star-Telegram* reporter noted that "handkerchiefs were out all over the courtroom and one juror used his." The audience never had a chance to pocket those handkerchiefs. It only got more maudlin, more melodramatic as he cranked up the rhetoric; it ran the full gamut from ridicule of the prosecution to denunciation of Al Boyce and the other men of the Boyce family.

He characterized the prosecution as "the cruelest he had ever seen." Turning his attention to the Boyces, McLean condemned them all:

> They tell us Beal Sneed killed an old, unarmed man. Al Boyce and Colonel Boyce and Henry Boyce helped to murder those two little girls a hundred times.

I would rather that a yellow-bellied moccasin crawled into the
bed and bit my boys than know that they were disgraced for life [as
Al Boyce had disgraced himself and the Boyce family].[26]

Then dramatically holding up a picture of the bullet-riddled
corpse of Colonel Boyce that the state had introduced into evidence,
McLean pointed to John Beal Sneed and the two Sneed daughters
who clung tearfully to their father and snarled, "For every wound
in his body, I can show a thousand bullet holes in the heart of John
Beal Sneed."

Next, the jury heard a heart-wrenching replay of the dreary 1911
Christmas at Henry Bowman's house. "Go get Momma," he quoted
the oldest daughter as pleading with her father. McLean then envisioned a scene that he assured the jurors was bound to occur if they
sent John Beal Sneed to the penitentiary: another dreary Christmas, this time with the two little girls clinging to Henry Bowman
pleading, "Go get Papa."

He paused theatrically for a long moment of silence while the
jury wallowed in the horror of that grim prospect, then intoned
his mantra:

Every time there is a home broken up, there ought to be a killing of all who assisted in it. When that's done homes won't be
broken up.[27]

Before the killing of Colonel Boyce, Beal Sneed had successfully leaned on the Canadian authorities to obtain an indictment
against Al Boyce for supposedly stealing the diamonds that Lena
took with her to Canada when they eloped. Lena's Canadian lawyer,
T. J. Murray, subsequently succeeded in persuading the prosecutor
to dismiss that grand larceny indictment on the ground of insufficient evidence. Although Colonel Boyce had little, if anything, to
do with getting this charge against Al dismissed, nevertheless, in his
argument, McLean took Colonel Boyce to task for his role in the
incident. He said:

They say that Captain Boyce was worse hurt over the fact that his
son was charged with the theft of diamonds than over his son

stealing another man's wife . . . I hope my two little boys will never steal, but if they do I would a thousand times rather they would steal diamonds than some other man's wife, for diamonds I could replace, but all the wealth in the world could not replace the jewel of a woman's virtue once it is taken from her.[28]

Winding down for a dramatic climax, McLean pointed out that if the jury sentenced Sneed to the penitentiary it would constitute grounds for a divorce, and if that envisioned calamity happened, then Sneed's "deranged wife" and all of Sneed's property and children would fall "into the despoiler's hands." McLean confided to the jurors that if convicted, his client would rather "be sent to the gallows" than spend a month in the penitentiary "without the power to protect the woman whom he has tried to protect so far."

Bill McLean concluded by noting that the prosecution had demanded that the jury render a verdict "that is right." He asked the jurors if they thought it would be right to return a verdict that would sentence "those innocent little girls sobbing on their father's breast to cringe through their young lives before Al Boyce's presence in the forests of Canada."

Again a long dramatic pause. Then:

I think I can see these little girls, in their little white gowns, saying their prayers tonight:

> *Now we lay us down to sleep,*
> *We pray the Lord our souls to keep,*
> *But let us die before we wake,*
> *Rather than Al Boyce our young lives take.*[29]

"Wild Bill" McLean then boomed: "Gentlemen, let your verdict be, 'We, the jury, declare that the homes of this country must and shall be protected.'"

Kitty Barry, the *Star-Telegram* sidebar reporter, recorded this scene as the jury departed the courtroom to deliberate:

Sobbing as though her little heart would break, Lenora Sneed sat on her father's lap, her arms thrown about his shoulders and

cried as W. P. McLean finished the last plea for Beal Sneed's life
and freedom . . . The gaping morbid crowd looked on and even
pointed at her and her father, both tear-stained. At that moment
Beal Sneed was a murderer to none . . .

　　The morbid had their highest hopes fulfilled—a little child
sobbed out her half-understanding sorrow on her father's arm.
Tear-dimmed, he strove to comfort her.[30]

Tear-dimmed though he was, John Beal Sneed didn't take very
long to recover his composure after the jury was out of sight. Soon
he was smiling and talking cheerfully with his friends and supporters. Barry, who observed all this, commented that he "showed by his
manner as plainly as by words that he had no fears of a conviction."[31]
Was this only a staged show of false bravado, a whistling in the dark
as he passed a graveyard, a contrived act of confidence designed
for public consumption? Or did he know something that only the
defense team knew? Sneed's sidekick, Henry Bowman, made a comment to the same reporter that heightened those suspicions. Bowman boasted, "The worse that can happen to us is a hung jury."[32]
A hope . . . an educated guess . . . or something more? Did the
Plano mule trader *know* that the defense had one ringer (or perhaps more) on the jury? Credence to that suspicion was magnified
by what had happened during the jury selection process of the trial
when accusations of attempted bribery of a prospective juror had
surfaced. Although the investigation was subsequently aborted for
lack of evidence, still, the suspicion lingered. Then, too, there was
the mysterious and defense-enhancing death of the state's key witness, Ed Throckmorton, on the eve of the trial. Even more suspicious events destined to happen later confirmed the likelihood that
skullduggery had indeed perverted the judicial process—including
something that happened only minutes after the jury retired to
deliberate its verdict.

　　The jury was supposed to "deliberate": that is, read and understand the court's lengthy written instructions setting out the applicable law as it related to the facts of the case and then carefully
review and weigh all the evidence. If done properly, that takes a

long time—at least several hours and, more often than not in complicated cases like this, jury debate usually lasts a number of days. Not just a few minutes.

But ten minutes was all the time it took for this jury to get hopelessly deadlocked: seven for acquittal and five for conviction.

The jury sent a note to Judge Swayne informing him that it was deadlocked. He instructed them to continue deliberating. Again and again, the jury kept sending notes back saying it was hopelessly deadlocked, and Swayne kept admonishing them to deliberate. Finally, he pleaded, "Pray to God Almighty that you may render a just verdict in this case." But it was no use. Not one of the jurors budged. Four days later, Judge Swayne gave up and, on February 29, 1912, he declared a mistrial, scolding the jurors for their obvious failure to perform their duty by seriously deliberating on the law and weighing the evidence.

Even though the defense didn't win an acquittal, the verdict was clearly a victory for McLean's team. The prosecution had started the trial with what appeared to be an airtight case: in front of credible eyewitnesses, the defendant had assassinated an elderly, unarmed prominent pioneer who had never threatened him—the victim being only an inconvenient obstacle in the way of the defendant's plan of revenge. Moreover, in view of that wanton killing in their community, public sentiment in Fort Worth at the beginning of the trial was tilted in favor of the state. It all amounted to an intentional killing for which the defense had failed to prove there was any justifiable defense to be found in the written laws of the state of Texas. With a lay-down hand like that, anything less than a guilty verdict spelled defeat. It was obvious that the prosecution was overconfident and almost serenely passive; the prosecutors were badly outlawyered by the fiercely aggressive defense team—and not only a fiercely aggressive, but also an unscrupulously creative team that came to court with an arsenal of dirty tricks it hesitated not a whit to employ. Then too, Judge Swayne, perhaps also sharing the state's overconfidence in achieving a successful prosecution of an obviously guilty defendant, allowed the defense free rein to do and say almost anything it pleased.

BEAL SNEED AND DAUGHTERS LEAVING COURT. John Beal Sneed and daughters Lenora (left) and Georgia Sneed departing Tarrant County Courthouse during the first Fort Worth murder trial for killing Colonel A. G. Boyce. Beal Sneed's two brothers are shown standing behind him slightly to his right: Joe T. Sneed, Jr. (left), and Marvin Sneed. *Photograph courtesy of the University of Texas at Arlington Library Special Collections.*

The defense also accomplished something else that would prove to be very important. During the entire trial, McLean and Johnson shamelessly courted the *Fort Worth Star-Telegram* reporters who wrote daily accounts of the trial. The courtship was successful. By trial's end those reporters had tossed objectivity to the winds and recast themselves as a cheering section for McLean, Johnson, Scott, and even the defendant, John Beal Sneed. In that relatively small, one-newspaper town, those reports circulated to most everyone in the community—the source from which the jury pool for the retrial would be selected.

Beal Sneed was released on bond pending a retrial.

The front-page headlines of the February 29, 1912, edition of the *Fort Worth Star-Telegram* trumpeted the sensational story of the jury-deadlocked mistrial of John Beal Sneed. Only three days later that newspaper carried another story about another development taking place on the front lines of the Fort Worth judiciary. While not as sensational as the Beal Sneed misfire, it was at least as interesting—and enlightening. Doctors Wilmer and Bruce Allison, president and manager, respectively, of the Arlington Heights Sanitarium, got themselves indicted by a Fort Worth grand jury for illegally restraining the liberty of a young woman named Irene George, in a case the article described as "strikingly similar" to that of the involuntary incarceration of Lena Sneed. As in the Lena Sneed case, the incarceration had been involuntary and accomplished at the insistence of her husband. True, in Irene George's case there had been at least a nod in the direction of legitimacy in her imprisonment—a lunacy hearing had been held resulting in a finding of insanity. But the court was more kangaroo than correct in that neither Irene nor any attorney representing her was invited, or permitted, to attend the induction ceremony. After confinement for a couple of weeks, Irene finally managed to contact and engage Senator O. S. Lattimore, the same lawyer who had represented Lena in her bid for freedom. Lattimore filed a habeas corpus petition during which the indignant patient was allowed to tell her story. She echoed Lena's complaints: against her will she had been confined to a locked room, deprived of her clothing, barred from her children, and besides that, she was quite sane, thank you very much. In the end, the jury agreed. She was adjudicated sane and ordered released.

For unknown reasons, the indictment of the Allison brothers seems never to have been called for trial.

CHAPTER 8

The Waiting Game

Ambush at the Death Cottage

JUDGE SWAYNE DECLARED A MISTRIAL in the prosecution of John Beal Sneed for murdering Colonel Boyce on February 29, 1912, and that was the day the waiting game began. Retrial of the murder case was scheduled to begin in the same Fort Worth district court in November 1912—eight months later. It would prove to be a very long eight months indeed.

Cone Johnson, in his closing argument for the defense, made a very curious comment: "There has been enough sorrow . . . The Boyces ought to be satisfied. The Sneeds ought to feel that there's been enough calamity." Perhaps. But that certainly didn't accurately reflect the sentiments of the three principals in the tragedy, none of whom were satisfied with the status quo. Lena was not satisfied. She wanted Al. But John Beal Sneed was in the way. Al was not satisfied. He wanted Lena. But, again, there was the John Beal Sneed impediment. Al also wanted to avenge the murder of his father—personally. Beal was not satisfied. He wanted more calamity. He wanted Al and Lena: Al dead, and Lena captured alive and forced to live with him, thus restoring, at least for public consumption, the image of his happy home that he had struggled so hard to portray during his murder trial. More than anything, and whatever it took, he was determined to vindicate his honor even if that included coercing the headstrong and unrepentant Lena to reunite—if not for love, at least for appearances' sake. Appearances' sake, that is, for John Beal Sneed's benefit.

Meanwhile, Beal, Lena, and Al moved warily in the shadows, stalemated. At least temporarily. Al was stuck in Canada, realizing that if he crossed the border he would probably be arrested under a federal white slavery indictment, courtesy of Beal's hired public official, Will Atwell. Or if not arrested, then likely assassinated by Beal himself. Al's family encouraged him to stay in Canada for the same reasons. In addition, they believed that more time and distance would finally cool Al's ardor for Lena. Too, they feared his return would lessen the chances of convicting Beal on his retrial.

Although the decision to remain in Canada was a wise one, it resulted in a traumatic experience for Al. He was alone. He had no friends. Nothing to do. Solitary confinement, exiled and isolated, Al suffered major depression in that bleak, cheerless, freezing Canadian winter. February 1912 was particularly painful. Less than a month ago Beal Sneed had murdered his father and now Sneed's trial was in progress in Fort Worth. A surging rage at Beal Sneed consumed him, that being aggravated by an agonizing sense of helplessness at his own inability to right that terrible wrong. Beyond all that he was tormented by a sense of guilt at having set in motion a chain of events that cost the life of his own father. Churning riptides of those powerful emotions gave him no peace. And thoughts of Lena haunted him constantly. How he yearned for her, needed her. Needed the solace that only she could give him. Yet boundaries of nations and circumstances kept them apart for now. And for how long? Forever?

Lending perhaps some credence to Captain Snyder's repeated rants that Al was a "whiskey-drinking fiend," Al went on a bender that lasted about a month during which time he didn't communicate with anyone. When he didn't respond to Lena's letters for some time, she became frantic. Finally Al wrote and explained that he had been "very sick" and apologized for failing to answer her letters. She wrote back expressing concern over his drinking problem:

> I want to write about you being sick—but oh Albert I *can't*—It almost killed me but my love for you is my very life—and I love

you just like you were my own little child and could never lose
faith in you—and I know the temptation was awful. And that
you have suffered as much as I have from it—and oh precious
heart I know you won't *ever do it again*— . . . and darling I thank
God you didn't drink very much . . . I won't say that it didn't hurt
me . . . but oh Albert I could never be mad with you—and where
a woman's love is her life there is no need to ask forgiveness.[1]

When Al wrote back promising to control his drinking, Lena
made this reply:

Your word and promise . . . is all I want—for you are *honor* itself
. . . Don't ever think I don't realize the horrible temptation . . . I
have never written about it before precious heart, because to me
your promises are sacred—but I want you to know how I understand, God bless you . . .[2]

Autocratic Beal was also frustrated by the stalemate. Immediate, direct, and often violent action was his preferred solution when
anyone dared frustrate his purpose. But that just wouldn't do now.
Not under these circumstances. Al was in Canada, out of rifle range.
Beal couldn't browbeat Lena into coming back home, even by keeping the children from her. After her sanity had been judicially determined, he couldn't again drag her off to some cash-friendly mental
asylum and cage her. Furthermore, since he had publicly portrayed
himself as the heroic martyr whose sole goal in life was rescuing and
nurturing poor Lena, he could hardly risk shattering that public
image by killing her, beating her, or using physical force to break
her and bend her to his will. Then, too, as Beal was well aware, he
would soon face another murder trial, and his very life and freedom
depended on his maintaining his heroic martyr image before the
public—and the next jury. His usual bulldozer tactics just wouldn't
work with Lena—or the public. Beal did take direct action on one
front: immediately after the mistrial, he hired a bodyguard named
John Blanton.

Lena, separated from her children, unable to reunite with Al, and
unwilling to reconcile with her husband, was in a state of anguished

limbo. Divorce, at least for the present, was out of the question for the simple reason that she had no grounds for divorce. The very idea of a "no-fault" divorce or anything remotely akin thereto was beyond imagination in 1912 Texas. If, however, Beal could be convicted and sent to prison, then she would have grounds, and the way would be cleared for her to obtain a divorce and marry Al. Yet, shortly after the mistrial, a despondent Lena wrote Al in Canada expressing the belief that no Texas jury would ever convict Beal. In Fort Worth, Amarillo, and for that matter, most of Texas, the sensational trial had caused a deep and bitter rift between the participants and their supporters.

The scandalous revelations publicly aired during the trial, as well as Beal Sneed's one-sided heroic-martyr version of the story, left Lena in a cauldron of unwanted notoriety, intrusive gawkers, newspaper reporters, and unrelenting gossip. The rumors were rampant, and they were vicious. One widespread report had it that Lena had had an affair with Beal's brother, Joe Sneed, and that he was the father of Lena's two daughters. There were also whispered suggestions that Lena was a nymphomaniac.[3] Less than two weeks after the mistrial, a desperate Lena wrote Al this:

> You are so far away . . . you don't realize . . . the intense feelings over the affair—all Texas is divided over it . . . I will die if I can't get away from this horrible talk . . . if I even sit on the porch people stop at the gate and stare at me . . . and it is killing me by inches—newspaper reporters come up here almost every day trying to interview me.[4]

Even though Lena's two daughters were then living with Lena's sister Eula Bowman and husband, Henry Bowman, in Plano (a short distance northeast of Fort Worth), the Bowman family forbade Lena from visiting her daughters, because she refused to repent and publicly confess that she was in the wrong for leaving Beal. The Bowmans also refused to pass on to the daughters' gifts and notes Lena sent them.

At first, she considered fleeing to Canada and joining Al there. However, Texas Senator O. S. Lattimore, who had represented Lena in her sanity hearing, advised against it. He warned Lena that if she

fled to Canada, "not only Texas but the whole U.S. would tear up creation" until she and Al were run to ground. An escape to Canada or
any other foreign country would be impossible, Lattimore advised.
Finally, Lena retreated to the only safe haven left—her sister Pearl
Perkins's home in Lake Charles, Louisiana. Meanwhile, she kept up
frequent correspondence with Al.

While the dilemma-conflicted principals were stewing in their distress
and indecision, the Sneed saga—already generously arrayed with the
outlandish and the unexpected—took yet another bizarre twist. Six
days after the mistrial, John Beal Sneed's father, Joe T. Sneed, Sr., was
murdered—shot down in his hometown of Georgetown, Texas, by
a tenant farmer named R. O. Hillard, who then committed suicide.
Initially most people assumed that it was a revenge killing somehow
connected with the Sneed-Boyce feud. Further investigation, however,
indicated otherwise. Hillard's wife produced a note from her husband
saying that he blamed the senior Sneed, his former landlord, for causing his "insanity." Still, to the public . . . there lingered an odor of
revenge, enhancing fascination with this ongoing theater of the fan-
tastic. But there was more to it—yet another twist, and a convenient
one for Beal who seemed to lead a charmed existence. His father
had advised him from the start that he should just forget Lena, get
a divorce, and get on with his life. But, as usual, Beal ignored advice
from anybody. His father, nevertheless, supported Beal through the
murder trial, including helping defray staggering attorneys' fees and
litigation costs. However, his father told him that in return for his
support he expected Beal to divorce Lena after the murder trial, failing which he intended to cut Beal out of his will. Thanks to Hillard's
timely intervention, the elder Sneed's will stood unrevoked at his
death, thus enabling Beal to inherit his share of his father's estate.[5]
Beal was now left free to deal with Lena as he saw fit and without the
elder Sneed's interference.

Although Beal's options were limited, and an immediate, direct-action solution was not one of them, his obsession to conquer any foe at any cost was relentless, and his clever mind and fertile imagination never ceased devising strategies to accomplish that purpose. It didn't take him long to concoct an alternative game plan, one perfectly tailored to take full advantage of his adversaries' weaknesses during this high-stakes waiting game. It involved steadily increasing the pressure on both Al and Lena—Lena in particular. He set about fraying her emotionally and squeezing her financially. He hired a platoon of spies and informants to keep Lena under constant surveillance, to intercept correspondence from Al, and to ensure that Lena and Al didn't once again elope. The threat of the white slavery prosecution would be enough, he believed, to keep Al at bay in Canada. If not, he would track Lena wherever she traveled and make sure she didn't reunite with Al. The plan also involved patiently waiting—as he steadily tightened the vise—for Al and Lena to make mistakes while taking care to make no mistake himself.

Although Beal was careful to maintain his public image of great concern for Lena's welfare, behind the scenes his maneuvers evidenced precious little consideration for her. He kept their children from her, refused to let her visit them, prevented any correspondence with the children, and intercepted any gifts she sent them. Plus, of course, he refused to send Lena any support money. That being the case, Lena should have stayed at her sister Pearl's home in Lake Charles and patiently waited out the months leading up to Beal's retrial. There she had love, safety, and support from her one true ally, aside from Al. Her mail would have been safe from interception, and Al had sent support money.

But Lena was distraught and restless. She hoped to go to a distant place where she could start all over again, away from all the ugliness and strife. Make a new life there and reunite with Al in a land where John Beal Sneed didn't have a license to kill. Senator Lattimore suggested that Lena go to California and establish legal residence there. Even if Beal was not convicted of murder, Lattimore (obviously misreading Beal's character) told Lena he thought that eventually, after tempers cooled, Beal would agree to a divorce.

Lena wrote Al of her plan and then notified Beal that she was going to California. That would prove to be a costly mistake; John Beal Sneed's plan was beginning to bear fruit.

By March 18, 1912, Lena had completed preparations for the California trip. Just before she left, Beal lured her to Dallas with the promise of a visitation with the children. Typically the crafty Beal Sneed had a plan: he was prepared with a carrot and a stick when they met. The carrot: if she would promise not to communicate with Al, he would send her children out to California in June for a visit. The stick: if she made one move to reunite with Al, he would "follow [them] to the end of the world." Meanwhile, Beal wanted to sell their home in Amarillo, and he needed her signature on the deed to do so. He promised her that if she would sign it he would send her one hundred dollars per month from the sales proceeds. She signed the deed, but, of course, Beal reneged on his promise and kept all the money. It wasn't the first time he reneged on a property promise. When Beal was in Canada he persuaded Lena to sign a release for the jewelry and diamonds she had taken with her, which allowed him to obtain possession of them from Lena's Canadian attorney, T. J. Murray. She never saw the jewelry again or any proceeds from any sale of them. After Lena left for California, Beal proceeded to sell not only their home but also all their household goods, furniture, and other valuables. Needless to add, Beal kept that money too.

However, just before Lena left for California, Beal generously offered to hire Nellie Steele to accompany Lena during her California stay. (Nellie was the unmarried sister of Billie Steele. Another sister of Billie Steele was married to Lena's brother, Tom S. Snyder, Jr.) It soon became apparent that Nellie Steele, like her brother, Billie Steele, was Beal's spy. Nellie kept Lena under constant surveillance.

For reasons that are not entirely clear, Al Boyce left Canada and came to California while Lena was there. Had he and Lena planned a rendezvous before she left Texas? Or did Al decide to risk leaving his safe haven in Canada when he learned of Lena's whereabouts in California? And what was the purpose of that much-anticipated reunion: a romantic interlude or a part of a plan to reunite and again elope to some distant land? Whatever their plan, the rendezvous was thwarted by Beal's steel-willed and ever-vigilant watchdog, Nellie Steele.

Al may well have had yet another motive—a darker, more sinister motive—for coming to California while Lena was there. J. Evetts Haley, noted West Texas historian, in a footnote to *The Flamboyant Judge*, suggests that Al may have gone to California hoping to lure Beal out there so he could kill him. In this cryptic and intriguing footnote, Haley wrote:

> Al Boyce left . . . for a visit with his distant relative, Ira Aten, the great Texas Ranger and once manager of the troubled Escarbada Division of the XIT Ranch, who had retired to a farm near El Centro, California. "We expected Beal to follow him out here," Mr. Aten recalled, "and, if he had, we were going to kill him."[6]

Whatever Al's plans were, Lena was left stranded and alone. Her communications with Al had become more sporadic thanks in major part to Nellie Steele, who was closely monitoring her mail. Once when Lena went to the post office and received a registered letter from her Canadian attorney, T. J. Murray, she opened the envelope and two blank sheets of paper fell out. Since Beal's spies were intercepting their mail in California and Texas, Al instructed Lena to destroy any letters he had previously written her and told her there would be no more letters from him. Hearing that Al would not write her any more letters was a devastating blow to Lena's already fragile psyche. Was she losing Al? Did he intend to end their love affair and abandon her?

Beal's strategy was working. Lena was stranded in a most inhospitable environment. She had no communication with Al, she knew no one in California, her only companion was the hostile Nellie Steele, and she had no contact with her children. Lena had not been well when she left Texas, and now her health deteriorated even more. In an April 6, 1912, letter to Al she complained that she was unable to eat, suffering from terrible headaches, backaches, pain, and insomnia. The symptoms were likely psychosomatic, aggravated further, it may be posited, by a sense of guilt in leaving her children and the fear of losing Al either by his loss of interest in her or by assassination by Beal. In that letter she sounded frantic: "Precious you *must* think and think what is best for your poor miserable girl and I will do just as you say." Continuing, she warned Al as follows:

> If he knew you were in Texas he wouldn't hesitate to hire someone to kill you or shoot you in the back—he carries two guns one a big automatic, he carries it in his front pocket + told me it would knock a man down fifty feet away—if he knew where you were + there is an indictment he would try + have you arrested + shoot you unarmed. John Blanton [his bodyguard] never leaves him one minute.[7]

If it had been a mistake to leave the safe haven of sister Pearl's home in Lake Charles and travel to California, Lena was now about to make an even worse mistake. She decided to return to Texas and check herself into a sanitarium (not a mental asylum) for her health problems. As a result of that decision, Al also made a misstep; he too decided to leave California and return to Texas. The change of venue for both couldn't have suited John Beal Sneed better. His relentless campaign was working—slowly but surely. He was winning the war of attrition. On April 21, 1912, Lena and her watchdog, Nellie Steele, boarded a train bound for Texas.

The waiting game was coming to an end.

When Lena arrived in San Antonio, Nellie in tow, she was met by Beal and their two daughters. After a brief visit, Lena traveled on to Fort Worth where she checked herself into a private sanitarium where she felt she would be safe from Beal. A nurse there, Miss Bridges, was a friend of the Boyce family, and Lena believed she could trust her. She begged Miss Bridges to get in contact with Al and have him write Lena in care of Miss Bridges. At long last, on May 18, 1912, Miss Bridges delivered a letter from Al. In that long-awaited letter Al expressed some concern—suspicion perhaps—about why she had met with Beal on her return from California, and he also complained about her not staying in California while he was still there. Lena had assured Al that she would kill herself before she would live with Beal. Now she reinforced that assurance with this reply to Al's letter:

> Oh precious please don't misunderstand me, I have done all the time what I thought was best for you—I could *never* have seen you in Cal—I was *never* alone a minute the *only* time was the day I went to Long Beach to see if I had heard from you + Billie [Steele] wired her [Nellie Steele] to watch me every minute . . . The last two days in Cal—she was so suspicious + saw *me* looking at the boy you had with you— + if I had staid [*sic*] out there it would have been dangerous for you. I told Beal I was coming here—he would have kept me from it if he could—but I knew you would be safe with me here . . . Of course Beal has no control over me + I could come back to Cal—but he would have my every movement followed— and watched . . . You say it hurts you for me to see him—Precious I hate him so I almost go wild when I look at him . . . I told Miss Bridges I must be an awful woman, but in my heart I wished he was dead— + she said well we are alike for that is my wish . . . [Beal] knows I'd die before I'd live with him again—and he had just as soon kill me as not . . .[8]

Three days later, on May 21, 1912, Lena wrote Al again, this time informing him that Will Atwell would have to dismiss the white slavery indictment but warning him against coming to Fort Worth.

According to Lena's May 18 letter to Al, her trusted friend, Miss Bridges, shared her wish that Beal Sneed were dead. Unfortunately, Lena's trust in nurse Bridges was misplaced. She betrayed Lena. Beal Sneed's spy and collaborator, Billie Steele, later testified that on or about June 20, 1912, he received a telephone call from Miss Bridges informing him that Al Boyce was in Fort Worth and warning him that Al and Lena might elope again. Steele immediately hurried to the sanitarium, loaded up Lena, and took her to his home in Dallas. Then he called Sneed at his farm in Paducah and informed him what had transpired. "Much agitated," Sneed soon arrived at Steele's home in Dallas, collected Lena, and set off for San Antonio.[9] For the next few weeks Beal, with Lena in tow, kept on the road, pausing briefly at various hotels in San Antonio, Dallas, and Fort

Worth. Then, on July 8, 1912, Beal rented a downstairs apartment at 4523 Reiger Street in Dallas for himself and Lena. He enlisted the assistance of two upstairs tenants, Mrs. L. A. Rogers and her sister, Mrs. C. Castleton, to keep an eye on Lena when he wasn't present, as well as to intercept her correspondence.

There is nothing in court records or surviving correspondence between the parties that indicated that Lena resisted Billie Steele when he checked her out of the sanitarium and took her to his home in Dallas. And, thereafter, she apparently made no objection when Beal arrived, collected her, and left town. Still later Lena consented to live with Beal when he rented the Reiger Street apartment and moved in with her on July 8, 1912. All of which leaves a mighty large question unanswered: What happened between May 21 and June 20 to cause Lena to leave the sanitarium and return to Beal? In Lena's May 21, 1912, letter to Al she had voiced her hatred for Beal (wishing he was dead) and had assured Al that she would "die before [she would] live with him again." So what was going on in the troubled and tide-churned caverns of Lena's psyche? Did an enraged Beal Sneed—his patience in playing the waiting game now totally exhausted—threaten to kill Lena if she didn't obey him? Was she now in fear for her own life? Was she experiencing serious doubts about Al's unwavering devotion? Was the initial white heat of their affair cooling in the continuing mundane demands of day-to-day existence? Did Lena finally decide that the glamour and the lust of her affair with Al were just not worth the freight? Was the social ostracism finally growing too oppressive? Was the guilt of neglecting her children becoming too much to bear? And where would she be if Beal killed Al? She had no career skills, and in that day the best job an unskilled woman could aspire to was employment as a maid, a waitress, or, at best, a low-paid secretary. Then, too, what self-respecting employer would hire a notoriously scarlet woman like Lena? One way or another, it seems clear that Beal's strategy of deprivation and intimidation was bearing bitter fruit. Much later, Lena confided to "close friends" that although she loved only Al, she had returned to Beal on account of her children and for financial support—an explanation that, given Lena's frail physical and emotional condition and her increasing insecurities, made a lot of sense. But it was another terrible mistake.

Sometime about mid-July, Al visited Lena's sister Pearl in Lake Charles. Pearl continued her wholehearted support of Lena and Al. On July 19, Pearl wrote Lena a letter inviting her to bring "her babies" and stay with her in Lake Charles. In the letter Pearl said that she was "crazy about" Al. Pearl added that if Lena came, she would hire an officer to guard their house, an officer whom Beal was "too big a coward" to stand up to. Beal's spies intercepted the letter, and on July 23 Beal showed it to Billie Steele. It is unclear whether Lena ever saw the letter.[10] If she did, she didn't act on it.

Somehow Lena and Al arranged for an extremely risky tryst on July 21, 1912. On that night, while Beal was gone, and despite the fact that Beal's two spies as well as Lena's mother were all present upstairs in the Reiger Street apartment house, they succeeded in spending at least a part of the night together. Whether intentionally or accidentally, they also apparently succeeded in getting Lena pregnant. Either way, it was not an unwanted pregnancy; Lena had often expressed a desire to have Al's child. But, again, what was Lena's motive—or motives? Was it insurance that Al would stay true and always be at her side? Her letters during this time (when communications between the two had been sporadic) had expressed a fear of losing Al's love and support. (In one she told Al that she knew "how it has hurt you me being in the same house with him—But oh, do you remember you wrote me you wouldn't write me anymore—and when I didn't get your letters . . .") Or, sensing an imminent showdown between Beal and Al, was it simply a means of hedging her bets on the outcome? Or was it to prove her love for Al? Or to spite Beal? Or some, or all, of the above? And . . . was she really pregnant? Whatever the motivation, the result was the same. In a letter dated August 10, 1912, Lena informed Al that she was pregnant and that it had resulted from their July 21 rendezvous.[11]

That August 10 letter is the last known correspondence between Lena and Al.

After the fateful tryst, Al left Fort Worth and went back to Amarillo. Surely, Al must have known that some of Beal's supporters in

Amarillo would soon get word to him that Al was there, openly living in the Boyce home. Was Al deliberately baiting a trap for Beal? In the same August 10 letter, Lena added this comment: "Of course if you stay in Amarillo—I believe Beal will finally come." In their previous correspondence Lena and Al both had discussed the subject of killing Beal. When Beal first brought her back to Texas from Canada, Lena wrote this to Al: "If they bring you back to Texas I want you to kill Beal."[12] But in another note, she equivocated: "Darling I don't want you to kill B or him you as it would be an awful thing + I will have to answer to God for it."[13] The subject came up again later that spring. In an April 6, 1912, letter she wrote:

> What did you mean by saying you would go to Texas as soon as the next trial was over—I think I know what you mean—I notice what you said precious about longing to give Beal every chance to kill you—I don't want you to give him one chance—and don't you take one chance for my sake—If he knew you were in Texas he wouldn't hesitate to hire someone kill to [sic] you or shoot you in the back.[14]

A comment in sister Pearl's letter of July 19, 1912, to Lena left little doubt about Al's intent to confront and kill Beal. The letter was written just after Al's visit to Pearl in Lake Charles. Pearl said: "I don't think the Jack [referring to Beal] is long for the world." It was that letter that Beal had intercepted. Assuming, as the evidence indicates, that Al anticipated Beal would track him to Amarillo and that a confrontation would result, the reader is left to speculate what was going on in Al's mind. Undoubtedly he wanted to avenge the cowardly assassination of his father, and, of course, he wanted Lena. But why now? Couldn't he have waited three months at least to see if Beal would be convicted at the retrial and imprisoned? But then, from Al's perspective, would a prison sentence, however long, have constituted a full measure of justice for John Beal Sneed? Was Al himself under the sway of the Code of Honor of the Old South and the western frontier to the extent that he felt that such a grievous outrage and public dishonor could never be properly vindicated except by direct and personal revenge? That frontier philosophy lends itself to intriguing reflections in irony. If, in the upcoming duel, Al killed Beal, and if a Texas jury still followed the Code of Honor's unwritten law, then shouldn't Al be exonerated for vindicating the slaying of his unarmed father? There was also another tenet of the unwritten law upon which Al could have relied for exoneration: If one man (as Beal Sneed had done) publicly threatened to kill another on sight, then the intended target was entitled to launch a preemptive and lethal strike to remove the threat as well as to vindicate his honor. If, on the other hand, Beal killed Al, shouldn't a Texas jury applying the same unwritten law exonerate Beal for killing the libertine who seduced and ran off with his wife?

What kind of a confrontation did Al imagine? Some cleverly orchestrated ambush? Or a classic western "high noon," face-to-face, fair-and-square gun duel on Main Street? Al was reputed to be the "crack shot" of the Panhandle, and this kind of showdown seems more characteristic of his straightforward personality. It was not, however, characteristic of John Beal Sneed's personality. Beal had little use for this "fair-and-square" nonsense.

All that aside, it is probable that impetuous Al had finally had enough of this frustrating cat-and-mouse game. It might have seemed to Al that it was time to end it—once and for all, one way or the other, even if it meant his death. He was not the only soul tormented by this agonizing ordeal. Tensions escalated: everyone knew that this business was not over, knew that the end was near. Lena was on the brink of a nervous breakdown, and Al's grieving mother was not much better off. Annie Boyce reportedly took Al out to the Llano Cemetery in Amarillo. She pointed to a spot on the ground next to Colonel Boyce's grave and said to Al, "There is your place."[15]

It had become clear not only that the waiting game was drawing to a close but also that the endgame was about to begin. In Amarillo.

In the deadly game that Beal and Al were playing, time worked to Beal Sneed's advantage. He was a patient, crafty, and calculating man. Al Boyce, the impulsive, fun-loving, devil-take-the-hindmost cowboy—although fearless and deadly with a pistol—was not well suited to this kind of match. As time passed, he became less cautious.

Returning to Texas was a foolhardy mistake that should have been obvious to Al, since Texas was the one place on the globe where Beal could, with almost assured impunity, bushwhack him and get away with it. Meanwhile, Beal Sneed never dropped his guard.

Shortly after he intercepted Pearl's letter of July 19 to Lena, Beal moved Lena and their daughters to his brother Marvin's central Texas farm near the small village of Calvert in Milam County, fifty miles or so southeast of Waco. There he left them while he plotted the fatal finale. Meanwhile he continued to practice his marksmanship with firearms. He also stopped shaving.

He sent his man, John Blanton, to Dallas to reconnoiter. In Dallas, Blanton ran into an appropriately named bartender—Joe Barr. Barr told him that Al and his friend Lucien Hughes had been in Dallas and that he had gone to their room in the Southland Hotel where he had seen "a regular arsenal" of firearms.[16] Blanton returned to Calvert where he reported this information to Beal, adding that he had also been told that Al had been seen driving by the Reiger Street house soon after Beal and Lena had left there. (Apparently Blanton gained this information from another of Beal's spies—Mrs. L. A. Rogers, the upstairs tenant in the Reiger Street apartments.)

Beal then left for Fort Worth. He registered at the Mansion Hotel under the name of John Wilson. His spies reported that the prey was now in Amarillo. After conferring with one of his lawyers, Beal sent for a tenant farmer named Beech Epting who worked on his farm near Paducah, Texas, some 130 miles as the crow flies southeast of Amarillo. When he arrived, Beal told Epting that he wanted him to go with him "to shut down his business operations in Amarillo."[17]

The "business" John Beal Sneed intended to shut down was Al Boyce.

By September 9, 1912, all the principals were in Amarillo.[18] Typically, Sneed had a plan—a carefully crafted plan. He had spent considerable time practicing his marksmanship with his guns; he had outfitted himself with a funky disguise; he had calculated the perfect location; and he had decided exactly how he would execute his plan once his prey walked into the trap. On the other hand, typically, Al seemed to be casually going about his affairs—business as usual. His only precaution was to stick a loaded pistol in his belt.

Several days earlier, Al left the family business in Dalhart and arrived in Amarillo, staying with his mother at the family home on Polk Street. On September 10, Al and his brother Lynn left town and drove to the Groom community east of Amarillo to look at a tract of land they were considering purchasing. They returned on September 13, but early the next morning Al accompanied Lynn back to that piece of land to retrieve their car, which was stuck in the mud. By early afternoon on September 14, they were back in Amarillo. As was his custom when in Amarillo, Al decided to go downtown. Although streetcar rails ran along Polk Street, Al usually walked along that street some four or five blocks to his destination. En route he passed an Amarillo landmark—the large and impressive Polk Street Methodist Church.

John Beal Sneed was well acquainted with that area of town. His own home on Tyler Street was located only three blocks from the Boyce home. He was also well acquainted with the route the Boyce family members usually took en route to downtown. And he knew that Al took that same route when he decided to go to town—strolled right past the Polk Street Methodist Church. That's why Beal Smith had instructed his associate, Beech Epting, to rent a small house across the street from the church—under an assumed name, of course. Epting followed his leader's instructions.[19] Folks would later call that small house the "death cottage."[20]

Beal Sneed arrived in Amarillo on September 9 in disguise, and a pretty bizarre one at that. He wore dirty farmer's overalls, a faded work shirt, and clodhopper work shoes; he had grown a full beard; he had dyed his naturally reddish hair black; and to top it all, he was wearing what one witness later described as "a pair of blue goggles."[21] He also brought along two automatic pistols, a shotgun loaded with buckshot, and a padded chest protector.

The gunmen themselves were, to understate the matter, an odd couple, cut from entirely different cloth: the leader, a wealthy pillar of his community; his deputy, a poorly educated tenant farmer. Nevertheless, they were united now, both dedicated to their kill-dead

AL G. BOYCE JR. Photograph from the January 13, 1912, edition of the *Fort Worth Star-Telegram*.

Polk Street, Looking South From Opera House, Amarillo, Tex.

POLK STREET METHODIST CHURCH IN AMARILLO, TEXAS, 1912. On September 14, 1912, John Beal Sneed shot and killed Al Boyce, Jr., as he was walking down Polk Street in front of the Polk Street Methodist Church (foreground right). *Photograph courtesy of Amarillo Public Library.*

mission. The small house they had rented for the intended ambush had no air-conditioning, but then nobody had air-conditioning in 1912 Amarillo. Still, most folks at least opened their windows to catch an occasional breeze. But not the assassins. They nailed the shades over all windows, leaving only a narrow space at the bottom of a front window to serve as a peephole. Then they punched a hole through the screen just large enough to poke a gun barrel through and pulled a cot up to the window so the scout could lie in bed while keeping a lookout on Polk Street.[22]

For four miserable days the pair sweated in the heat of early September without sighting their target. Days dragged slowly by: one . . . two . . . three . . . four. Still nothing.

But the leader was patient. And he was determined. Perhaps, as the long hours of waiting gradually turned into days, he reflected on the strange turn of events that had led him—a card-carrying member of pioneer Texas cow country royalty and a college-educated lawyer—to this ironic juncture in his life. Already indicted for one murder, he now was hell-bent on committing another. Worse, his intended victim had been a friend from years back. Philosophical reflection, however, was not John Beal Sneed's long suit, and the word irony was probably not in his working vocabulary. He was totally focused on the bloody mission ahead.

Beal was well aware that his intended victim always went armed, and he was also aware that Al Boyce was reputed to be a crack shot, one of the best in the Texas Panhandle. That was why Beal had spent so much time of late practicing his marksmanship. Even so, in a fair fight he would likely come in dead last. He knew that. But then he had no intention of fighting fair.

He did, however, have every intention of winning. This contest or any other contest. Whatever it took.

September 14, 1912, marked a tragic anniversary. It had been almost nine months ago to the day that John Beal Sneed had assassinated Colonel Boyce. The afternoon of September 14 was a pleasant day. The sun was shining, but there was a hint of fall in the air; the temperature had cooled a bit. Al Boyce was enjoying his stroll downtown. As he approached the Polk Street Methodist Church he recognized the

pastor, the Reverend Ernest Robinson. The minister had been shopping and was carrying an armload of groceries. "Howdy-do," Al called
to the preacher. Robinson returned the greeting, and then made some
remark about the weather, noting that the heat had moderated. "Yes,"
Al replied, "it's getting to be the fall of the year."[23]

About then Beal Sneed—sweating profusely in the steamy death
cottage and peering out his peephole—spied Al. Cold, grim, and
determined, Beal slipped both pistols in his belt and grabbed his .12
gauge shotgun. It was loaded with buckshot. This business was going
to be settled right now. Now and forever.

Leaving Epting in the cottage, he quietly opened the front door.
Al had passed—his back now to the cottage. He didn't see Beal
approach. Beal silently stalked his prey, quickly closing the distance
between them. He intended to use the shotgun—a lot less chance
of missing his target with a splatter-barrel. But then there was one
limitation to manhunting with a shotgun: the hunter had to get very
close to his prey. He couldn't risk shooting too quickly from too
great a distance. He couldn't afford to simply wound Al. If he did,
Al would turn, draw his own pistol, and return fire. Beal knew Al
was lethal with his pistol. Beal continued his swift, stealthy stalk. Just
before he reached the streetcar rail, he had closed the distance to
within a few yards. Close enough. He raised the shotgun and began
firing. He fired three times, and he didn't miss a one.[24]

Reverend Robinson heard the shots and saw what was happen-
ing. The terrified minister raced pell-mell up the church steps,
throwing groceries to the wind, and disappeared into the safety
of his parsonage. The preacher later testified that Al never said a
word.[25] But then, in his panicked flight to escape danger, he might
have missed something.

There was another eyewitness—probably a more reliable one—
who told a slightly different story of those final seconds in Al's life.
A young boy named Earl Jackson was riding his bicycle nearby on
Polk Street when he heard the shots and saw what was taking place.
In his excitement, the boy ran his bicycle into a hitching post and
fell in a mud puddle. But his attention continued to be riveted on
the horrifying spectacle. He would later testify that when Al finally

realized someone was behind him, he turned, recognized Beal, but didn't have time to draw his pistol. He pleaded, "Don't shoot me! Please don't shoot me![26] But Al might as well have saved his last breath. John Beal Sneed was not about to show any mercy. Mercy was another word that was not in Sneed's working vocabulary. According to Earl Jackson, just after he finished firing three shotgun blasts at point-blank range into Al's body, Sneed muttered, "I guess you are dead, you son of a bitch."[27] Al never said another word; his undrawn Luger pistol was still tucked inside his belt.[28]

A doctor was called, but there was nothing he could do for Al. His body was taken to the Boyce home where the doctor counted thirty pieces of buckshot in his body and then stopped counting.[29] The distraught Annie Boyce shook her fist in anguish and frustration and demanded that somebody "show me the man who killed this man." Then she reached over, brushed Al's hair back, and moaned, "If only my boy could speak to me."[30]

Meanwhile, Beal, unruffled, ambled north on Polk Street to the Potter County courthouse and jail. En route he greeted an acquaintance, but because of Beal's disguise, the man failed to recognize him. Another man, seeing people rush to the scene of the killing, asked Beal, "What's the trouble?" to which Beal coolly replied, "Nothing, I have got him."[31] As Beal passed the Magnolia Hotel, one of the inhabitants witnessed him making his way toward the jail. Her name was Georgia O'Keeffe. She would later become a famous artist, but, at the time, she was just beginning her employment as an Amarillo schoolteacher.[32]

When John Beal Sneed reached the sheriff's office still in disguise, he identified himself, surrendered to the startled officers, handed over two pistols and a shotgun, and then calmly stated that he had just killed Al Boyce, Jr. But he declined to elaborate. Or, as lawyers of that day in their formal and stylized legalese would have phrased it: "Further, the defendant sayeth naught."

At the appropriate time, however, the defendant would sayeth much.

When the doctor examined Al Boyce's body, he also examined his clothing, and that's when he made an astonishing discovery: a letter that clearly and unequivocally documented the fact that John Beal Sneed and his attorneys (Scott and Johnson) had bribed at least one of the jurors in Beal's trial for the murder of Colonel Boyce. The letter was dated June 24, 1912, shortly after the conclusion of the murder trial. It was a registered letter written by one Earl McFarland and addressed to John Beal Sneed. How Al Boyce ended up in possession of the letter was not documented. The content of the letter, especially when taken in context of the bribery allegations aired during the trial, speak convincingly of its authenticity. McFarland's letter to Beal read:

> My objective in seeing you was in regards to the settlement made by your attorneys for my services rendered in your case . . . Your attorneys told me to come + after having a talk with Mr. Scott, also Mr. Johnson they told me to go ahead with my plan which I did, + that you know of. I told Mr. Johnson that I had an agreement to pay the Juror $100. He said that would be satisfactory. My expense there, train fare + hotel bill for 23 days came to $76.00. When the settlement was made Mr. Scott gave me $150.00 saying that was all you had allowed. Which made me $26.00 looser [sic]—regardless of my time.[33]

Later events, as they continued to unfold in the incredible saga of John Beal Sneed, lent even more credence to the belief that this letter was indeed authentic.

Meanwhile, John Beal Sneed, having wisely retreated and surrendered himself to the Amarillo sheriff, languished comfortably in the Potter County jail. An ambitious reporter for the *St. Louis Post-Dispatch* attempted to interview Amarillo's most notorious inmate but Beal declined to comment.[34] He was safe there, at least for the time being, while he was out of range of the guns of Al's three brothers, Henry, Will, and Lynn—Lynn being "the big westerner"

who, during Beal Sneed's Fort Worth trial, had once dropped his whittling knife and lunged at Bill McLean when McLean berated Lynn's mother during cross-examination. As soon as Lynn heard that Beal Sneed had killed his brother, he grabbed a Winchester rifle and roamed the streets of Amarillo stalking the assassin. But he was too late. Beal beat him to the safe haven of the Potter County jailhouse.

Many a blood feud had erupted in Texas on a lot less provocation than the ambush killings of a man's father and brother. Now it seemed that all Texas was holding its collective breath in anticipation of what appeared to be the inevitable—the next revenge killing. Or killings.

The conviction that more bloodshed was inevitable reached far beyond the borders of Texas. The September 16, 1912, edition of the *New York Times* ran a story headlined: "Boyce-Sneed Feud Feared: Clans of Hostile Families Gather in Amarillo." After listing all the key players of the Sneed, Snyder, and Boyce families who had arrived in town, the *Times* story portended the gathering storm:

> With a score of members of the feudist families here, city and county officers established a strict surveillance to prevent any clash, for while matters were quiet on the surface today, it was feared that a hasty word or a suspicious movement might make mischief . . . Armed deputies were constantly at [John Beal Sneed's] side.

However, there was calm at the eye of the storm. The *Times* story continued:

> Sneed showed the utmost indifference in his cell today. He ate three meals, smoked cigarettes, conferred with his attorneys, and refused to issue any public statement. Service was held as usual today in the First [*sic*] Methodist Church, whose front steps and walls were bespattered with Boyce's blood yesterday.

As if all the above was not sufficient to satisfy the cravings of the most avid of dime-novel addicts, another bombshell exploded. Only twelve days after John Beal Sneed killed Al Boyce, the September 26, 1912, edition of the *Fort Worth Star-Telegram* carried a story in which it reviewed the latest developments in this ongoing tragedy. One sentence in that story, seemingly added as an afterthought, must have astonished even those closest to the principals—John Beal Sneed in particular. The reporter noted that Lena would "shortly be a mother."

"Because This Is Texas"

The Second Fort Worth Murder Trial of John Beal Sneed

LODGED IN THE POTTER COUNTY JAIL in Amarillo under indictment for the murder of Al Boyce, John Beal Sneed once again petitioned for bail.[1] The Amarillo district attorney, H. S. Bishop, opposed it. District Judge J. N. Browning agreed, finding that "proof was evident" that Sneed was guilty of having committed the offense of premeditated murder. As Sneed's defense lawyers had done only nine months earlier in Fort Worth, they contended that proof was *not* evident that Sneed had committed premeditated, first-degree murder. Just as they had done in the Colonel Boyce murder case, McLean did not deny that Sneed killed Al Boyce or deny that Sneed had killed him intentionally. Nevertheless, McLean contended, the most that the state could prove against Sneed was a manslaughter charge, and therefore, Sneed was entitled to have appropriate bail set for his release. In making this argument, McLean relied on the "insulting words or conduct" directed toward a "female relative" statute as he had during Sneed's first murder trial. The effect of that statute was to reduce the grade of that offense from what would otherwise have been premeditated murder to manslaughter, two to five years, provided that the defendant killed the libertine at their "first meeting" after the enraged relative learned of the insulting words or conduct.

Although Sneed had learned of the affair between Al and Lena some eleven months earlier, McLean contended that John Beal Sneed shot Al Boyce upon their first meeting after Sneed learned of it. Alternatively, McLean relied on a second Texas manslaughter statute contending that the sudden appearance of Al Boyce incited in his client a "sudden passion arising from adequate cause." Judge Browning didn't buy either argument, so on September 28, 1912, he refused to set bail. Sneed appealed the ruling and, in a split decision, the Texas Court of Criminal Appeals agreed with McLean, reversing Judge Browning's ruling and setting bail.

One appellate judge wrote a brief dissenting opinion agreeing with Judge Browning. He didn't believe the facts of the killing of Al Boyce fit within the intent of either manslaughter statute. Noting that Sneed, in disguise and secreted in the death cottage, had waited patiently for several days to ambush his prey and then shot Al Boyce in the back, the dissenting judge wrote that this hardly qualified as a "first meeting" as contemplated by the law. Furthermore, he continued, the second manslaughter statute obviously envisioned a scenario in which the encounter incited the defendant to fly into a sudden passionate rage at the libertine's outrageous conduct toward his wife. The dissenting jurist also wrote that whatever passion and outrage that Sneed felt upon learning of the affair some eleven months earlier had "fully passed out and away before the killing, and the [premeditated] *passion of revenge* completely took its place."[2]

John Beal Sneed killed Al Boyce on September 14, 1912. On October 30, 1912, the Court of Criminal Appeals set his bail at $20,000. After having served approximately one and a half months in the Potter County jail, Sneed posted bond and was released just in time to appear for his retrial back in Fort Worth for the murder of Colonel Boyce scheduled to begin on November 11, 1912.

The November 9, 1912, edition of the *Fort Worth Star-Telegram* informed its readers that John Beal Sneed arrived in town "looking fresh as a daisy," that he was in a congenial mood, and that he laughed and joked with the Fort Worth lawmen who had escorted him from Amarillo to Fort Worth.

The Murder Trial Begins

One sensational headline chased yet another across the front pages of Texas newspapers that month. On November 9, 1912, the front-page headline in the *Fort Worth Star-Telegram* screamed: "Christians Face Massacre if Constantinople Falls." The next day's front page carried this sensational headline: "Europe with Armies Fifteen Million Strong Now Facing a General War." On a lighter note, another headline told of "Joyous Democrats" celebrating the election of Woodrow Wilson as president. Another headline announced that Southern Baptists revealed plans to raise a whopping one million dollars in 1912. Catholics were not so fortunate, however. The Texas textbook board rejected a protest filed by Catholics complaining that a Texas history textbook discriminated against them. On November 12, the day the Sneed trial began, the lead story announced that a nut case named John Schrank pleaded guilty to wounding third-party candidate and ex-president Teddy Roosevelt during a campaign speech in Milwaukee. Other headlines announced that Mexican president Madero planned to distribute lands to peasants and that suffragists were planning to hold their next national convention in Texas.

However, not even such exciting stories as those could galvanize the Texas public like daily updates on the John Beal Sneed murder trial. The day before the trial started, the front page of the *Star-Telegram* headlined the upcoming drama, telling its readers this: "All the United States is watching the trial that begins Monday. So far as Texas is concerned, no criminal case ever was so important." Backgrounding the tragedy, the story continued:

> College chums at Georgetown, John Beal Sneed, Al G. Boyce, Jr., and Lena Snyder formed a three-sided acquaintance that they never dreamed would be their undoing. The girl chose Sneed. The pathways of Mrs. Sneed and young Al Boyce parted . . . until they met again in the spring of 1911 when Boyce visited his girl friend of college days.[3]

Tarrant County Attorney John Baskin was the elected official in charge of the prosecution. However, once again facing the fiercely aggressive defense team headed by "Wild Bill" McLean, Baskin welcomed all the help he could get. With his consent and approval, the Boyce family beefed up the prosecution team by once again hiring not only Senator W. A. Hanger but also another state senator, D. W. (Weldon) Odell of Cleburne. Renowned West Texas frontier lawyer and legal historian, Charles Coombes, called Senator Odell "one of the greatest orators I have ever known."[4] Obviously, the Boyce family hoped that Odell would checkmate the defense team's master spellbinder, Cone Johnson. Dramatic Jordan Y. Cummings was also hired to assist County Attorney Baskin.

Not to be outdone, John Beal Sneed hired another celebrated defense lawyer to bolster his roster. Defending those accused of murder was A. J. Fires's specialty, and during his long career in the trenches of the criminal courts, he represented one hundred and twenty-three defendants in murder trials with only four of them departing the courthouse in chains. In several of his high-profile criminal cases around the turn of the century Fires teamed up with the colorful and eloquent Temple Houston, youngest son of Texas hero Sam Houston. Although Fires might not have been as eloquent as Temple Houston, the "Bible-quotin', gun-totin' lawyer," he made up for it with his bulldog determination. Fires, like McLean, was of the "whatever-it-takes-to-win" school of jurisprudence, and he rarely permitted mere ethics to get in his way. Fires and McLean were alike in another respect. It was well understood that his enthusiasm and dedication to a client's cause kicked in only after Fires had collected a king's ransom of a fee. Contemporaries at the bar often snickered (outside of Fires's hearing) that he had two fee schedules: a stiff fee if a client furnished his own eyewitnesses to the murder but a much higher fee if A. J. had to furnish the eyewitnesses. Still others remarked—sometimes with a chuckle, but more often with a grumble if they were on the opposing side—that old Amos Fires might not actually commit murder to win an acquittal, but that he'd probably damn sure consider it.

A. J. Fires hailed from Childress, Texas, on the southeast cusp of the Texas Panhandle, and nearly all of his cases were tried in courts of that area. Since John Beal Sneed killed Al Boyce, Jr., in Amarillo, it was apparent that the murder trial (as well as the murder trial of his sidekick, Beech Epting) would be held either in Amarillo or in a nearby county. Hence, Sneed's strategy in hiring Fires was clear: not only would he be a valuable addition to the defense team in this Fort Worth trial, but also he would gain helpful insight and experience for the upcoming Al Boyce murder trial to be held on Fires's home turf.

When Amos Fires joined the Sneed defense team, he realized that he was signing on for at least two murder trials after Fort Worth. What he did not realize at that time was what his association with John Beal Sneed would lead to outside of the courtroom after these trials were over. If A. J. Fires had had the benefit of a crystal ball, he might have glimpsed yet another one of John Beal Sneed's future shooting sprees—one in which he would be more than just a bystander.

The second Fort Worth murder trial followed the same basic pattern as the first: the same basic contentions from both the prosecution and defense teams, the same basic trial strategies, same judge, and, mostly, the same lawyers on both sides. However, there would be significant differences and surprises in store for the throngs of courtroom spectators as well as newspaper readers across the nation.

One question that occurs to any legal historian who studies the first trial has to be: what can we make of Judge Swayne? Much of the blame for allowing McLean and the defense team to run wild during the first trial had to be laid at the doorstep of the somnolent prosecutors for their failure to make timely and proper objections. However, there was much Judge Swayne could have done, but didn't, to rein in the excesses of the defense lawyers. After all, it was his court, and he was in charge. Was he incompetent? Was he bribed? Was he intimidated by the combined brilliance, force, and imposing presence of "Wild Bill" McLean, Cone Johnson, Walter Scott, John Beal Sneed, and the elder William McLean, the respected Texas statesman?

During the course of the second John Beal Sneed trial, it became apparent by Judge Swayne's actions as well as by his comments thereafter that he was not intimidated or bribed nor did he intentionally attempt to help the defense team win. So why then did Judge Swayne allow the defense team to figuratively "get away with murder" during the first trial? In all probability his reticence was due to two considerations. First, the judge likely granted the defense considerable latitude in hopes of denying the Sneed team any possible reversible error to complain about on appeal of the guilty verdict he expected. At that time the prosecution had absolutely no right to appeal any "not guilty" verdict while the defense had the right to appeal any "guilty" verdict, and, in a long and complicated criminal trial such as the Beal Sneed case where the trial judge was required to make scores of calls, the chance of committing an error was multiplied. Furthermore, the risk of committing a reversible error was greatly enhanced in those days because the Texas Court of Criminal Appeals viewed almost any trial error—however trivial—as just cause to reverse the conviction. (In 1900, for example, the Texas Court of Criminal Appeals reversed convictions in an astounding 68.5 percent of all criminal convictions it reviewed, not counting prohibition and liquor convictions.[5]) That had the unfortunate effect of encouraging trial judges to make rulings favorable to the defendant when any close legal question was raised during the trial, all in hopes of avoiding the embarrassment of a reversal.

Second, Judge Swayne's lengthy legal career as a private lawyer, as a prosecutor, and as a judge was most notable for his ongoing personal crusades against crime and injustice. He was a man of high principles and lofty ideals, and sometimes that caused him to fail to make a down-to-earth assessment of issues. For instance, earlier in his career, when he served as Fort Worth city attorney, he once launched a doggedly determined campaign to clean up "Hell's Half Acre," a section of town notorious for its saloons, brothels, and gambling establishments. Unfortunately for Judge Swayne's crusade, it turned out that a majority of Fort Worth residents were not yet ready to renounce Cowtown's rough and rowdy frontier ways. No convictions resulted in the fifty-odd criminal cases he filed.[6]

It therefore seems probable that Judge Swayne's lofty ideals and failure to make accurate appraisals of judicial reality led him astray in the John Beal Sneed murder trials. Very likely his naiveté caused him to believe that no reasonable jury could possibly acquit a killer who had intentionally shot an unarmed old man who had never threatened him regardless of whatever bombast and out-of-order tricks the defense came up with. So believing, he tended to allow the defense team additional latitude to ensure against a reversal of the conviction he felt certain would be returned.

Judge Swayne was obviously surprised when the jury in the first murder trial failed to return the anticipated "guilty" verdict: deadlocked seven to five in favor of an acquittal. Consequently, during the second murder trial Judge Swayne tightened the reins on McLean and company, thinking no doubt that doing so would avoid another hung jury and ensure a guilty verdict. Unfortunately for the prosecution, he didn't tighten those reins nearly enough.

The questioning of prospective jurors proved almost as interesting as the trial, and it certainly gave unmistakable clues as to where the trial was headed. Although Judge Swayne seemed basically in sympathy with the prosecution, he nevertheless, inexplicably, allowed the defense to get away with a thinly disguised appeal for a "not guilty" verdict by reason of the unwritten law. For example, when the prosecutor Weldon Odell asked a juror if he understood that there was "no such thing as the unwritten law" and that jurors were expected to abide by the law and the evidence, the man answered in the affirmative. But then in response to McLean's question, he stated that he believed killing another man was justified if done "to protect the home." The prosecution challenged the juror for cause, but Judge Swayne overruled the challenge, forcing the state to use up one of its fifteen peremptory (reason-free) challenges to keep him off the jury. However, the prosecution soon ran out of peremptory challenges and had to accept some unwanted jurors, such as Walter Portwood. McLean had asked Portwood if he believed the "home should be protected against slander of the old as well as the young," to which the prospective juror replied, "It would be a sorry man who wouldn't."[7]

Another example of Judge Swayne's leniency during jury selection was demonstrated during the questioning of T. W. Cole by McLean. McLean asked him this: "Do you believe in a man's right to kill an old man as well as a young man for slandering his wife?" Even the archaic "slander of a female relative of the killer" statute did not grant the offended relative a "right" to kill anybody, young or old. County Attorney Baskin correctly objected to this question. He said: "That question is not fair. The law does not give one man a right to kill another for slander." Once again Swayne overruled Baskin's valid objection, whereupon when prospective juror Cole answered that he did believe slander of one's wife gave the offended husband a right to kill the insulter, the prosecution was forced to take Cole as a juror.[8] Having to accept Cole and Portwood on the jury (as well as others expressing similar sentiments) did not augur well for the prosecution. Their responses to McLean's questions also provided a not-so-subtle hint of the prevailing sentiment in the community.

On the other hand, prospective juror A. A. Porter seemed to be headed for the jury box until McLean found out that he had been born in the state of New York. "Too far north," McLean growled—and got rid of him with a peremptory strike. Then there was E. L. Craig, a farmer. When Odell asked him whether news accounts of the first Sneed trial had caused him to form an opinion as to the defendant's guilt or innocence, Craig assured him that it hadn't. In fact, he added, he hadn't read a newspaper in all his life. "I never had curiosity to read newspapers," he added. McLean welcomed him to the jury. And so the defense ended up with a jury that suited its criteria to a tee: twelve married men, all with children, all farmers, all born and raised in the South, and all of whom believed in "protecting the home." If ever the state was forced to construct its entire prosecutorial edifice upon a foundation of sand, this had to be Exhibit A.

Judge Swayne obviously believed that one or more jurors on the first Sneed murder trial had been bribed because when the jury was finally seated he instructed the jurors to "knock down and spit on anybody who tried to talk to them about the case." He went even further and ordered the jurors not to kiss their wives in the courtroom during the trial.

McLean's questioning of each venireman was a clear signal that McLean and Sneed intended to rely on the "insulting words" statute. Even though the defense had no intention of settling for a manslaughter verdict, still the "insulting words" statute did open wide the gates of evidence, allowing the defense to present to the jury all the demeaning things that Colonel Boyce had allegedly said about Lena. It would go a long way toward allowing the defense to sidetrack the jury—to focus its attention on trying Colonel Boyce for slander instead of trying John Beal Sneed for murder. In reality, then, in its grand design, the defense team relied on the "insulting words" manslaughter statute only as a stalking horse to reach its real defense: the unwritten law. And exoneration.

To their credit, Hanger, Odell, Cummings, and the prosecution team did wake up and make an effort to keep McLean and company from injecting at least some of the inadmissible and emotionally laden irrelevant testimony that it had injected into evidence during the first trial. Once when the defense attempted to smear Colonel Boyce for the supposedly "vulgar" remark he had made about Lena, Senator Hanger objected: "Testimony in this trial ought to be limited to the actual slaying of the deceased and the guilt of the defendant." But McLean was not having any of that: "If it's true Captain Boyce connived at, aided in, and advised the elopement of Mrs. Lena Sneed with Al Boyce, Jr., these men who have to pass on Beal Sneed's liberty ought to know it." Once again, McLean got away with tacking his own inadmissible, unsworn, jury-courting sidebar allegations onto his response to a legal objection.

Judge Swayne, although not limiting the evidence to the actual slaying as Senator Hanger requested, nevertheless did restrict the defense considerably more than he had done in the first trial. For example, he didn't allow the defense to permit Sneed's banker friend, W. H. Fuqua, to read the maudlin, self-pitying letter Beal had written him while the search for the missing Al and Lena was in progress. And he didn't let the defense get Colonel Boyce's famous "stand hitched" letter into evidence this time, nor did he let Johnson ask Colonel Boyce's bank officer, Ed Farwell, if Colonel Boyce had instructed him to furnish the money for his son's elopement with Lena. When Cone Johnson arrogantly persisted in attempting to ask that question in the jury's presence after being instructed not to do so, Judge Swayne found him in contempt and fined him $100. Judge Swayne also refused to allow any witness to testify as to any "insulting" remarks Colonel Boyce allegedly made about Lena unless it could be shown that those remarks had been repeated to Beal Sneed prior to the time Sneed killed the Colonel.

Even more important, Judge Swayne reversed the incorrect ruling he made during the first trial and, over a defense objection, allowed the prosecution to introduce the testimony the deceased Ed Throckmorton had given during Sneed's first bail bond hearing. This jury thus got to hear Throckmorton's account of the fatal confrontation between Sneed and Colonel Boyce, including Beal's final words while standing over Colonel Boyce's body, Sneed saying, "Now you're out of it—you're done for." Judge Swayne also ruled out all correspondence from the Boyce family to Al Boyce after the elopement, as well as Colonel Boyce's letter appealing for Canadian authorities to allow his son to remain in Canada. (This was the same letter in which he had described Lena as being "mean as a snake.")

However, the judge did once again allow McLean and company to get away with some egregious trial sins. The defense called as its first defense witness Lena's father, Thomas A. Snyder, for the purpose of blaming Colonel Boyce and his wife for failing to stop the affair before it got out of hand. To bolster his contention, he testified as to conversations he had had with Colonel and Annie Boyce. The state repeatedly objected that it violated the hearsay rule to let Snyder quote what the Colonel or Annie Boyce allegedly said during these conversations. Despite these repeated objections and some attempts by Swayne to exclude this hearsay testimony, Captain Snyder, from the stand, loudly demanded that the court and the lawyers leave him alone and "let me tell my story." Finally, Swayne relented and allowed Snyder to make a rambling, ranting stump speech—hearsay and all. However, when the prosecution finally called Annie Boyce and questioned her about conversations she had had with both Lena and Captain Snyder, McLean strenuously objected on hearsay grounds, and Judge Swayne sustained his objection. Therefore, Annie Boyce never got to "tell my story," and the jury only heard a one-sided version of those conversations. The *Star-Telegram*, by this time having abandoned any pretense of objectivity in its adoration for McLean, Sneed, Johnson, and the defense theory, gave a glowing description of Captain Snyder, describing him as:

> A picturesque figure, iron gray hair, short and bristly, shoulders erect, commanding respect of the court who looks out of place in court . . . [and would] look more in place as master of an antebellum plantation in his native state of Mississippi.[9]

As expected, the defense called John Beal Sneed's private lawyer, Will Atwell, who was also the U.S. District Attorney. Again, the prosecution failed to force Atwell to own up to his flagrant conflict of interest. And, once again, the artful dodger avoided any potentially embarrassing cross-examination questions. His memory seemed to fail him on those occasions. He repeatedly answered: "That isn't just clear, so I'll say I don't remember."

Beal's sidekick and brother-in-law, Henry Bowman, was called once again, the high point of his testimony being a recital of the bleak 1911 Christmas at his home in Plano shortly after Al and Lena had eloped. The *Star-Telegram* reported that "tears stood in the eyes of jurors, lawyers, and women spectators" when Bowman described how the two Sneed daughters cried and begged their father to go and find their mother. Bowman went on to praise Beal Sneed as a model father and husband.

To lay the groundwork for Beal Sneed's much-anticipated appearance as the defense's star witness, McLean called a down-on-his-luck Oklahoma lawyer named W. A. Weaver. Weaver testified that he was present in the lobby of the Metropolitan Hotel when Sneed killed Colonel Boyce. Weaver told the jury that just before Sneed pulled his pistol and started firing, he heard Colonel Boyce make this "vile" remark to his comrade, Ed Throckmorton: "Here comes the _____ now." (Once again, in deference to its readers' tender sensibilities, the *Star-Telegram* refused to print the "vile" part of that remark.) That, according to Sneed's testimony in the first trial, was the straw that finally broke the camel's back, causing him to fly into a rage and begin firing away.

With that the defense cleared the stage and put the spotlight on its stalwart spellbinder, John Beal Sneed. No one on either side of the aisle doubted that his performance would be worthy of its billing. On the day before Sneed's eagerly awaited appearance on the witness stand, the *Star-Telegram*, in a headline story, once again forsaking impartiality at the throne of hero worship, surrendered page one to the defense. Bill McLean gave the credulous reporter a masterful spin-doctoring scoop. The jury, he predicted, would get an earful of sensational testimony when John Beal Sneed related what Lena had told him after he rescued her in Canada and brought her home. He was quoted as confiding this to the reporter: "Mrs. Sneed, repentant over her elopement with Al Boyce, Jr., told her husband about statements that Colonel Boyce had made to her."

McLean later added other helpful background information. He said that although Lena and Beal were not living together as man and wife, Sneed was supporting her and said that he would support and protect her for the rest of her life because she is the mother of his children and because he still believes her insane in spite of a finding to the contrary of a jury here.

Cone Johnson also got in his licks on the same front page. He said:

> The prosecution is weakening its cause. It is succeeding in excluding our testimony that would show Captain Boyce was implicated in a conspiracy to take Beal Sneed's wife from him. The jury will wonder what that testimony is.[10]

One also has to wonder if McLean and company didn't somehow manage to slip a copy of that edition of the *Star-Telegram* to the jury. It had all the earmarks of a carefully calculated, surreptitious plot by the defense, not only to outflank the prosecution but also to get before the jury all the testimony that Judge Swayne had outlawed as inadmissible during the trial. And wasn't the timing just too convenient—right on the eve of John Beal Sneed's appearance on the witness stand? In view of all the other extralegal shenanigans that McLean and associates had concocted and successfully implemented, the slipping of a copy of that *Star-Telegram* edition to the jury via a friendly court bailiff or deputy seems very likely. It all failed to pass the smell test—and the foul odor was more than merely the stench of journalistic malpractice.

When John Beal Sneed testified the next day, he once again constructed his tale of woe—including all his selfless sacrifices, as well as the reasonableness and necessity of the assassination of Colonel Boyce—upon the foundation of Lena's moral insanity. In fact, he was even better this time than he had been during his first trial, doubtless due to much storytelling practice, additional time to reflect on it all, and additional "memory-refreshing suggestions" courtesy of his inventive attorneys. The sky, after all, was the limit, since there was a total absence of prosecution witnesses available to refute any such refreshed recollections. Improvements in the new hearsay-laden version of Sneed's tale included these revisions:

1. He now claimed that he, and not the expensive Burns Detective Agency, had finally succeeded in finding Al and Lena in Canada, and this only after his unrelenting and lonely ordeal. Sneed detailed his long, painful search for Lena including "walking the streets of St. Louis tirelessly and scanning the faces of all the hurrying people in hotel lobbies, vainly hoping to find his wife."

2. Beal's account of his picture-perfect family life B.A. ("Before Al") got even rosier this time around. Looking directly in the faces of the jurors, he said: "My family life was all that a man could wish for . . . my wife used to come to me and tell me she was so happy she feared it couldn't last long, she feared something would happen."

3. Beal told the jurors that after the elopement, Colonel Boyce had publicly "made fun of him." Beal said he "couldn't go down Main Street so great was my humiliation. I took the back streets."

4. Beal claimed that he had learned that Colonel Boyce had not only approved of the elopement of Al and Lena, but had actually furnished the money for their flight to Canada; that he had sent his bank officer, Ed Farwell, with the money to Fort Worth to "help Al take my wife away."

5. During the first trial, Sneed testified that while he was bringing Lena back from Canada she confessed to him that she, with Al's approval, had planned to sneak back to Texas, kidnap their two daughters from the Bowman home in Plano, and take them back to Canada. As unlikely as that story sounded the first time around, it got even more incredible this time. Sneed refined it and added a bit to the story of Lena's "confession." According to this version, Lena confessed that it was Colonel Boyce himself who was going to kidnap their daughters and bring them to Dallas where Lena, in disguise, could take possession of the children and then return with them to Al in Canada.

6. Beal's new and refined version of Lena's purported confession (asserting that Colonel Boyce had volunteered to kidnap Lena's daughters from the Bowman home and then deliver them to her and Al) was totally inconsistent with other parts of Beal's testimony—such as, for example, Beal now saying that his friend W. H. Fuqua informed him that Colonel Boyce was making "remarks [about Lena] so vile that he [Fuqua] wouldn't make them about the vilest woman in town." That and other derogatory remarks about Lena attributed to Colonel Boyce.

7. Finally, Beal repeated his claim that when he came into the hotel lobby just before the shooting, he heard the Colonel say to Ed Throckmorton: "Here comes the _____ now." According to Beal, this insult was what finally pushed him over the edge. Trouble was, nobody else in the lobby seemed to have overheard this remark—*except* the Oklahoma lawyer W. A. Weaver whom the defense had called ahead of Beal to lend credibility to Beal's claim that the Colonel had indeed made that "vile" remark.

This time, however, the state was ready for Weaver's lie. After Beal's testimony, the state, in rebuttal, called seven witnesses who proved conclusively that Weaver couldn't have heard such a remark, or any other remark made in the hotel lobby that night, since he was nowhere near the Metropolitan Hotel at the time of the killing. And, by the way, it also surfaced that lawyer Weaver had recently been ejected from his hotel room in Oklahoma for failure to pay his rent. Weaver was promptly charged with perjury and carted off to jail.[11]

Much embarrassed by this revelation, the defense had to deal with the crisis somehow. Cone Johnson was assigned the unpleasant task. Johnson took the stand and denied any prior knowledge that Weaver's story was false. He said that Weaver voluntarily showed up at McLean's law office and told his story and that he had believed him. On cross-examination by Senator Hanger, Johnson was called upon to explain how come, *after* Weaver had been proven to be a liar and had been jailed for perjury, the defense lawyers nevertheless posted a $1,000 bail bond to get him out of jail. Johnson, rather lamely, explained, "Because he was a stranger in town, and I didn't want him to go to jail, and I felt I owed it to him to keep him out of jail after he had offered to help my client."[12]

One has to wonder if Senator Hanger didn't find Cone Johnson's explanation much too disingenuous to swallow. According to Johnson, this broke lawyer from Oklahoma wandered in off the street one day and claimed he just happened to have been in Fort Worth on January 13, 1912, and just happened to have been an eyewitness to this sensational murder, and then, instead of reporting his eyewitness account of this tragic incident to the authorities, he decided to seek out the defense lawyers and tell them a tale that, amazingly enough, just happened to dovetail perfectly with the defense script—the same version, in fact, that John Beal Sneed intended to sell to the jury, including the exact epithet that Beal now claimed to have heard. According to Johnson, he, McLean, and Scott didn't bother to check out Weaver or his story; they just wound him up, put him on the stand, and let him go. According to Cone Johnson, it was only after the prosecution unmasked Weaver that the defense realized that their witness was a fraud and a liar.

Perhaps if Senator Hanger had reflected on the matter, another scenario might have occurred to him, one with the ring of truth to it—a scenario that played out something like this: the defense found this ne'er-do-well four-flusher under a rock somewhere and put him up to telling this convenient fabrication. Even more convenient was the fact that Weaver was broke and no doubt his witness fee was very reasonable. But the prosecution exposed this scam. It provided the prosecution with a marvelous opportunity to magnify this audacious ruse and cast doubt on the credibility of the defense lawyers as well as all the other defense witnesses, including John Beal Sneed. That is, if the prosecutors had been astute enough to recognize the potential of this weapon the defense had so generously presented them and had been skillful enough to exploit it. Bad as all that was—if the above supposition is correct—then there was a far more serious time bomb a-ticking in the defense camp. Regardless of what a despicable reprobate Weaver might have been, the defense just couldn't afford to let him swelter and stew in his jail cell and become disgruntled with his fate. He just might begin to feel that his erstwhile friends and fellow conspirators had abandoned him. If so, he might also decide to start talking to the wrong people; just might decide to cut himself a deal with prosecutors: drop the perjury charge against me, and I will give you the big fish. If such were the case, then it is no wonder that Cone Johnson broke speed records getting to the jail with a $1,000 bail bond for their debunked eyewitness. It is a better than even bet that Weaver hit the street posthaste and headed out of town with plenty of traveling money in his pocket.

Back in the courtroom, one can only imagine the devastating cross-examination that would have been in store for Cone Johnson after telling that whopper had "Wild Bill" McLean been on the prosecution's team. But Senator Hanger was no Bill McLean, so he didn't bother to challenge Cone Johnson's absurd explanation. Was it professional courtesy? Or did Senator Hanger, a Fort Worth politician, have his eye on his next bid for reelection, and therefore stop to consider the political clout of the McLean firm in Fort Worth as well as that of U.S. senatorial candidate Cone Johnson? Or did Hanger just . . . go to sleep again?

The state again called John W. Covey in rebuttal. Covey, the druggist who rode with Colonel Boyce in the ambulance after the shooting, testified that he asked Boyce who shot him. Boyce replied, "Beal Sneed."

Covey: "Did you have any words?"

Boyce: "Not a word."

As it had during the first trial, the prosecution called the *Dallas Times-Herald* newsman E. R. Hambrick, who had caught Atwell off guard the night Boyce was killed. Atwell told Hambrick that the reason Sneed killed the Colonel was that Sneed was enraged at him for getting the Fort Worth indictments against his son dismissed. In addition, the prosecution found one new witness who gave incriminating testimony. Ernest Thompson, a next-door neighbor of Sneed's in Amarillo, testified that prior to the killing he had a conversation with Sneed during a train ride in which Sneed blamed Colonel Boyce for all his troubles, and commented, "I ought to kill the old _____," adding that he and Al would "have to shoot it out."[13] Beal Sneed, of course, swore to the jury that he never made any such statement to Thompson. Beal's denial that he told Thompson that he and Al "would have to shoot it out" gave Senator Hanger another opportunity to take a verbal jab at the witness. By the time of the second trial, Sneed had already "shot it out with Al," and everybody knew all about it. But Hanger let it slide.

The overwhelmed prosecution also failed to take advantage of, and vigorously exploit, a glaring inconsistency in the defense's case. In one breath, Beal Sneed contended that he had the right to kill Colonel Boyce because the Colonel had encouraged and financed the romance and elopement of Al and Lena and later conspired to reunite them, and yet in the next breath Beal claimed that Colonel Boyce was going around Amarillo calling Lena "the vilest woman in town" and, according to Atwell, Colonel Boyce threatened to "drag her through the slime" for the rest of her life. How could the prosecution have overlooked such an obvious contradiction? Also, as in the first trial, the prosecution missed the boat by not vigorously attacking the cornerstone of the entire defense structure: Lena's alleged "insanity," moral or otherwise. Why didn't Hanger call expert witnesses to testify to her sanity; why didn't Hanger emphasize, over and over, the Fort Worth jury's finding at Lena's habeas corpus hearing that she was in fact sane; and why didn't Hanger speculate, loudly and frequently, about the defense's reasons for being so afraid of placing Lena on the stand?

One of the most remarkable things about the second trial is the almost unanimous and unquestioning acceptance (by the press, spectators, and jurors) of Beal's version of the events as well as the motives he attributed to himself, Lena, Al, Colonel Boyce, Mrs. Boyce, and the Boyce brothers. Even more puzzling is the feminine reaction to Beal. The pictures of Beal Sneed, as well as the reports of his words and actions, combine to depict Beal as a decidedly stern, cold, arrogant, unsexy man—the same man who had taken his wife's children away from her and locked her up in an asylum, a man who had ambushed the unarmed Colonel Boyce and then ambushed and killed his son. Nevertheless, he seems to have charmed reporter Kitty Barry and the female spectators. The courtroom was made up, in large part, of women showing their support of and belief in Beal Sneed! At noon recesses many of the women fought for a chance to shake Beal's hand. Even more disturbing, when Beal was scheduled to testify, Kitty Barry noted that a large portion of the audience were girls ten to fifteen years old accompanied by adult women. The idea of Beal Sneed being an early-day teen idol seems totally preposterous. Maybe it was simply the fact that in those days this was one of the few types of dramatic entertainment available.

Jordan Y. Cummings opened the arguments for the state—opened with a roar, and it only got louder after that. Meanwhile, Beal Sneed's two daughters—Lenora, age eleven, and Georgia, age six—sat next to their father only a few feet from the jury. Cummings had hardly begun shouting denouncements of Sneed when little Georgia broke into tears and had to be led out of the courtroom.

Cummings ridiculed attempts by the defense to compare Beal Sneed to Jesus Christ. He related the biblical story of the "woman of shame" who was brought before Jesus who forgave the harlot and told her to "go and sin no more." But, Cummings demanded, what did John Beal Sneed do? Beal Sneed, he bellowed, never forgave anybody for anything. When his wife strayed, he had her locked up in a madhouse and wouldn't let her see her own children.[14]

Cummings then scoffed at the defense assertion that Lena was morally insane, pointing out that it took a $50-a-visit expert, Dr. Turner, three visits with Lena before he finally discovered that she was "morally insane." "Moral insanity," he continued, "has no support in psychology nor in law."

About that time little Georgia Sneed, still sniffling, was brought back into the courtroom and seated on Beal's lap where her older sister, Lenora, began ministering to her. Sneed sat with bowed head while Cummings shouted that nothing could save him from the gallows. That's when, according to the *Star-Telegram* report, Lenora "studied the troubled face of her father [and] threw her little bare arms about his neck, drew his face to her and kissed him."

"It's an awful thing," Cummings observed, "to bring those little girls in here to hear the story of their mother's shame in order to protect the man that killed old man Boyce." Cummings did little, however, to make it any easier on those little girls when he ended his oration, still shouting, with this demand to the jurors: "I ask you to administer justice to this defendant and if you do you will break his neck."

The November 29, 1912, edition of the *Fort Worth Star-Telegram* carried the story of Cummings's jury argument on its front page under this headline: "Sneed Prosecutor Pleads To Jury for Death Verdict." Ironically, on the same front page adjacent to that story, was another article—this one about a hanging in Waxahachie, Texas, headlined "Oates Smokes On Way to Scaffold; Denies His Guilt." It related the gruesome details of how a black man named Oates had been hanged before a large and enthusiastic crowd after having been convicted of murdering a Dallas grocer. The story noted that after Oates was pronounced dead, officers had to beat back the large crowd that rushed the gallows.

Cummings was followed by defense attorney Walter Scott. The ever-theatrical Scott lived up to expectations. "This defendant," he intoned, "stands before you today as a man without a home." He continued: "You remember the evidence showed that this homeless man walked the streets of St. Louis and New York at the dead hour of midnight, hunting his wife, while Al Boyce, Jr., was with her up in Canada and was receiving letters from old man Boyce." All that was emotional enough for most any jury master, but what really brought tears to the eyes of the jurors was when Scott played the "children card." In high drama, Scott reenacted for the jury the dreadful and cheerless 1911 Christmas that Beal and his children spent at Henry Bowman's home with Beal's daughters crying and pleading with their father to "Go get Mamma."

Cone Johnson for the defense was next. First came the obligatory denunciation of Al Boyce, that "cigarette and whiskey fiend" for "lying around Beal's house and wrecking his home." Then came the denunciation of Colonel Boyce, whom Johnson accused of attempting to put Lena "back in the embraces of Al Boyce, and Beal killed him for that. He thought it was the only way."

Once again Cone Johnson compared John Beal Sneed to Jesus Christ, adding that Sneed was "the one man in Texas whose every act commands the admiration of all honorable fathers and husbands." He went on to praise his client for "defying the miserable doctrine of free love," which, he added, "is what is the matter with society."

Waxing even more eloquent, Johnson contended that "the state doesn't build scaffolds for the likes of Beal Sneed," characterizing him as a "man of religion, a man of morality, and a man of peace." It was only when Colonel Boyce—just before the shooting—made that vile remark that finally pushed Sneed over the "precipice," and that was, as Johnson, mixing a metaphor, phrased it, "the feather that broke the camel's back." After all, Johnson pointed out, "a man has a right to protect his home, to protect his wife from debauchery, and to keep her from being taken away from him." Continuing his litany, Johnson confided that the ordeal his client had endured in protecting his home had proved to be "a mill of sorrow that has crushed every fiber of his being." Then it was time for Johnson to play the children card. He said:

> Mr. Cummings said it was cruel to bring these little girls here to influence you jurors. They are motherless, homeless. Where else is there for them to be except beside their father on trial for his life and liberty by you twelve good men. He is all that is left to them; they are all that is left to him. . . . Their tender little hands are not asking for blood. All they ask is that you give their father, all that is left for them, into their little arms. . . . Do not tear Beal Sneed from the embraces of these tearful little children.

Then, standing within arm's reach of the jurors, looking them in the eye, in hushed, reverential tones, playing shamelessly on the fears and prejudices of those rural Victorian Texans, he said this:

> May God protect every one of you good men; may the guardian angel protect your home; may you never meet your [wife] on the gallery [of your home] and have her tell you that she doesn't love you anymore.

It was a powerful and persuasive closing, doing credit to Johnson's reputation as a first- class orator. Yet, just before that closing, he made a remark that, perhaps unintentionally, may well have revealed a clue as to what this whole bloody melodrama was really all about, may have laid bare John Beal Sneed's real motivation. Johnson said, "Are you going to crucify a man who stood by his wife and children through all the outrages *at the risk of his own reputation?*"[15]

Next up for the state was Weldon Odell. Though touted as a spellbinder in the same class as McLean, Scott, and Johnson, his opening arguments were less than riveting—at least as far as the spectators were concerned. When Odell launched into an extended discussion of the applicable statutes, the spectators grew restless and impatient. They had not come to be bored with legalese; they had come to be entertained. With the spectators talking among

themselves and shifting in their seats, Sheriff Rea had to interrupt
Odell several times to call for order. Finally, Odell shifted gears and
came to life. He dealt with the children issue first:

> We all sympathize with the children, but it is sad and it is true that
> every time a criminal is brought before the bar of justice, there is a
> sorrowing and broken-hearted mother, wife, sister, or children. If
> we are to listen and heed the appeals for them, let our law books
> be abolished and let anarchy reign supreme.

Continuing his appeal for primacy of law over maudlin sentiment and lawless revenge, he reminded the jurors that "this is the
most important case ever tried in Texas." He told the jurors that "no
twelve men ever held the destiny of law and order in their hands as
you do." Then Odell said this:

> Don't mistake a swaggering bully with a six-shooter and spurs
> on his heel, a man who shoots out life, as representative of the
> highest citizenship of Texas. We have stood for the Jameses and
> the Youngers for a long time. That kind of citizenship has been
> builded [*sic*] in the minds of too many men.

Odell then raised an interesting point by urging that Texans get
beyond violent self-redressment of wrongs in favor of lawful admin-
istration of justice in the courts. He phrased it this way:

> The law should protect all life. We seldom have difficulty enforc-
> ing our laws against theft, arson, seduction, and rape, but why is
> it that murder goes unpunished so frequently? Why should we
> sympathize with him that takes that which God only gives and God
> only should take?

Odell reminded the jurors that John Beal Sneed's motive for
killing Colonel Boyce was pure revenge triggered by the Colonel's
successful effort to get the indictments against his son dismissed. It
had nothing to do with "protecting Sneed's home," he concluded.
Returning to the children issue, Odell noted that many tears had
been shed for the little children, but that there were no tears shed
"for old Captain Boyce, his life blood flowing."

Odell closed with a demand that the jury break Beal Sneed's neck, saying:

> Divest yourselves of maudlin sentiment and sympathy and you will realize that Beal Sneed has forfeited his right to live, and you'll not hesitate to say so.

Incredibly, the next day's *Star-Telegram*, in an appalling example of biased journalism, depicted Odell's argument as a "merciless attack on a man on trial for his life and liberty." The reporter went on to describe the "tragedy" that had befallen Beal Sneed when his wife ran off with another man. Nothing, however, was mentioned about the "tragedy" that the Boyce family had suffered.

Fiery Bill McLean had the last word for the defense, and he made the best of it with this exhortation:

> I ask no sympathy, though they say we do. We just ask for right and justice, and when you have returned a verdict of that kind no one will have a right to criticize you and no gentleman will. And when you return home and take your children in your arms, clasp your wife to your bosom, and kiss them, be prepared to tell them you returned a verdict that you are not ashamed of that you have said that a man has the right to protect his home; and though there is little probability of such a thing happening, should some scoundrel have entered your home and despoiled it while you were away attending to business, may you take your shotgun, go after him, get him, and I will defend you.[16]

Senator Hanger had the final argument in the trial. He reiterated the contentions advanced by Cummings and Odell, but his closing was, well . . . rather lackluster compared to that of the stars of the defense team: Hanger was simply not up to scaling the rhetorical mountain peaks of a Cone Johnson or of matching the melodramatic thunder of a "Wild Bill" McLean.

The prosecution's jury arguments raise an interesting tactical question. The state expended much of its final time allowance demanding that the jury assess the death penalty. Wouldn't it have been better tactically for the prosecution to have focused all its firepower simply on winning a guilty verdict? By insisting that the jury inflict the death penalty, wasn't the prosecutor risking a hung jury or possibly even an acquittal in the event that some jurors believed Sneed was guilty but were opposed to the death penalty? By insisting on a verdict of guilty of first degree murder and punishment by hanging, didn't the state risk blocking a compromise verdict of second degree murder or manslaughter, neither of which carried the possibility of a death penalty and both of which allowed punishment to be assessed at a lesser term of years in prison?[17]

Wouldn't even a fairly light prison sentence have been enough? It would have been a prosecution victory, and more than that, to the proud and pompous Beal Sneed, just being convicted and having to serve any number of years in prison would have been a fate worse than death. It would have forced him to sit behind those prison bars day after day, agonizing not only over his public disgrace, but also over the sure knowledge that Lena was out there somewhere— divorced, free at last, and having fun.

Still, in that day when public hangings were considered great family entertainment, perhaps the prosecution team thought that insisting on the death penalty was not only appropriate, but that it actually enhanced the state's chances of obtaining a conviction. Was the prosecution fearful that it would appear weak or uncertain of its case if it didn't insist on the death penalty? In that culture—and for even a decade or so later—Texas prosecutors seemed to feel it was obligatory in almost every murder trial to demand that the death penalty be assessed—even in cases where the killing was not particularly heinous.

Even so, in this case it was still a terrible tactical mistake for Cummings and Odell to continue to shout demands that the jury "break his neck" while Beal's two small daughters were clinging to their father and crying hysterically only a few feet from the jury box. That had to have been counterproductive.

That, in turn, brings up another tactical mistake the prosecution made. Why, oh why, did Hanger let the defense get away with that maudlin stunt in the first place, at least without a fierce protest? True enough, in that time, sensitivities as to children's psychological well-being were primitive by today's standards, but even so why didn't the prosecutors demand that Judge Swayne ban all children under twelve from the courtroom, at least during those bombastic and melodramatic jury arguments. Or, at the very least, why didn't Hanger demand that Sneed's two little daughters be prohibited from sitting in Sneed's lap, creating such a scene, and disrupting the prosecution's jury arguments? Even absent an objection from the state, why did Judge Swayne tolerate such egregious disorder in the court?

Judge Swayne's actions during the Sneed trial provide another remarkably revealing comment on the culture of 1912 Texas. On the one hand, the judge was very solicitous about protecting the tender sensitivities of ladies in the audience and took every precaution to have them excluded from the courtroom when any cursing or salacious testimony was anticipated. On the other hand, the judge seemed totally oblivious to the tender sensibilities of children— even children less than 10 years of age—and made no effort to protect them from what had to have been a terribly scarring emotional experience. Particularly the two little Sneed daughters—lambs sacrificed by their own father on the altar of his struggle to get away with murder. That it had to have been a terribly scarring emotional experience for them seems obvious from this twenty-first century vantage point, but then it obviously wasn't obvious from Judge Swayne's vantage point. After all, as noted, parents of that yesterday saw nothing at all wrong with treating their children, of whatever age, to the holiday spectacle of a public hanging.

In modern practice, the trial judge prepares the court's jury charge before the jury arguments. The instructions contained in the charge explain the applicable criminal laws to the jurors and tell them what they may and may not consider. Then the attorneys argue their cases. That is certainly a logical sequence: first read the judge's instructions to the jurors, then have the jury arguments. However, at the time of the Sneed trial, the practice was different. Illogical as it seems, the trial judge didn't prepare and read the court's instructions until *after* the attorneys had completed their jury arguments.

Judge Swayne's jury charge in the second Sneed trial was a blockbuster that caught the defense flat-footed. "Wild Bill" McLean and his cohorts howled in protest. The judge instructed the jury that it must find Beal Sneed guilty of murder (either first or second degree)—or acquit him. And he refused, over vigorous objections from the defense, to give the jury the option of finding Beal guilty of the lesser offense of manslaughter. Worse yet, he refused to give the jury the option of finding Beal not guilty by reason of insanity or self-defense. Judge Swayne declared that the evidence did not raise either of those defensive issues. Insanity and self-defense were the only two defenses under the laws of Texas and the facts of this case that could have justified the killing of Colonel Boyce. This surely appeared to be a mortal blow to the defense, leaving the jury, in effect, no place to go—except conviction. That is, *if* the jury followed the evidence *and* followed the court's instructions spelling out the applicable *written* law of Texas.

The defense attorneys wailed and wrung their hands in frustrated disbelief. But to no avail.

The Verdict

The jury retired for deliberations at five thirty on Monday afternoon, December 2, 1912, taking with it to the jury room Judge Swayne's lengthy written instructions. The defense attorneys were so appalled by the judge's jury charge that Cone Johnson immediately set about drafting an appeal of the anticipated conviction.

The jury, for its part, didn't bother reading all those pages of Judge Swayne's legalese; didn't bother going over all the evidence either. They simply took a quick vote and found themselves in unanimous agreement. However, since it was late in the afternoon the jury had to wait until the first thing the next morning to announce its verdict.

Cone Johnson should have saved the paper and ink he used in drafting an appeal. When the "not guilty" verdict was announced,

John Beal Sneed let out a loud "cowboy yell" and jigged about the courtroom. "Wild Bill" McLean and his partner, Walter Scott, joined in, whooping it up and sailing their hats over the courtroom chandelier, a most indecorous judicial exhibition for which they were both fined $50 for contempt of court by the disgusted Judge Swayne.[18]

The judge shook his head in disbelief at the verdict: "I don't see how they could have done it . . . under my charge."

The *Dallas Dispatch* reported that the state's attorneys had also expected a "guilty" verdict and were "thunderstruck" when they learned Sneed had been acquitted.[19]

It was obvious that the jurors had paid no attention to Judge Swayne's instructions, had taken the bit in their teeth and ignored the criminal laws of the State of Texas in favor of their own notions of justice. Today that's what we call "jury nullification."

Although Cone Johnson was startled by the jury's rapid and unexpected response, he quickly recovered and announced to the press that public sentiment had been with John Beal Sneed throughout the state all along and that the jury's verdict was receiving overwhelming support. Explaining the jury's rejection of the prosecution's plea for adherence to statutory law when it failed to adequately "protect the home," Johnson added, "This may go on in the North, but, thank God, it hasn't reached the South yet!" Then, in a real head-scratcher, he volunteered that John Beal Sneed's "forbearance was wonderful." Meanwhile, John Beal Sneed shook hands with all the jurors, took their names and addresses, and promised to send each a picture of himself and his children. But not one of Lena.

The jury was quizzed as to why it returned a "not guilty" verdict in the face of overwhelming evidence of guilt. Jury foreman J. W. Crane, an honest man, didn't mince words. He explained it this way:

> The best answer is, because this is Texas. In Texas we believe in protection of the home at any cost. We in Texas believe a man has the right to safeguard the honor of his home even if he must kill the person responsible.[20]

Could any lawyer or social historian have better articulated the unwritten law's "honor defense" and its potency in 1912 Texas?[21]

Sneed, Jurors and Judge Before Whom He Was Tried

Left to right, bottom row: Joe Gaston, J. C. Gaither, Walter Portwood, J. D. Crone, Judge J. W. Swayne; middle row, T. P. Blanton, Weaver Birch, J. M. Fitzgerald, S. B. Austin; top row, T. H. Bird, J. W. Dunlap, Walter Winnett, I. W. Cole.

JUDGE AND JURY IN SECOND FORT WORTH MURDER TRIAL Judge James W. Swayne is seated, far right. The jurors were a very homogeneous group that suited the defense lawyers perfectly. All were white, married males with children. All were small farmers residing in rural Tarrant County. Five of the twelve were native Texans and the others were natives of southern states who had migrated to Texas: two from Tennessee, two from Mississippi, and one each from Alabama, Missouri, and Arkansas. *Photograph from the November 17, 1912, edition of the* Fort Worth Star-Telegram.

JOHN BEAL SNEED. Picture taken the day a Fort Worth jury acquitted him of the murder of Colonel A. G. Boyce. *Photograph from December 3, 1912, edition of the* Fort Worth Star-Telegram.

190

A reporter asked Mrs. Annie Boyce if she had a statement to make about the trial and its outcome. She refused, saying only, "No, I'm too heartbroken."

Lena was shopping in downtown Fort Worth when the verdict was announced and didn't learn about it until she returned to her hotel. When a reporter informed her that her husband had just been acquitted, she displayed no emotion. "Is that so?" Lena asked quietly. She refused any further comment and retreated to her hotel room where she barricaded herself. A reporter's phone call brought only the response that "she did not care to express her feelings in regard to her husband's acquittal." A Sneed relative, contacted in Sneed's headquarters, however, gave the reporter a very different take on Lena's reaction: "She is happy over the verdict, and she loves her husband and her children." The Sneed spokesman also denied reports that Lena had been "closely guarded" during the trial by Sneed's henchmen lest she make any inappropriate comments.

So ended the trial of John Beal Sneed for the murder of Colonel Albert Boyce. There was, however, the matter of the indictments still pending in Amarillo against him and his cohort Beech Epting for the murder of Al Boyce, Jr.

It would appear that if John Beal Sneed could get away with murdering Colonel Boyce, surely he could get away with killing Al Boyce. After all, it was Al who started it all by running away with Beal's wife. But the murder trial for the killing of Colonel Boyce had been held in Fort Worth. Beal's trial for the killing of Al Boyce would be held in the Amarillo area, and the well-respected Boyce family was a presence to be reckoned with on their home turf. Colonel Boyce had not only been a venerated Confederate veteran, a Texas pioneer, a longtime manager of the XIT Ranch, and president of banks in Dalhart and Amarillo, but he was also an esteemed citizen. Could the McLean team, even if bolstered by the estimable A. J. Fires, pull another rabbit out of the hat and exonerate Beal Sneed for the ambush assassination of Al Boyce?

"Making 'em Believe in Ghosts"

The Beech Epting Murder Trial

A MONTH AND THREE DAYS AFTER the Fort Worth jury cleared John Beal Sneed for the killing of Colonel Albert Boyce, he was involved in another murder trial. But he was not the defendant in this one. His cohort, Beech Epting, was on trial for his role in the killing of Al Boyce, Jr.

Al Boyce was killed on September 14, 1912, in Amarillo, and a Potter County grand jury had promptly indicted Beal Sneed and Beech Epting, jointly, for murder.[1] "Wild Bill" McLean once again was captain of the defense team, and he wasted no time in winning three major tactical victories during pretrial proceedings.

First, McLean argued for a change of venue to transfer the trial out of Potter County. With considerable water under his paddle, he argued that on account of the sensational nature of the killing as well as the massive publicity that followed, it would be impossible to get an "unpolluted" jury in Amarillo. There was another factor of which McLean was mindful: although a hung jury was a victory for the defense in the first Fort Worth murder trial, nevertheless, he and Beal Sneed were determined to win this trial—12 to 0 for the defense. In Amarillo, sentiment was bitter and split down the middle between Boyce partisans and Sneed partisans. Hence, it seemed most unlikely that any twelve Amarillo jurors could be found who would agree, unanimously, on any verdict.

Nobody was surprised when the Potter County judge granted a change of venue. No doubt the judge had his own personal reasons for wanting to get rid of that hot potato. Not only would the trial be long, onerous, and unpleasant, but there was another very practical reason for handing the trial off to an out-of-town judge. In Texas, now as then, district judges are elected officials, their jobs dependent on a favorable outcome in the next election. Hence, being caught in the middle of a bitter and divisive battle between two community factions would be a no-win predicament that any sane politician would avoid at all costs.

Next, McLean filed a motion to sever, seeking separate trials for Sneed and Epting. He argued, again logically, that very different issues would be presented as to each defendant. The judge granted McLean's motion to sever.

Then the problem arose: which defendant to try first. McLean contended that Epting should be tried first, arguing that if Sneed were tried first a lot of very sordid testimony would probably be aired which, when it became public, would tend to prejudice Epting when he was tried later. That was true . . . as far as it went. But was McLean really as concerned with Epting's welfare as he was with that of Sneed? As we shall soon discover, it was primarily for Sneed's benefit that McLean wanted Epting's head on the block first. Since McLean represented both Sneed and Epting, a very serious issue involving a conflict of interest existed. Every client is entitled to have his own independent lawyer whose only duty is to look out for the client's best interest. But then Epting, the uneducated and inexperienced tenant farmer, probably was not aware of that. Besides, he had no money to hire his own lawyer anyway. The judge granted McLean's motion. Epting would be first up to bat.

All those pretrial issues settled, there remained only one to be decided. If the trials of Epting and Sneed were not to be held in Amarillo, then where? The Epting trial was transferred to the tiny town of Memphis in Hall County some eighty miles southeast of Amarillo,[2] and the Sneed trial was transferred to the slightly larger town of Vernon in Wilbarger County located ninety miles southeast of Memphis.[3] Both counties were a part of the sprawling ten-county Forty-Sixth Judicial District of Texas, and that's the reason that a popular and personable young district attorney named Hugh D. Spencer suddenly found himself as head prosecutor of the two most sensational criminal trials in the State of Texas. A rising young star on the firmament of the Texas Panhandle judiciary, Spencer was serving his third two-year term as district attorney of the Forty-Sixth District.

When Spencer learned that Epting was going to contend that he had no idea what Sneed was up to during those five days he and Sneed patiently waited in the death cottage while peeping through the peephole, young Spencer scoffed: "If Epting's attorneys succeed in making a jury believe that Epting didn't know Sneed was going to kill Boyce, then they can make 'em believe in ghosts."[4] But then Spencer was still a young, rural prosecutor who had never seen the likes of "Wild Bill" McLean and his cohorts at the bar.

When the news got out that the venue of these cases was to be changed out of Amarillo, many area towns vied for the location, since hosting the trial would prove a healthy boost to the struggling economy of these small towns. The secretary of the Memphis Commercial Club gleefully predicted that the trial would be worth the whopping sum of $5,000 to the town. Memphis was agog with this sudden attention as well as the anticipated thrill of having the drama of a notorious murder trial played out right there in that sleepy frontier community. All this, plus reaping the harvest of a badly needed economic injection. But the Memphis folks suddenly discovered they had an unexpected problem: where would they put all those out-of-towners? The two small local hotels could not even accommodate the 150 witnesses who were subpoenaed for the trial, much less the horde of lawyers, court personnel, lawmen, and families of the parties, as well as the spectators. Private citizens were pressed to open their homes. But there was yet another urgent problem: entertainment. No radio. No television. No motion picture show. Domino games in the hotel lobbies were about the extent of it. But that too was limited: no domino playing was permitted after 10:30 p.m., and the curfew was strictly enforced.

To their credit, however, the town fathers did make a heroic effort to welcome the visitors. Although snow flurries were falling and the temperature hovered near zero on the eve of the trial on January 5, 1913, the Memphis Commercial Club's "booster band" braved the elements and held a free outdoor concert on the courthouse square. Later, on another evening after the trial began, local thespians put on a play called *The Rosary* held in the Memphis Opera House. The district judge even permitted the jurors to attend, but only after lining them up on the courthouse lawn and making each swear that he would not be influenced by anything that he might see or hear during the excursion.

The cast of locals for *The Rosary* might have been impressive, but it paled in comparison to the cast waiting backstage to appear in the upcoming courtroom drama. A Hollywood casting director could not have done a better job. In addition to the young stalwart Hugh D. Spencer, the prosecution team included the local county attorney, S. A. Bryant, who would also prove a valuable and articulate advocate for the state, as would veteran Amarillo trial lawyer H. H. Cooper, whom the Boyce family hired to bolster the team. The family also enlisted the services of a local Memphis lawyer named A. S. Moss to assist in jury selection. But the high-dollar lawyer hired by the Boyce family was the popular and garrulous state senator, D. W. (Weldon) Odell, who had assisted state senator W. A. Hanger in the failed Fort Worth prosecution of John Beal Sneed. When Senator Odell arrived in Memphis, the *Fort Worth Star-Telegram* described him as being "brilliant and picturesque." The senator proudly showed off his brand-new cowboy boots to the reporter and bragged that they cost him the astounding sum of $17. The *Star-Telegram* reporter made this droll comment: "The senator is keeping his ankles warm, and is not neglecting his vanity." Senator Odell was certainly "picturesque," and he may have been a "brilliant" politician, but the question remained, would he be a match for the defense team? Rounding out the prosecution team was Will Boyce, Al Boyce's brother, who was reputed to be one of the best lawyers in the Texas Panhandle.

As impressive as was the array of lawyers representing the prosecution team, it would be facing major league all-stars of the criminal

trial bar: Bill McLean, A. J. Fires, and Walter Scott. To add depth
to the roster, Beal Sneed also hired W. D. Berry, R. D. Brown, and
a local Memphis lawyer, J. M. Elliott, who would prove valuable in
selecting a jury. Lawyer Brown lived and practiced in nearby Paducah, Beech Epting's hometown. Paducah was also the community
where Beal Sneed owned the large farm upon which Epting was
a tenant farmer. W. D. Berry hailed from Vernon and was already
recognized as the best trial lawyer in that town. (He would soon be
elected district attorney, the position now held by Hugh Spencer.)
Then, too, Vernon was to be the site of the upcoming trial of Beal
Sneed. The defense, always looking ahead to the next trial, must
have viewed the Epting trial as a learning experience for Berry.
There was still another reason to add Berry to the defense team:
the presiding judge in the Epting trial was to be James A. Nabers,
who also hailed from Vernon, and Berry would have insight into his
character, biases, and courtroom predilections.

The *Fort Worth Star-Telegram* reported that it had learned "on good
authority" that the Beech Epting trial was costing Beal Sneed more
money than both of his own trials in Fort Worth. Never one to skimp
on expenses when it came to gaining any edge in a fight, Sneed considered it money well spent. He once told one reporter: "Any man
who's a man will fight and fight to win all the time.[5] Sneed realized that the outcome of the Epting trial was important to him. He
needed to ensure that Epting was not found guilty. If Epting were
acquitted it would give the defense a leg up in Beal's trial. Everyone
would have heard about the acquittal by then and that could augur
well for Sneed's chances. Moreover, the odds were that McLean
and his team could win the Epting trial since the prosecution's case
against Epting was much weaker: Epting had never fired a shot, had
never even poked his head outside the door of the death cottage
while all the carnage was going on. Besides, Epting had no criminal
record or any prior violent incidents in his past; he was just a poor,
hardworking, tenant farmer with a large family.

That said, there was still a more important reason for wanting Epting to be tried first. Even if he were convicted, it would nevertheless provide McLean with a crucial advantage when he defended Sneed. Epting was to serve as a stalking horse for McLean. Epting's trial would be a dress rehearsal for the defense in preparing for Sneed's trial. During the Epting trial the defense would have the opportunity to review the prosecution's case and probe for weaknesses. Besides, learning the testimony of each adverse witness in advance would afford Beal Sneed a wonderful opportunity to tailor his own testimony in order to exploit any inconsistency or weak spot in the state's case when he was tried. On the other hand, the defense would not have to expose much of its hand during Epting's trial. Beal Sneed would not testify. He would be protected by the constitutional safeguards against a defendant's right against self-incrimination under the Fifth Amendment to the U.S. Constitution. In fact, since Epting and Beal were indicted for the same offense, it would have been reversible error in Epting's trial for the prosecution to even call Sneed to the witness stand and force him to claim his Fifth Amendment rights.

The same edition of the *Star-Telegram* that reported Sneed's trial expenditures also furnished insight into the character and style of the opposing attorneys. It reported that during a Sunday break in the trial, all the lawyers enjoyed "touring the countryside in automobiles"—except Bill McLean, who borrowed a horse and took a twenty-mile horseback ride through the prairie.

Another edition of the *Star-Telegram* printed a sidebar tale that allowed its readers to savor an authentic sample of the flavor of the time and place of the Epting trial. There was a missing witness whom the defense sought—that bartender with the very fitting name of Joe Barr. Barr was finally located in the little town of Dalhart near the top of the Texas Panhandle. Subpoenas were sent ordering him to appear. Barr simply ignored them. The defense team demanded that the trial be postponed because of the absence of this witness.

Then came "Scandalous John" McCandless to the rescue. He was the sheriff at Dalhart. He had been a cowboy on the XIT ranch when Colonel Boyce was the ranch manager, and it was Colonel Boyce who had affixed the "Scandalous John" moniker on him. Later, he became a Texas Ranger and then sheriff of Dallam County.

The trial judge solved the Joe Barr problem by issuing a "writ of attachment" for the reluctant witness, ordering sheriff Scandalous John to physically seize the body of Joe Barr and haul him to court. The legendary old rough-and-tumble lawman didn't experience much difficulty in accomplishing his assigned mission, and thus balky Joe Barr reluctantly made his court appearance. As a result of the laconic lawman's notoriety, a *Star-Telegram* reporter covering the trial latched on to the opportunity to interview Scandalous John about his adventurous career on the lawless West Texas frontier. It went like this:

> **Scandalous John:** I used to have one God-awful time with them cattle thieves in those days.
>
> **Reporter:** Were you ever shot?
>
> **Scandalous John:** Nope.
>
> **Reporter:** Were you ever shot at?
>
> **Scandalous John:** Several times a day.
>
> **Reporter:** Did you ever get any of them?
>
> **Scandalous John (with a grin):** Oh, now and then I got one.[6]

Rounding out the cast of colorful courtroom characters in the Beech Epting trial was District Judge James A. Nabers of Vernon. Nobody, even W. D. Berry, knew quite what to expect when Nabers mounted the bench. He was the loose cannon on that judicial deck because he had only presided over one other trial. In addition, his legal training and experience was almost nonexistent. Nabers was not a lawyer by trade; he was a surveyor. He had previously managed to get himself elected as the county judge of Wilbarger County, but that afforded little judicial experience. County judges in Texas—then and to this day—are not required to be lawyers. Furthermore, when speaking of county judges, the term *judge*

Left: A. J. FIRES, bulldog defense lawyer of Childress, Texas, was one of the lawyers who represented John Beal Sneed in his murder trials. *Photograph courtesy of the Panhandle-Plains Historical Museum, Canyon, Texas.*

Bottom Left: **STATE SENATOR D. W. "WELDON" ODELL** was employed by the Boyce family to assist in the prosecution of Beech Epting and John Beal Sneed for the killing of Al Boyce, Jr., on September 14, 1912, in Amarillo. *Photograph from* A History of Texas and Texans, *Vol. IV, by Frank W. Johnson, published by the American Historical Society, Chicago, 1914.*

Bottom Right: **JUDGE JAMES A. NABERS**, district judge of the Forty-sixth Judicial District Court of both Hall County (Memphis, Texas) and Wilbarger County (Vernon, Texas), presided over the Beech Epting murder trial for the killing of Al Boyce, Jr., held in January 1913, in Memphis and the John Beal Sneed murder trial held in Vernon in February 1913, also for the killing of Al Boyce, Jr. *Photograph from the January 10, 1913 edition of the* Fort Worth Star-Telegram.

is somewhat of a misnomer. Texas county judges are basically the county's chief executive officer who also presides over the county's legislative body (called the "Commissioners Court," another misnomer since it is a "court" with absolutely no judicial function). The county judge's judicial duties are limited to a few misdemeanor criminal cases and small claims civil disputes. After serving several terms as county judge, Nabers was defeated for reelection by a local mail carrier. Undeterred, however, he filed for the office of district judge and won the election on his promise to save taxpayer money.

Shortly after the Epting trial began, McLean and company must have realized that they didn't have to look their gift horse in the mouth to verify that Christmas had indeed come early that year. Whether due to inexperience or bias, or both, Judge Nabers was proving himself a very defense-friendly judge. Jury selection had hardly begun when that became apparent. Beech Epting was being tried as John Beal Sneed's accomplice in the murder of Al Boyce. Hence, unless the jury believed that Sneed, as principal in the killing, was guilty of murder, then how could it find that Epting was guilty of being an accomplice to murder? Therefore, when one prospective juror expressed an opinion that John Beal Sneed was innocent, the prosecution challenged him for cause, but Judge Nabers overruled the challenge. Senator Odell protested, saying, "But we must prove Sneed guilty to convict Epting." Judge Nabers waved him off. "Never mind, they [the jurors] are trying Epting and not Sneed."

During the two Fort Worth trials, the defense had carefully avoided telling the jury—explicitly at least—that their real defense was bottomed on the unwritten law, instead euphemistically referring to it as the "protecting the home" defense. Not so, however, in Memphis, Texas, in Judge Nabers's court. No pussyfooting about here. It was "the unwritten law" from gavel to verdict. That became clear during the questioning of one of the first veniremen, C. F. Bromley. He stated that he believed in the unwritten law "in certain cases." The state challenged him for cause, whereupon Judge Nabers took over the interrogation. Bromley said he understood that the unwritten law was usually invoked when the deceased victim had wronged the defendant or his family. Judge Nabers then took it a step further. Would Bromley consider exonerating a man on grounds of the unwritten law where neither he nor his family had been wronged by the victim? Bromley replied, "Not necessarily." That was good enough for Judge Nabers. He overruled the prosecution's challenge for cause, and Bromley ended up on the jury.

The state had given notice that if Epting were convicted, it would seek the death penalty. Therefore each juror was questioned as to whether he had any scruples against assessing the death penalty "in a proper case." A Memphis barber, C. H. Hooks, replied that he was opposed to the infliction of the death penalty. A. J. Fires, for the defense, then asked Hooks this question: "Suppose that a Negro would rape a white woman and you were on the jury that found him guilty—"

"Hanging would be too good for him," Hooks interrupted. "I'd burn him at the stake."

If there had been any question about whether sentiment in Hall County was tilted toward the Boyce family or John Beal Sneed, it was quickly dispelled during jury selection. When only two jurors had been selected from the first venire of one hundred men summoned, the court instructed the county sheriff to select another hundred men at random from the county. The sheriff, after an exhaustive roundup, finally returned with another hundred. It was then that one of the Hall County Commissioners, T. N. Baker, who lived in the country some nineteen miles west of Memphis, told a *Star-Telegram* reporter this: "They sure were rustling nesters [prospective jurors] out in my part of the county today, and they kicked like broncos at serving on this jury. Nearly all of them have expressed their partiality for Sneed a thousand times." It was also revealing that, out of the first two hundred summoned for the jury panel, only one man said he had never heard of the Boyce-Sneed bloodletting. In view of that obviously polluted jury pool, why didn't the prosecution scream for a mistrial and plead for a change of venue to some point across the wide expanses of Texas? Perhaps the prosecution realized that begging Judge Nabers to change the venue would almost certainly have been an exercise in futility considering the enormous expenditure of taxpayer money that it would have cost, plus taking into account

Judge Nabers's campaign pledge to the voters—a promise to save taxpayer dollars.

∼‿◦

Finally, on January 14, 1913, the jury was selected, and the trial began. Beech Epting's family was there—his wife and all six of their children, ages two to eleven, "littering the courtroom floor with ginger cake crumbs."

Already at a disadvantage after jury selection, the state suffered another setback when Judge Nabers refused to allow the prosecutors to present a "realistic staging" of the killing of Al Boyce by John Beal Sneed during the eyewitness testimony of Rev. Ernest E. Robinson, pastor of the Polk Street Methodist Church in Amarillo. Robinson was allowed, however, to testify that he witnessed Sneed kill Al Boyce.

The case against Epting was based wholly on circumstantial evidence. None of the eyewitnesses saw Epting at the scene when the shooting happened. But evidence was produced to show that Epting had rented the death cottage under an assumed name, that he had stayed in the death cottage with Sneed for several days before the killing, that Sneed was heavily disguised all this time, that there were several guns kept inside the cottage, that Sneed did not transact any legitimate business during those waiting days, and that Epting fled the scene of mayhem immediately after Al Boyce was killed. P. L. Wilkes, a hotel clerk from Quanah, Texas, some 140 miles southeast of Amarillo, was called by the prosecution. He testified that several hours after Al Boyce was killed, Beech Epting showed up at his hotel and told him that he had witnessed one man kill another in front of the Methodist Church in Amarillo earlier that day and that he had fled the scene immediately to avoid being called as a witness. Taken together, the state's circumstantial evidence seemed to bear out District Attorney Spencer's prediction that the prosecution's evidence would bind Epting to the crime so tightly that he couldn't wiggle free, and that if the defense could manage to convince a jury that Epting was an innocent victim of circumstance then it could indeed make them believe in ghosts.

Spencer was probably right about that. The jury probably was convinced that Epting was John Beal Sneed's accomplice. But that was only half the battle for the state, and the other half was uphill all the way. The prosecutors had labored in vain to explain to Judge Nabers that to convict Epting of a crime, they first had to prove that Epting was an accomplice to a murder. It is no crime to be an accomplice to a justifiable homicide. In any event, at this point in the trial, the state turned its focus on attempting to prove the guilt of John Beal Sneed. Eyewitnesses had already testified that they saw Sneed ambush and kill Al Boyce. It was not an accidental killing. No mistaken identity. No temporary insanity. No self-defense. In the end, there was no room for a justifiable homicide plea under the written laws of Texas. Only the unwritten law—the "honor code"— could save Sneed. And Epting.

As in the two Fort Worth trials, the Sneed defense team used the archaic manslaughter statute ("insulting words or conduct toward a female relative") as a tool to open evidentiary doors and thus lay the foundation for its real defense—the unwritten law. Therefore the defense replayed much of the testimony it had adduced in the Fort Worth trials: the affair between Al and Lena, Lena's alleged "moral insanity," her institutionalization by Beal, her escape and elopement with Al to Canada, Sneed's "rescue" of her from the clutches of her evil seducer, and so on. Lena's father, Captain Tom S. Snyder, was again turned loose to rant about the "cigarette and whiskey fiend" who had corrupted his daughter and to repeat hearsay statements allegedly made by Colonel and Mrs. Boyce. Lena's brother-in-law John A. Pace, the New Mexico attorney, testified that Lena stayed with them after being returned from Canada. Pace said that he forbade Lena to go out onto the streets because "the whole affair was so nauseating." He did admit that Lena begged not to be incarcerated in the insane asylum again. The porter on the Frisco train carrying Lena and Al away from Fort Worth when they eloped testified that they had slept together on the train.

Calling on his trademark flair for the dramatic, McLean's partner, Walter Scott, was permitted (over the state's hearsay objection) to read two letters Al had written Lena while he was still in Canada.

The first one was written on the day Al learned that Beal Sneed had killed his father in Fort Worth. In it Al told Lena that he felt it would be his "pleasure and duty" to return to Texas and avenge his father's murder, calling Sneed "a brute."[7] Two days later he wrote Lena again, signing his letter "Your Grief Stricken Boy, Albert."[8] In it he expressed a wish that they could be together in their sorrow and begged Lena to comfort him all she could.

Although Beal Sneed's father had been killed after the last Fort Worth trial, Judge Nabers (again over a hearsay objection) allowed defense attorney Berry to read a portion of a letter he had written in which he expressed his suspicion that Colonel Boyce was "abetting" his son in taking Sneed's wife from him and quoted Colonel Boyce as proposing that Sneed allow his wife a divorce and alimony.

Over another hearsay objection, Judge Nabers permitted the reading of a portion of another letter from Al to Lena that Sneed's spies had intercepted. In it Al mentioned an intention to kill Beal Sneed. Then he wrote: "I sometimes believe I am losing my nerve, but when I realize I must do it for the sake of your liberty and your children's, I regain my nerve."[9] Predictably, the defense called Henry Bowman who, once again, gave a teary replay of the dreary 1911 Christmas when the Sneed daughters were crying for their gallivanting mother. Dr. John Turner was called to explain why it took him three analysis sessions with Lena before he finally arrived at the desired diagnosis: Lena was insane—or, more accurately, "morally insane." On cross-examination, Dr. Turner again struggled mightily to explain the difference between "moral insanity" and "general depravity."

Finally, Beech Epting testified in his own defense. He said, "Sneed misled me . . . If I had known he was going to kill Boyce I never would have gone there with him." He admitted that he had rented the death cottage under a false name, that he had stayed in it with Sneed for several days before the killing, that Sneed wore a garish disguise all this time, and that they had nailed shades over the windows. All this, he continued, was because Sneed was afraid of the Boyce family, and so had to take these precautions while he was "winding up his business" in Amarillo. Epting also admitted that under orders from Sneed he had made a trip to Amarillo shortly before the killing and that he had registered at the hotel under the name of John G. Cross. He explained the use of the alias by saying Sneed had sent him out to find stolen cattle and had told him not to tell anyone his real name and not to tell anyone his business.

Judge Nabers allowed each side six hours to make their final jury arguments. H. H. Cooper opened for the state by arguing premeditated murder and contending that manslaughter was not an option because the killing was not done as a result of a "sudden passion." Cooper pointed out that the undisputed evidence negated any notion of "sudden passion," instead proving a cold, premeditated plan, and he called attention to several things that Sneed did in carrying out his plan: "He grew whiskers, bought breast protectors, armed himself with automatic pistols and shotguns, rented houses, and hired men to help him kill Al Boyce." He continued:

> Sneed's mind was calm, cool, and deliberate. He walked away from the scene of the homicide as calmly as any farmer would walk away from the hog pen after killing a hog. A greeting was on his lips for every friend he met.

At that point in his argument, Cooper dared go where no other prosecutor had gone before in all the Sneed trials. He defended Al and Lena and their love affair. He told the jury this:

> Any woman would rather live in a hovel with a man she loves than in a palace and all its splendor with a man she hates. I never heard it argued before that because a woman is married to a man she becomes his slave and chattel. Mrs. Sneed was slammed from sanitarium to sanitarium just because she loved another man. If Al Boyce did love her, as his letters indicated, what manner of man would he have been not to respond to her call for him to rescue her from John Beal Sneed.[10]

Bill McLean, in his argument, returned to his familiar "protecting the home" theme. He said:

> This case is the most important case in the annals of Texas courts
> because not only is a human life involved, but on it depends
> whether Texas homes are to be protected . . . whenever a home
> is wrecked, the despoiler should be killed.[11]

McLean then proceeded to denounce the rich Boyce family "with their thousands and hundreds of thousands" of dollars dedicated to prosecuting Beech Epting, "this poor ignorant tenant farmer. They know it would bleed Beal Sneed's heart to have his faithful servant convicted." Then, as he had done in the two Fort Worth trials, McLean played his ace: "the poor little children" card. Pointing to Epting's wife and the six little Epting tykes seated in the front row of spectators, he said that Epting was a far happier man than Sneed "because Epting's home is not broken up and will not be unless you take him away from his dear little wife and six little ones." McLean then turned his guns on Al Boyce, the villain who had broken up Beal Sneed's happy home. How could Beal Sneed possibly be blamed for vindicating the terrible wrong that Al Boyce had done him? "Put yourself in Sneed's place," he challenged the jurors. In answer, the Hall County Attorney, S. A. Bryant, for the prosecution told the jurors he would accept McLean's challenge. He said:

> Sneed had no right to the custody of his wife, even if he thought
> her insane. They say she is insane just because she didn't love
> Sneed for giving her a fine home and diamonds. She was a bird in
> a gilded cage. She was born in a land of freedom and she yearned
> for the freedom that was rightfully hers. The defense has not yet
> shown that Al Boyce wrecked Beal Sneed's home. They have not
> shown that Mrs. Sneed ever loved her husband.[12]

After all the melodramatic claptrap about the righteousness and necessity of taking gun in hand and slaying all licentious home wreckers, the arguments of Cooper and Bryant were as refreshing as a spring breeze—or at least it would seem to most twenty-first-century jurors. Not so, however, for 1913 rural Texas jurors. Once again, McLean was in tune with his time and place, and he knew what would resonate well with these jurors.

The final defense argument also underscored what played well to that audience. Roland D. Brown of Paducah (Epting's home-town) quoted the Bible liberally as authority for exoneration by application of the unwritten law. Among other biblical stories, he called attention to the bloody aftermath of the seduction of Jacob's daughter. She had been seduced, Brown said, by the princes of the tribe of Hamor, and when her brothers found out about it, they (disregarding father Jacob's counsel) not only killed their sister's seducers but also "nearly wiped out the whole Hamor tribe, and God protected them."[13]

District Attorney Spencer objected to this reference, saying that Brown was not quoting from a proper legal authority, namely, the laws of the State of Texas. The objection was good. Judge Nabers should have sustained it and then admonished the jury to disre-gard the reference. Instead, in a highly improper comment from the bench, he said, "It seems to me that the Bible is high enough authority."[14] Perhaps Judge Nabers had overlooked that provision in the Texas Code of Criminal Procedure (if ever he had bothered to read it) that commands that at no time during a trial is the judge permitted to "make any remark calculated to convey to the jury his opinion of the case."[15]

Regardless of the law, the jury agreed with Judge Nabers. It took the jurors only thirty minutes and one ballot to find Beech Epting not guilty. The courtroom spectators heartily approved. The next day's *Star-Telegram* reported this: "Every spectator in the court-room including many church women of Memphis, Texas shook hands with Epting and kissed his wife." The verdict was returned on January 23, 1913. John Beal Sneed was reported to have been very pleased with the verdict, as well he should have been. His own trial for the killing of Al Boyce was scheduled to begin in less than a month in Vernon, Texas, some ninety miles southeast of Memphis, and 170 miles southeast of Amarillo. Judge James A. Nabers would again be presiding.

Few observers doubted what the outcome of that trial would be.

11
CHAPTER

"No Trial for the Dead"

The Vernon Murder Trial
of John Beal Sneed

The Scene: The district courtroom in Vernon, Texas, February 11, 1913.

The Billing: The State of Texas v. John Beal Sneed, a murder trial.[1]

That billing, however, was somewhat misleading. What the packed courtroom witnessed when the curtain parted was less of a solemn, dignified, dispassionate judicial pursuit of truth and justice than . . . well, what would you call it? Part tragedy, part comedy, part farce, part melodrama, part pathos, part bare-knuckle brawl? Whatever you called it, it was well larded with generous helpings of hyperbole, nonsense, and old-fashioned tent-revival-style hallelujahs and hellfire damnations.

The judicial cast for both sides was the same as it had been during the Beech Epting trial except the prosecution added Vernon lawyer Cecil Story to its roster while the defense added Vernon lawyer Harry Mason. Judge James Nabers again presided.

Jury selection proved both entertaining and revealing. Each prospect was tested on his views on the unwritten law. Several candidly admitted that they believed the unwritten law was higher than any written law. Another voiced the opinion that "in some cases a man ought to take the law into his own hands." Surprisingly, Judge Nabers excused these candid souls. H. Eggenberg was also a forthright fellow. He was a native of Missouri and said he had never heard of the unwritten law until he had recently moved to Texas. Plus, he denied having heard anything about the Sneed case, explaining that he had been too busy repairing a broken corn shucker to bother listening to gossip. Eggenberg was definitely not Bill McLean's kind of guy, and McLean promptly got rid of him with a peremptory challenge. When S. C. Hawley was asked if he had already formed an opinion as to Sneed's guilt or innocence, he replied, "He ought to be acquitted." He was excused by the court. The court also excused N. R. Heath, a Vernon jeweler, but for the exact opposite reason. Heath said, "Sneed should not go free."

As Heath was leaving the courtroom, Bill McLean said, "Wait a minute. Where were you born?"

Heath: "Pennsylvania."

McLean: "I thought so."[2]

When the panel was selected, ten of the twelve were farmers, all but one was married, and all but two were fathers. No Yankee imports made the cut. It was apparent that most of the panel had pro-Sneed predispositions.

Much of the trial was a replay of the Epting trial. The Methodist minister, Rev. Ernest Robinson, gave his eyewitness account of the killing of Al Boyce. Then the state called a number of witnesses to underscore Beal Sneed's murderous premeditation, including the painstaking plotting and the precise execution of his plan to kill Boyce. W. M. Burwell, the Potter County sheriff, testified that about thirty minutes after the shooting he saw Sneed when he turned himself in. He said Sneed had the appearance of a tramp, wearing dirty overalls, a black derby, and a beard that was stubby. Burwell had known Sneed for several years but testified that he didn't think he would have recognized him if he had met him on the street. After the shooting, the owner of the death cottage, Mrs. T. B. McKibbon, entered the house and found that the only furniture there was one cheap iron bed, a few pieces of clothing marked "J. B. S.," and a breastplate that was designed to cover the body from shoulders to waist, looking "much like a bullet proof vest."[3]

The defense opened its case with a surprise: McLean called Lynn Boyce to the stand as an adverse witness. Lynn admitted that immediately after he heard that his brother had been killed, he grabbed a Winchester rifle and roamed the streets of Amarillo searching for Beal Sneed. By that time, however, Beal had prudently retreated to the safe haven of the Potter County jail. Lynn Boyce further testified that neither he, nor his brothers, nor his parents could dissuade Al from continuing his torrid affair with Lena, and that finally, before the elopement, he had bought Al's business interests for the sum of $60,000.

Defense witnesses were called who told of the love affair, its discovery, and the aftermath, as well as Lena's commitment to the insane asylum, her elopement with Al, Sneed's pursuit and recapture of Lena, and her recommitment to the asylum. The Frisco train porter again testified that he observed Al and Lena sleeping together on the train during the elopement.

McLean then called as witnesses Beal Sneed's spies, who had tracked Lena and Al and intercepted their correspondence after her return from Canada in January 1912 until Al's death in September 1912. Mrs. L. A. Rogers, who lived upstairs from the Reiger Street apartment, testified that around July 16 or 17, 1912, at a time when Beal Sneed was on a trip to the family farm at Calvert, Texas, Al visited Lena at that address. Lena introduced him as her brother. Mrs. Rogers was also monitoring the correspondence between Lena and Al, and she told of the contents of their letters.

In yet another surprise move, Sneed's team raised the defense of temporary insanity. Dr. J. E. Dodson, a local doctor who admitted on cross-examination that he had never treated insane patients and that he had never even seen Beal Sneed prior to this trial, nevertheless testified that when Beal Sneed saw Al Boyce walking down the street just before the killing his "reason was dethroned," and therefore his mind was not capable of forming a criminal intent. "Loss of sleep and worry over his troubles" was the cause of Sneed's temporary insanity according to Dr. Dodson.[4] He added that temporary insanity was a mental disease "as are all other forms of insanity." Senator Odell interrupted to ask if this "disease you speak of" wasn't really just "old-fashioned revenge." Dr. Dodson denied that it was.

Mildly amusing as was Dr. Dodson's questionable diagnosis, the defense's next insanity expert's testimony shaded off into pure burlesque. The defense called Dr. D. C. Darnell, who spent considerable time touting his professional credentials on the causes and treatment of insanity. Then he focused in on "moral insanity." When McLean asked him how long he had known of such a thing as moral insanity, Dr. Darnell replied, "It dates back to the beginning of the world. I think old Mother Eve was morally insane."[5]

Whatever remaining credibility the jury may have attached to Dr. Darnell's testimony must have been weakened considerably when, upon cross-examination, the good doctor asserted that by his own diagnostic criteria, about 80 percent of all people in the world were morally insane—a startling new scientific breakthrough that undoubtedly accounted for the survival of the human race. But Dr. Darnell was not done yet. He volunteered the opinion that not only was Lena morally insane, but John Beal Sneed himself was afflicted with "moral insanity." Darnell then refined his diagnosis a bit. He said Beal Sneed was temporarily morally insane at the time he shot Al Boyce. When Odell asked Dr. Darnell if Beal Sneed was still insane, he replied: "No. The cause of his insanity was removed when he killed Boyce, and he is cured." It finally got so outlandish that some spectators started snickering. Judge Nabers hammered his gavel and announced that he would not tolerate any disorder. But it was too late. The crowd broke into an uproar. Judge Nabers hammered away again. "You people must not laugh," he began sternly, but before he could finish his admonition he himself lost control and, as the *Star-Telegram* reporter noted, the judge, the spectators, and the jury all "hee-hawed" away.

To restore some gravity to the proceedings, the defense once again summoned to the stand Dr. John S. Turner, Beal Sneed's "$100-a-day" sanity expert, to give a more dignified "moral insanity" diagnosis. Turner, however, limited his moral insanity diagnosis to Lena.

Next it was Captain Snyder's turn. Through practice, he had improved his rant against Al, that "whiskey drinking cigarette fiend." "I would have killed Al Boyce as if he had been a yellow dog without the least compunction of conscience." Then he shifted his rant to include all the Boyce family, blaming Colonel Boyce and Annie Boyce for not putting a stop to the affair and saving his family from disgrace. It became clear that Captain Snyder was much more concerned with damage to his pride than with the welfare of his daughter. He broke down and sobbed, "God only knows what I've suffered. I'm getting old and this trouble has been hard on me."

His anguish soon turned to rage, however, when Senator Odell interrupted him with a hearsay objection. He shouted his defiance at Odell and insisted that he be allowed "to tell my story." Finally, despite continued objections from Odell and admonishments from Judge Nabers, once again, as he had done in the two previous murder trials, Captain Snyder succeeded in telling it his way—hearsay and all—including a history of the three families from their early Georgetown days. He denied that Al and Lena had ever been childhood sweethearts.

The appropriately named bartender, Joe Barr, was the next defense witness. Barr had been a bartender at the saloon in the Southland Hotel in Dallas during the late summer of 1912 about a month before Al was killed. Apparently, Al and his friend Lucien Hughes went on a spree that lasted several days during which time they headquartered at the Southland Hotel. Joe Barr said that he had visited their hotel room once and noticed Al and Lucien Hughes had "a regular arsenal" up there. It made him nervous, he said, when he saw a very intoxicated Lucien Hughes "monkeying around" with all those pistols. A shadow of a doubt, however, was cast upon the accuracy of bartender Joe's opinion as to the intoxication of Lucien Hughes—or anybody else for that matter—when, during cross-examination, he admitted that he himself had "eight or ten drinks since two-thirty that afternoon" and then went on to mention that he customarily knocked back two or three shots of whiskey every morning before breakfast—just to get the day kicked off right.[6]

To ramp up the pathos yet another notch, the defense called another veteran of the witness stand, Henry Bowman, to retell the story of the motherless children's desolate Christmas of 1911. The prosecution objected on grounds of relevancy. It was beyond dispute that Beal Sneed intentionally killed Al Boyce, so how could this sad story be relevant to any issue in this trial? The defense contended that the story was relevant to demonstrate that at the time Beal pulled the trigger he was in the throes of a "sudden passion," thus entitling the jury to consider the lesser offense of manslaughter. The prosecution, in turn, argued that whatever happened at Christmas 1911 was too remote to arouse a violent "sudden passion" in Beal's mind on September 14, 1912. Nevertheless, Judge Nabers overruled the state's objection, and Bowman proceeded to tell his heart-rending tale again.

At this point in the trial, Judge Nabers's bias in favor of the defense had become abundantly clear. While it was also clear that Judge Nabers was way yonder shy of being a legal scholar, still it appears very doubtful that all his erroneous rulings could be attributed to his ignorance of the law since his calls always favored the defendant. Which raises the question: why? Was Judge Nabers so imbued with the mores of the Old South and the frontier West that, regardless of what the written laws of Texas provided, he believed that Al Boyce got what he deserved because he ran off with another man's wife? Or, as a politician, was he acutely aware that his constituents were almost unanimously in favor of the unwritten law and therefore in favor of John Beal Sneed's method of administering frontier justice? Or, was he bribed? Or, was he simply overwhelmed by the combined, dynamic presence of "Wild Bill" McLean, Walter Scott, A. J. Fires, and the rest of the defense team—not to mention John Beal Sneed himself? Or, was it a combination of some, or all, of the above? In any event, Judge Nabers's outrageous calls had to have been more than a little exasperating to the prosecution team. But there was little they could do about it other than register foredoomed objections: the trial judge was king of the trial court, and the prosecution had no right to appeal to a higher court even if the defendant was found not guilty as a result of demonstrably erroneous rulings by the trial judge.

Then it was time for the star of the defense performance to take stage center. Beal Sneed, nimble of wit, glib of tongue, and a superb actor, had polished well his theatrical talents during his first two tours of duty on the witness stand in the Fort Worth trials. With that experience behind him, he was a peerless performer, exuding such an earnest and sincere blend of self-righteousness, self-pity, and self-sacrifice that would have brought tears to the eyes of Jack the Ripper—pushing syrupy melodrama to the brink of unadulterated farce. He recounted the traumatic scene that followed his discovery of his wife's affair—the sleepless nights that followed and his desperate entreaties to Lena to reconsider, begging her not to run off to South America with Al and take the precious children with her. The *Star-Telegram* reporter noted that at this point "there was hardly a dry eye in the jury box" and that one young juror who had been married only ten months, buried his face in his hands. Meanwhile, the reporter continued, "Sneed at times all but broke down and when he pulled himself together he would fairly shout his story to the jury."[7]

Then came the long recital of what a happy home he and Lena had before Al; how often she told him how much she loved him; told him how lucky she was to have him as a husband; and so on. Then followed his account of having to perform his reluctant duty to institutionalize his wife when he became aware how mentally ill she was; that followed by his account of how the licentious Al Boyce had kidnapped her from the asylum; that followed by the story of his lonely trek all over the United States to find and rescue her, ending with the recapture of his wayward wife in Canada.

Although the newspaper reporter covering the trial seemed not to have noticed, during Beal's seven-hour tour de force on the witness stand, his testimony was occasionally inconsistent. Beal testified that after he rescued Lena from Al's evil spell and brought her back from Canada, she was repentant and told him how much she loved him. Referring to her later decision to leave Johnson's Sanitarium with Billie Steele in the spring of 1912 and live with him at the Reiger Street apartment in Dallas, Beal testified that Lena had told him afterward that "she cried every night for him" and that "she had the baby's shoes about her neck all the time and kept a picture of him on her wall."[8] (Ironically, it was during this time frame that Lena apparently became pregnant by Al Boyce during a secret tryst at the Reiger Street apartment one night in July 1912 when Beal was out of town. Of course, the jury never got to hear anything about that.) Although Beal claimed that Lena joyously reunited with him at the Reiger Street apartment during the summer of 1912, he later confided to the jury that he and "Mrs. Sneed" had not lived together as husband and wife since her elopement with Al Boyce back in the fall of 1911 and that he was caring for her only as he would a sick child. Forlornly, he unburdened himself of another painful secret: Lena sent Valentine's Day cards to the children . . . but not to him. (Let's see now: Lena so happy to reunite—loved him so much—yet didn't bother to send him a Valentine?)

Then too, Lena's mental condition seemed to change to suit Beal's current melodrama. At times, when it suited his purpose he portrayed her as lucid and rational (e.g., told Beal she was "repentant," happy to reunite, had "cried for him every night," etc.), but in another context she was "deranged." At one point defense attorney McLean gently elicited this tear-jerking testimony from Beal:

Q: Do you now believe that your wife is mentally deranged?

A: (Facing the jury and speaking with deep feeling in his voice) I know it, gentlemen, better than I know I'm living, that this is all that has kept me in the world—just to care for and protect her.[9]

Another inconsistency involved Beal's stated reason for coming to Amarillo. He denied that he had come to Amarillo with the express intention of killing Al Boyce. He had gone there to see his friendly banker, W. H. Fuqua, and to "wind up his business affairs." Further along during the trial, however, Beal seemed to recall that something entirely different compelled him to go to Amarillo. He told the jury: "These people had taken all I had but my little children, and they were still trying to kill me, and *something* just took me to Amarillo."[10]

Divine guidance, no doubt.

Initially Beal claimed that he killed Al on impulse after unexpectedly seeing him. Beal testified:

> On that afternoon of the killing, I was lying across the bed brooding
> over what I had gone through and wishing I was a thousand miles
> from nowhere. I hadn't heard from my children since I'd been in
> Amarillo and I hadn't seen Boyce. I had been there nearly a week.
> I thought maybe he was right then down at [the Sneed family farm
> near] Calvert taking my little girls away from me. Then, when I saw
> him coming up the street, I rushed out and killed him.[11]

Later, when Sneed decided to claim that he shot Al Boyce in
self-defense, he modified his account of the killing. He testified
that after he rushed out of the death cottage Al Boyce turned and
saw him. He said that he and Boyce looked at each other, and then
Boyce reached for his pistol. Only then, Beal testified, did he fire
the fatal shotgun blasts.[12]

To no one's surprise Beal Sneed was not dented on cross-examination—he ducked, he dodged, he deflected, he parried, and often he
was simply unresponsive. Like Senator Hanger during the Fort Worth
trials, Senator Odell never pursued him vigorously or pinned him
down on any controversial point or forced him to give a "yes" or "no"
answer when it didn't suit Beal's fancy. For example, this exchange
between Senator Odell and Beal Sneed on cross-examination:

Q: What did you rent that cottage for?

A: I knew this, that he was going to kill me.

Q: Don't you know that you rented that cottage to lie in wait
disguised and kill Albert Boyce?

A: My disguise was to keep other people from recognizing me.
It was not for Al Boyce.[13]

During direct testimony Sneed had testified that he had seen
Al's brother Will Boyce armed with a shotgun when he went past
the Boyce home and therefore he carried a shotgun. Senator
Odell, on cross, then asked Beal if he really expected Will Boyce
to go about "totally unarmed" after what Beal had done to Will's
father in Fort Worth.

Beal answered: "I didn't want to harm Will Boyce, but I knew the Boyces wanted Al to kill me and were willing to help him. They were either going to do it themselves or hire someone to do it."[14]

Sheriff Burwell had testified that Sneed was so well disguised that he didn't recognize him when he first saw him at the jail shortly after his arrest. He also testified that Sneed had blackened his naturally reddish hair with something like coal dust. After Sneed was jailed, Sheriff Burwell searched the death cottage, and discovered some "blacking" and a camel's hair brush as well as a false mustache. He also found a canteen and a breastplate. When Senator Odell cross-examined Beal Sneed about these unusual items, Beal Sneed gave these explanations:

Breastplate: bought it in Dallas for Beech Epting's eight-year-old son who liked to play baseball.

False mustache: bought it in Dallas and intended to wear it in Fort Worth as a part of his disguise to "slip" his "shadower." (Beal contended that the Boyce family had hired someone to "shadow" him wherever he went.)

Canteen: Epting bought it for him when he said he was going to his Potter County ranch.

Blacking and camel's hair brush: said the first time he ever saw them was in the courthouse in Amarillo.[15]

Senator Odell's cross-examination was desultory at best. Granted that Beal Sneed was intelligent, articulate, and a very elusive artful dodger, still, it is hard to imagine "Wild Bill" McLean—had he been on the prosecution team—allowing Sneed to get away with such evasive nonsense. A skilled cross-examiner could have exposed Sneed's disingenuous responses for what they really were: absurd and ridiculous. Plus asking simple questions such as: "By the way Mr. Sneed, what legitimate business goals were you pursuing during those four days you spent, alone with Beech Epting, sweating in the death cottage?" And on and on and on.

When the defense rested its case, the prosecution offered rebuttal evidence. First on the list was a letter Lena had written to Al. It was the letter she had written to Al shortly after Beal had incarcerated her in the Allison brothers' insane asylum. In it she begged Al to come rescue her. The letter certainly seemed most relevant to several disputed issues in the trial: relevant to prove that Lena was not insane, that she really loved Al, and that Beal was not the loving, self-sacrificing husband he portrayed himself to be for the jury. Nevertheless, Judge Nabers sustained McLean's objection on the grounds that the proffered exhibit was not relevant, and besides, it was hearsay evidence. And so the jury never saw it.

Earlier in the trial, however, Judge Nabers overruled a prosecution objection on the same grounds when McLean offered a transcript of Beal Sneed's father's testimony during the first Fort Worth murder trial. (It will be recalled that the elder Sneed was murdered shortly after that trial by an insane tenant farmer.) His previous testimony was offered to show that Colonel Boyce and Annie Boyce had failed to do all that they should have done to break up the romance between their son and Lena. That testimony might have been relevant in the earlier trial to prove a motive for Beal to kill Colonel Boyce, but how was it relevant to the overriding issue in the case: why did Beal kill Al Boyce? And so the jury was allowed to hear Sneed the elder speak from the grave.

"Dressed in deep mourning," according to the *Star-Telegram* report, Annie Boyce was called as the state's final witness. Odell asked her, "Your home is in Amarillo, Mrs. Boyce?"

"My home is closed," she answered. "The house is there."

She told of a conversation she had with her husband and Captain Snyder just after the affair was discovered. She said that Captain Snyder admitted he didn't believe his daughter was insane, but he would rather keep Lena in confinement the rest of her life than have her threatening disgrace to his family. Annie Boyce claimed that Beal Sneed knew about the infatuation between Al and Lena before she and her husband did.

When McLean began his cross-examination of Annie Boyce, he obviously didn't wish to make the same mistake he had made when cross-examining her during the first Sneed trial in Fort Worth—didn't want it to appear to the jury that he was an overbearing bully to a woman who had recently lost her husband, and now her son, also. So he gently inquired, "You have lost your husband and your son, haven't you, Mrs. Boyce?"

"Yes," she retorted, "one by murder and one by assassination." When pressed further, she bitterly commented on the tragedy. The defense lawyers leaped to their feet in a chorus of protest, objecting, "not responsive!" Judge Nabers sustained their objections, but it took her son Henry Boyce to finally silence her. In her last appearance on behalf of her slain husband and son, she demanded that, like Captain Snyder, she be allowed to tell "the whole story." Judge Nabers then instructed her to answer McLean's questions directly and without comment "because everything is not admissible under the rules of evidence." Annie Boyce then said this to the judge:

> This is just a trial for the living, and there is no trial for the dead. Why can't I tell the whole story as Captain Snyder did. He hasn't the sorrow and the trouble that I have. I can't cry, but my heart is dripping blood.[16]

Final jury arguments were a gourmet feast of melodrama properly seasoned to the taste of 1913 Texans. Judge Nabers granted each side seven hours in which to baste its turkey. District Attorney Hugh D. Spencer led off for the state by denouncing not only Beal Sneed but also Lena's father, Captain Snyder, and her brother-in-law Henry Bowman for their mistreatment of Lena. He said:

> They placed her in a madhouse to punish her; took her away from her children and all her loved ones and locked her up with insane people and pellagra patients.
>
> . . . Sneed didn't want her back as a wife . . . He wanted her back to punish her. Sneed determined that if he couldn't have her, Al Boyce, the man she loved should not.[17]

McLean for the defense responded by justifying Sneed's act in killing Al Boyce without giving him a chance because, he contended,

Sneed knew that he wouldn't stand a chance against Al Boyce in an "open" fight. Sneed, he continued, couldn't stand the thought of his little children living under the same roof with a man like Al Boyce, "the despoiler of his home." He said:

> There was but one thing to do, and that was to kill him.
>
> Were the penitentiaries made for such men as Beal? If they were, then I want to go to the penitentiary and associate with home protectors. Whenever a home is despoiled, gentlemen, I say there ought to be a killing.[18]

Special prosecutor Hugh H. Cooper of Amarillo then grasped the baton for the prosecution and told the jury that long before the elopement, John Beal Sneed had no home left to be protected or destroyed. "Silks, fine raiment, and elegant furniture do not make a home," he said. "You enforce the law and the homes will take care of themselves."[19] Lena's love for Al was "genuine" and Al's love for her was "true." Al's only wrong, he contended, was his love for Lena and its tragic consequences. He concluded by telling the jury "if you decide [this case] according to the law and the evidence . . . you will call this the most cold-blooded murder and assassination ever depicted by pen or in life."[20]

Harry Mason, the Vernon lawyer recruited by the defense for this trial, finally got his opportunity to appear on the courtroom stage. He told the jury that Sneed had every right to kill Al Boyce, Jr. Mason proclaimed that if any man ever attempted to ruin his home, he would "camp out on his trail, shoot him down, and bend over him to watch his last agonized pain as his foul soul winged its way to the depths of hell." He then turned to Sneed and told him that he had every right to kill Boyce. The only thing that he had against him, Mason said, was that he didn't do it sooner.

Nevertheless it was Walter Scott for the defense who stole the show. According to the *Star-Telegram* report of the trial, Scott had a "national reputation" as a trial lawyer with theatrical talents of Shakespearean proportions.[21] In a previous murder case Scott and McLean represented a woman indicted for killing her husband's mistress. The defense did not deny she was the perpetrator, and self-defense was not a serious issue. Rather, Scott—written law notwithstanding—relied on the tried and true "protector of the home" defense, and in his final jury argument Scott assumed the role of the defendant-wife. He, portraying the wronged wife, pretended to gather the woman's poor children about her, and with arms draped protectively about her imaginary brood, treated the jury to a doleful, forlorn baritone version of "Home Sweet Home." It worked. She walked.

Scott once again laid it on thick for John Beal Sneed in this murder trial: "The best shots ever fired in Texas were the shots that took Al Boyce's life, and I hope every home destroyer in the land meets the same fate."[22] Scott commended Sneed for "saving" Lena from herself. Had he let her go, Scott assured the jury, it would have been but a short time before Lena would "be in the red light district of some big city, flitting about dark corners as a shadow, then gone."

Proof was plain, Scott told the jury, that at the time Al Boyce was killed he was planning a "second elopement" with Lena, and that he was also plotting to "take the life of the man whose home he had already wrecked." If that had happened, Scott shuddered to reflect, the poor little children would have been doomed to a fate worse than death: life under the same roof with the despicable Al Boyce.

Walter Scott ended his argument by enacting one of his trademark dramatic skits for the jurors. He played the part of a juror coming home after having voted to convict Beal Sneed and send him to prison. He climbed up on the witness stand and, using it as his stage, pretended he had just returned to his home after the trial. He took his imaginary little daughter on one knee and his imaginary little son on the other. The children asked him where he had been. He explained that he had been a juror trying Beal Sneed. The little boy asked him what Sneed had done, and he replied that Sneed killed the man who took his wife and his little children away from him.

"Well, you let him go, didn't you, Papa?" the little boy asked.

"No, son," the juror sadly answered, "we sent him to the penitentiary."

With that, Scott sprang from the witness chair and confronted the jury. "Men," he warned, "those little children would walk away from you in shame."[23]

WALTER B. SCOTT and his law partner, W. P. "Wild Bill" McLean, represented John Beal Sneed in his three murder trials. *Photograph from the January 30, 1912, edition of the* Fort Worth Star-Telegram.

It took only about twenty minutes of discussion and one ballot for the Vernon jury to declare John Beal Sneed not guilty of the murder of Al Boyce. Upon hearing the verdict, the defendant leaped from his chair and clapped his hands. Applause broke out from the entire courtroom, and Sneed was carried toward the door of the district clerk's office by the press of the crowd eager to shake hands with him.

It was apparent that the verdict came as no surprise to the other side. None of the Boyce family was present when the verdict was returned. All of the special prosecutors were also gone. Only District Attorney Hugh Spencer remained in the courtroom and did so only because he was occupied with the trial of a minor criminal case. He sat impassively at the counsel table when the verdict was read and then resumed trial of the other case as soon as order was restored.

That the jurors had already heard all about the facts of the case and had made up their minds before the trial ever began was evidenced by the remarks of one juror after the trial. That juror told a *Star-Telegram* reporter that the verdict would have been the same if the defense had not presented a single witness. He noted that "about all the prosecution had proved was that Sneed killed Boyce," adding that the jury already knew that because Sneed had admitted it and that they, the jury, "had a general idea of Sneed's provocation."

During the Vernon trial, a startling fact came to light. And even more startling was the fact that nothing came of it.

The prosecution produced, and attempted to introduce into evidence, the Earl McFarland letter. It was the letter found on Al Boyce's body just after he was killed. Addressed to John Beal Sneed, the letter was written shortly after Beal's first murder trial in Fort Worth. In it, McFarland had demanded additional payment for his services in bribing a juror. The letter also implicated Beal's defense lawyers, Cone Johnson and Walter Scott, in the bribery scheme.

It will be recalled that it was during jury selection of the first Fort Worth murder trial that allegations of attempted jury bribing arose but were not proven. It will also be recalled that while the jury was deliberating on a verdict in that case, Beal Sneed's sidekick, Henry Bowman, bragged to a reporter that the worst that could happen to Beal Sneed was a deadlocked jury.

During the Vernon trial the prosecution offered this letter in evidence on grounds that it tended to prove a motive for the killing of Al Boyce by Beal Sneed, namely to avoid being prosecuted for bribing a juror. Judge Nabers, however, upheld a defense "relevancy" objection, obviously feeling that the prosecution's "motive for murder" theory was too far-fetched. Although Judge Nabers eventually ruled out presenting the McFarland letter to the Vernon jury, Senator Odell was permitted to question Beal Sneed about it at a hearing outside the presence of the jury. Beal admitted that he had received the letter from McFarland, but said he just passed it on to his lawyers. And, of course, Beal Sneed denied that he had bribed any juror or had authorized anybody else to bribe a juror. Apparently Odell let it go at that, thus once again allowing Sneed to shrug off an embarrassing—and potentially incriminating—subject. Since Walter Scott was present in the courtroom, why didn't Odell call him to the stand and demand an explanation? One can speculate with assuredness that, had McLean been captain of the prosecution team, and had this nugget fallen into his lap, there would have been hell to pay for the defense.

Still, two mysteries remain unsolved by the incident. First, even though the letter was properly denied admission into evidence during the Vernon jury trial, why didn't Odell, or even Judge Nabers, deliver that letter to the Tarrant County district attorney in Fort Worth and demand that a criminal investigation be instigated? The proper procedure would have been for the district attorney to call a grand jury. The grand jury could have subpoenaed witnesses, put them under oath, and thereby discovered what really happened. McFarland, as well as Sneed, Walter Scott, Cone Johnson, and all twelve of the jurors in the Fort Worth trial should have been grilled by the grand jury. Had a vigorous prosecutor put McFarland in the hot seat, it is a better than even bet that he would have rolled over to save his own skin and disgorged the whole story. That a prosecution was not pursued suggests more than just ineptitude on Odell's part. Didn't fidelity to his clients, the Boyce family, require Odell to launch a vigorous attack to redress what appeared to be a gross miscarriage of justice—one that possibly allowed the killer of Colonel Boyce to escape just retribution? Just retribution not only for assassinating Colonel Boyce, but also just retribution for corruption of the judicial proceeding if the McFarland allegations proved to be true. To say the least, the whole episode reeked of flagrant malfeasance on the part of lawyers on both sides, as well as the judge and the prosecutor.

The second unanswered question is this: how did Al Boyce end up in possession of the McFarland letter? It was addressed to Beal Sneed, and Sneed testified that he had received it but had turned it over to his lawyers, McLean and Scott. If that had been the case, it is for sure and for certain that that letter would never, ever, have seen the light of day thereafter. So how did Al Boyce get it? The only logical surmise is that after Lena went back to live with Beal in the summer of 1912, she must have found that letter in Sneed's effects and given it to Al Boyce.

The Public Weighs In

Widespread publicity, as well as the sensational nature of the case, sparked considerable public debate about invoking the unwritten law. Fairly typical was one widely reprinted opinion—that of Reverend M. T. Tucker, pastor of the First Baptist Church of Dublin,

Texas, who weighed in on the side of the unwritten law. Reverend Tucker, a self-proclaimed biblical scholar (who apparently never got past the Old Testament), advocated a legislative effort to transform the unwritten law into statutory law. He wrote:

> Under the Divine law, adultery was punished by death, and organized society should punish it with a penalty at least sufficient to rebuke its frequency and to prevent so much bloodshed. But until this is done resort will be had to the unwritten law and properly under such circumstances. And if such men as Sneed . . . are to be reduced by our courts to the level of criminality, then it seems to me that our processes of law have become a miserable farce of pretended justice.[24]

As observed above, the Sneed trials may have sparked a public debate about the propriety of invoking the unwritten law as a defense in murder trials, but, judging from the results of those trials, it must have been—at least in 1913 Texas—a rather one-sided debate.

District Attorney Hugh D. Spencer sat silently in the Vernon courtroom on February 25, 1913, and heard the jury pronounce John Beal Sneed not guilty. He must have been disappointed. Still, the result was not much of a surprise to anyone—especially after the Fort Worth jury had already exonerated Sneed for the murder of Al's father, Colonel Boyce. Spencer may have been disappointed, but he probably was not crushed by the defeat. The handsome, thirty-eight-year-old bachelor was honorable, well respected, and riding the crest of a successful career. He could not have imagined what a tragic twist of fate was in store for him before the year 1913 was out—a fate that, as we shall explore later in Appendix One, would turn out to be even more bizarre than the John Beal Sneed saga. And, just as it had been with the John Beal Sneed story, when the Hugh Spencer tale unfolded, a woman would be at the center of it all.

The John Beal Sneed Wars Continue

Combat in the Courts, Firefights in the Streets

JOHN BEAL SNEED walked out of the Vernon courthouse a free man on February 25, 1913. For almost two years he had soldiered on through physical, mental, and emotional ordeals that would have worn out the body and crushed the spirit of an ordinary man—all the confrontations, the bloodletting, the killing of two human beings, and then being run through the emotional wringer during four murder trials—in three of which his own life hung in the balance. On top of all of that, his family life had been devastated.

In the end, John Beal Sneed's iron will, his callous disregard for anyone except himself, and his grim determination to prevail, whatever the cost, did prevail. He had succeeded in ending the love triangle between his wife and Al Boyce; he had publicly vindicated his wounded pride by killing Colonel Boyce and Al Boyce; he had forced a woman who hated him to remain his wife and live with him; and finally, he had defeated all the criminal charges lodged against him. It would seem that any mortal man who had been through all that John Beal Sneed had just endured would have been more than content to lead a life of peace and quiet forever after—devoted, if not to family, at least to his agricultural pursuits. But not John Beal Sneed. He was not content unless he was fighting with somebody over something—in court or out of court. And, as he had candidly admitted earlier to a reporter, if he got into a fight, he intended to win it. By whatever means it took.

John Beal Sneed's vendetta against the Boyces nearly ruined him financially. He had ignored his father's sensible advice to simply throw Lena out: divorce her and be rid of her. But, as we have seen, that didn't satisfy Beal Sneed's rage for vengeance. Although he had gone against his father's advice, still his father agreed to finance his defense in the first Fort Worth trial—the one that ended in a mistrial. However, he warned his son that if he didn't divorce Lena after that trial was concluded he would cut Beal out of his will. Fortunately, for Beal Sneed, one of his father's tenant farmers shot and killed Joseph Tyre Sneed, Sr., on March 6, 1912, before the Fort Worth retrial of Beal Sneed, and before Beal killed Al Boyce, and before the two murder trials that followed that killing—and before Beal's father got around to rewriting his will and disinheriting Beal. Even so, Beal had to fork over a king's ransom for all those expensive lawyers, witnesses, and court costs incurred in the last three murder trials. Consequently, Beal was forced to liquidate most of his holdings, including his mansion in Amarillo.

Beal did manage to salvage one asset devised to him through his father's unrevoked will: a large tract of land in Cottle County, Texas, some 130 miles southeast of Amarillo and some eleven miles south of Paducah, Texas. In 1887, Joseph Tyre Sneed, Sr., had purchased this block of land located along Buford's Creek, a tributary of the North Wichita River. Although rainfall was scanty there, still the land was fertile, and, except in droughty years, it usually produced good cotton crops.

Over the years following the elder Sneed's purchase of the large farm in 1887, a small rural community developed. They named it

"Sneedville."[1] Soon it boasted a school, a cotton gin, a general merchandise store, and a post office, and by 1915 Sneedville had a population of 100. After the last murder trial in 1913, John Beal Sneed established a modest home for himself, Lena, and their two daughters in Sneedville. The tiny, remote farming village of Sneedville on the parched, desolate, windswept plains must have seemed— particularly to Lena—quite a comedown from vibrant Amarillo, the bustling "Queen City of the Panhandle," but John Beal Sneed had no time or inclination to waste indulging in such sentimental claptrap: he immediately built a few shacks for farm laborers and launched into raising cotton and buying and selling rural properties.

Since Beal spent considerable time traveling and making land trades, he hired a young man by the name of David "Wood" Barton to manage his Paducah farming operation. He was Beal Sneed's kind of guy—an arrogant, overbearing, and violent bully whose idea of dispute resolution was to issue an ultimatum and then enforce it with a good, old-fashioned pistol-whipping (or worse) if the directive was not promptly executed to his satisfaction. In 1921, Wood Barton, age thirty, married Beal and Lena's youngest daughter, Georgia, age sixteen.

It didn't take Barton long to earn an unenviable reputation for himself in the Paducah community. A neighboring farmer, Ed Carnes, would later say that he was so appalled by Barton's mistreatment of his Mexican cotton pickers that he voluntarily appeared before the Cottle County grand jury and testified that Barton was beating his workers. When Barton heard about it, he jerked Carnes off his wagon seat one day in downtown Paducah and beat him soundly. Not satisfied with that, Barton proceeded to bite a chunk out of Carnes's ear.[2]

Next, he got into a squabble with another neighboring farmer and Baptist minister, Rev. Albert A. Green. Barton had imported a large number of illegal Mexican immigrants to help harvest Sneed's cotton crop. The workers were housed in some shacks on Sneed's farm, and Sneed's manager hauled them to town every Saturday for groceries and supplies. So naturally, Sneed charged the Mexicans for "lodging and transportation" expenses. They were paid a penny or two a pound for picking the cotton, but not before Sneed deducted the "lodging and transportation" expenses from their meager earnings. Meanwhile, Green hired some of these workers to come over to his farm and pick cotton for him. Problem was, at least according to Barton and Sneed, these cotton pickers still owed Sneed $150 for housing and transportation—such charges supposedly accruing while they were still picking Sneed cotton. On January 18, 1920, Barton demanded that Reverend Green deduct $150 from the wages he owed the workers and reimburse Beal. An argument erupted, ending with Barton pistol-whipping Green and knocking him down. Then he threatened to kill Green if he didn't pay up immediately. Green protested that he didn't have any money with him. A bystander, J. E. Etheridge, interceded on Green's behalf and wrote a $150 check on his own account, payable to J. B. Sneed.[3]

The next day, however, Green filed charges of "assault with intent to rob" against Wood Barton.[4] On May 9, 1920, a Cottle County jury found Wood Barton guilty and sentenced him to two years in prison. Barton appealed and the appellate court reversed his conviction, sending the case back for a retrial. It was during this time frame that Barton assaulted Scott Jolly, one of the jurors who had voted to convict him. Jolly later testified that he was in a drugstore buying a soft drink when Barton slipped up behind him and knocked him down, exclaiming, "By God, I'm not a robber."[5] A frightened Scott Jolly fled the scene. Retrial of Wood Barton on the assault with intent to rob charge never happened and for a very good reason: Wood Barton did not live that long.

Barton didn't learn from his experience with Reverend Green. Perhaps he was also emboldened by his successes in and out of court. Anyway, he soon got into another cotton-picking dispute with yet another neighbor. But there was a decidedly different outcome.

C. B. Berry, a Cottle County farmer and Paducah businessman, dealing with Wood Barton, bought Sneed's cotton crop in the fall of 1922 for $2,000. He secured some Mexican pickers to harvest the crop. Barton sent some additional workers to help. Later, Barton claimed that Berry owed him $38 for some unspecified expenses. Berry declined to pay. A few days later, an angry Barton confronted

Berry in the Campbell barbershop in Paducah in the presence of witnesses. Barton threatened Berry, but Berry again refused to accede to his demands. One barbershop witness later testified that after Berry departed Barton said, "By God that _____ will pay me that $38 or I'll kill him." Another said he heard Barton make this threat: "I believe I'll go and beat the brains out of that _____."[6] The witness said that he communicated this threat to Berry. Two or three days later Barton encountered Berry's twenty-one-year-old son, Charles Berry, on the street. He called young Berry over and said, "I'm going to get that $38 one way or another and you can tell your old man that I said so." Other locals communicated threats that Barton had made against Berry. Then a few days after the barbershop encounter, Berry testified that he saw Barton standing across the street. "He had one glove off and was slapping it against his hand. He looked at me sneeringly, started walking toward me, but then turned and walked off." After that episode, Berry armed himself with a .32-caliber pistol.

A few days later, November 11, 1922, he again encountered Barton at the entrance to the First National Bank in Paducah. Berry was talking to another man and tried to ignore him. Barton said, "Come out here Berry, I want to talk to you." Berry followed him a short distance down the sidewalk. Barton stopped with his back to the wall of the bank building, put his right hand under his vest near his armpit.

"Berry, when are you going to pay me the money you owe me?"

"I don't owe you anything."

"You're a s_____ and a liar."[7] With that Barton pulled his hat down with his left hand and, according to Berry, thrust his right hand deeper under his arm. Berry stepped back, pulled his .32 automatic and fired twice. Then his pistol jammed. But twice was enough. He hit Barton once in the heart and once in his stomach.[8]

Berry walked away. Soon John Beal Sneed arrived at the scene and ordered the undertaker to examine Barton's body and clothing. No weapon was found. He had been unarmed. Berry would later testify that he was aware of the prior episodes of violence in Barton's brief career. Barton was thirty years old when killed. Berry was forty-five.

Naturally, Beal Sneed sought revenge and did so in the way he knew best. Some four months later, on March 7, 1923, while Sneed was standing on the corner of a crowded downtown street in Paducah visiting with his friend and courtroom defender, A. J. Fires, he saw C. B. Berry walk past. Sneed drew his pistol and shot Berry five times while Berry was walking away from him. Berry was hit three times in the right arm, once in the left arm, and once in the right leg. Although badly wounded, Berry took refuge by lurching into an adjacent store.[9] Quick action by A. J. Fires in grabbing Sneed as he was blazing away saved Berry's life. In its next edition, the nearby *Quanah Tribune-Chief* weekly newspaper gave this account of the shooting:

> Sneed stopped [on Main Street in Paducah] to talk to Judge A. J. Fires, and his left hand rested upon Fires' shoulder when Berry passed them. [Berry] had not gone half a dozen steps when Sneed drew his revolver and began shooting. That such a good marksman did not kill his man outright was wholly due to Fires' quick wit, which spoiled his aim.[10]

After the shooting, Fires scolded his former client, saying, "Now you've played the devil!" Sneed shrugged it off. He said, "Didn't you see [Berry's] gun?" Fires told him that he hadn't seen any gun.

The *Quanah Tribune-Chief's* account of the shooting also mentioned Sneed's legal and financial reversals over the preceding few years, and ended by noting that Sneed had become "heavily indebted to the merchants of neighboring towns." Meanwhile, the Cottle County district judge, J. H. Milam, alarmed by the escalating violence that inevitably followed in the wake of John Beal Sneed, summoned Texas Ranger Red Burton in hopes of quelling any more outbreaks.[11] Ranger Burton came, but he failed to stop the bloodletting.

Berry survived, although he spent several months regaining enough strength to get out of the Quanah hospital. When he did, however, he came after Beal with a vengeance. Berry slipped back into Paducah unannounced and secreted himself in a small unoccupied brick shed behind the First National Bank building. The hut had a view of the main street of Paducah. There Berry stashed food, water, a blanket, a six-shooter pistol, a Winchester rifle, and a .12-gauge shotgun loaded with buckshot—and patiently waited. On July 2, 1923, Beal eventually showed up in downtown Paducah and parked near the bank building in sight of the brick hut where Berry was hiding. About noon Beal returned to his car and was about to open the car door when the first shotgun blast roared. Buckshot pellets hit Beal in the back of the head and neck. Dazed, but still standing, he thought at first there had been a blowout of an automobile tire. Then he realized he had been shot, and drew his .45-caliber automatic pistol. However, he didn't know where the shot came from, and he couldn't locate the shooter. About that time Berry fired a second blast. This one hit Sneed in the back and legs. In all some twenty-five to thirty buckshot pellets penetrated him, one of which punctured a lung. Nevertheless, Beal still didn't go down. He staggered across the street to the Ellis tin shop and collapsed. He was rushed to the hospital in Quanah some forty-five miles away.[12]

Meanwhile, the attention of a ten-year-old boy, Wayne Smith, had been attracted by the first shotgun blast. He looked across the street and saw C. B. Berry with the shotgun standing in front of the door of the brick building at the rear of the bank. The boy watched Berry fire the second shot. He told authorities, and the Cottle County Sheriff W. T. Patterson was summoned. Sheriff Patterson knocked on the locked door of the brick shed. He got no answer. After kicking the door open, he discovered C. B. Berry inside, hiding behind some bales of hay. He also found the shotgun, the pistol, the rifle, the blanket, and the cache of food and water. The sheriff arrested Berry and took him to jail.[13]

A shotgun, especially when loaded with buckshot (large-size pellets), is an awesome weapon and the shooter doesn't have to worry much about taking a fine bead on his target. Still, the shotgun does have one distinct limitation: the shooter must be fairly close to the target to do lethal damage. Berry, unlike Beal when he bushwhacked Al Boyce, Jr., failed to get close enough to his victim before firing. Although Beal was splattered with multiple buckshot pellets, he was not critically wounded. His wounds were serious enough, however, to keep him hospitalized for approximately two weeks.

Berry was indicted for murdering Wood Barton;[14] Beal Sneed was indicted for assault with intent to murder Berry;[15] and Berry was indicted once again, this time for assault with intent to murder Beal.[16] All indictments were returned in Cottle County. Venue was changed in all three cases—the murder case against Berry was transferred to Seymour in Baylor County, and both of the assault with intent to murder cases were transferred to Benjamin in Knox County.

The trial of C. B. Berry for the murder of Wood Barton began in Seymour on July 10, 1923, in the Baylor County District Court, and it made headlines all across Texas.[17] John Beal Sneed was unable to attend because he was still in the hospital recuperating from Berry's shotgun attack. However, Sneed hired the old courtroom warhorse, A. J. Fires of Childress, to assist District Attorney J. Ross Bell of Paducah. Sneed also hired a local lawyer, Joe Wheat of Seymour, to assist in the prosecution. Not to be outdone, however, Berry got his own renowned trial lawyers: the imposing former district judge Jo A. P. Dickson and the former district attorney Isaac O. Newton, both popular hometown Seymour lawyers. Berry also added to the defense team J. B. Shirtliffe, who, ironically, had been a college classmate of John Beal Sneed.

The Baylor County courthouse couldn't accommodate the crowd of spectators who wanted a ringside seat to hear a detailed account of the killing of Wood Barton. The little village of Seymour couldn't accommodate all those spectators plus the eighty-nine witnesses who had been subpoenaed to testify. Many were forced to camp out in the tourist park at the edge of town.[18]

The first thing that District Judge J. H. Milam did when he called the court to order was to direct the sheriff and his deputies to search all spectators, witnesses, and parties for weapons. That accomplished, the trial began.[19] The prosecution's case didn't take long. The state called two eyewitnesses who had seen C. B. Berry shoot Wood Barton on a street in downtown Paducah on November 11, 1922. The prosecution also proved that Wood Barton was unarmed at the time of the shooting.

The defense didn't challenge any of that, but Berry's lawyers did parade a host of witnesses to enlighten the jurors about the background of the deadly feud and to prove that Barton had instigated it. In addition, many Cottle County farmers and businessmen plus the sheriffs of Cottle and King counties were called to attest to Wood Barton's bad reputation as a dangerous man with an explosive temper and that Barton was the kind of man who would likely carry out any threats to kill.

Then the defense called witnesses who were in a position to give the jury specific examples of Barton's brutality—witnesses who had been the target of Barton's wrath:

Reverend A. A. Green: told of being pistol-whipped and knocked down by Barton over a $150 cotton-picking dispute and then being threatened with death if he didn't immediately pay up.

J. E. Etheridge: told of witnessing Barton's attack on Green and saving Green from further attack or death by paying Barton the demanded $150.

Scott Jolly: told of being waylaid by Barton in retaliation for Jolly's service as a juror who voted to convict Barton for his attack on Green.

Ed Carnes: told of the retaliation Barton had administered when he discovered Carnes had told a grand jury about Barton's brutal mistreatment of his cotton-pickers; how Barton jerked him off his wagon seat and soundly thrashed him and then bit a chunk out of his ear. Carnes created such an outburst from jurors and spectators that Judge J. H. Milam had to gavel them down when Carnes backed up his testimony by exhibiting his partial ear.[20]

In the end, it all came down to the classic "unwritten law" defense in frontier Texas murder cases: "the sorry SOB needed a damned good killing anyhow" defense, thinly veiled, of course, by an obligatory nod in the direction of a legal defense—statutory self-defense. To that end, C. B. Berry took the stand and testified that he thought (mistakenly as it turned out) that Barton was armed during the fatal encounter and that, just before he triggered the fatal shot, he witnessed Barton "thrust his hand under his vest" and therefore assumed he was reaching for his pistol.

Special prosecutor Joe Wheat would later, during final jury arguments, sarcastically remark: "Now that's a new wrinkle in an old suit. It is usually a hip pocket play."

A news account of the trial noted that the recently widowed Georgia Sneed Barton displayed much emotion during the trial, often hiding her face and "making frequent use of her handkerchief." Lena also attended the trial. The same news account had this to say about Lena's demeanor:

> Mrs. Sneed sat motionless and listened attentively, only permitting herself to be disturbed by a tug on her skirt made by her grandchild, the eighteen-month-old child of Wood Barton.[21]

As a criminal defense lawyer, A. J. Fires was almost unbeatable, having won acquittals in 121 out of 124 murder cases in his long and illustrious career. But old Judge Fires just wasn't cut out to play offense. More likely, however, in view of Wood Barton's unsavory reputation, coupled with the unsavory facts of this case, there probably lived no trial lawyer in the whole United States who could have persuaded that West Texas jury to convict C. B. Berry. Prosecutor Isaac O. Newton summed it up for the jury this way:

> A bad character can get by for some time. He can hit a man over the head with a pistol; he can strike a man while his back is turned; and he can jerk a young man off a wagon and bite off a piece of his ear; but sooner or later he will reach his grave through such actions, and that is what occurred in this instance.[22]

At the conclusion of the trial, the jury took only twenty-five minutes and one ballot to come back with a not guilty verdict.[23]

On February 27, 1924, after John Beal Sneed had recovered sufficiently to stand trial, he was tried in neighboring Knox County for attempting to murder C. B. Berry. The shooting had occurred on a downtown street in Paducah on March 7, 1923. Prosecution witnesses said that Beal Sneed and his friend and attorney, A. J. Fires, were standing on a street corner talking when C. B. Berry walked past them. Berry was only a few feet past Sneed and Fires, still walking away, when Sneed suddenly drew his .45 automatic and shot Berry five times. Although Berry was armed with his own pistol, the witnesses said he never made any attempt to draw it. Fires, meanwhile, when Sneed began firing, grabbed Sneed by the shoulder and spoiled his aim, resulting in Berry escaping with five non-fatal wounds.

The *Wichita [Falls] Daily Times* reporter covering the trial noted that throughout the trial, John Beal Sneed maintained a "calm and quiet attitude" and that he seemed "confident and at ease." To no one's surprise, Sneed, when he testified, claimed self-defense; said that after Berry passed him, he turned and made a motion with his right arm indicating that he was reaching for his pistol. Sneed testified:

> I know positively that he was going to kill me. I knew it was going to be a swap out game, and I pulled my gun and started shooting.[24]

Sneed added that "numerous persons" had told him that Berry had been making threats to kill him. However, he did not explain what motive Berry could have had to go gunning for him. Then Beal Sneed's testimony took the same cloying blend of self-pity and self-aggrandizement that he had so masterfully perfected during his three prior murder trials. Still believing that Berry, for whatever reason, had it in for him, Sneed told the jury that he had done all in his power to avoid meeting Berry. Beal added:

> I wasn't afraid of him, but I had been in trouble enough during my lifetime and I didn't want to get into trouble and thought that by avoiding meeting him face to face I would not be inviting trouble. Besides I had further responsibilities now because you might say I had a little child to bring up.[25]

The *Daily Times* reporter added this observation: "Tears came to his eyes as he explained that he meant his little grandchild, the Barton baby."

That Beal Sneed would play his "poor little child" card sometime before the trial ended would have been a sure bet.

Sneed called his friend and lawyer, A. J. Fires, an eyewitness to the shooting, but Fires's testimony seemed more harmful that helpful to Sneed's cause. Perhaps Sneed thought—hoped—his friend would provide a more defense-friendly version. In any event, Fires testified that immediately after the shooting he said to Sneed, "Now, you have played the devil." He said Sneed replied, "Didn't you see that gun?" But Fires testified that he told Sneed that he hadn't seen any gun.

Berry's version was very different. He had passed Sneed on the street and was walking away when Sneed began firing at him. No words had passed between them before the shooting. He further denied he had made any prior threats to kill Beal.

When Berry took the witness stand to testify, he looked Beal directly in the face. The *Daily Times* reporter described it this way:

> Just before the examination began, the eyes of Berry and Sneed met. Both fixed their gaze for fully two minutes when both turned their heads simultaneously. The little bit of play was noticed by all those who happened to be inside the far railing.[26]

The brief trial came to a halt later that same day, and the jury left to make a decision. Twenty-five minutes later the jurors filed back into the courtroom with their verdict: "Not guilty." The trial of C. B. Berry for assault with intent to kill John Beal Sneed was set to begin the next day, February 28, 1924, in the same courtroom.[27]

Beal Sneed, for the prosecution, testified that he was ambushed—shot twice with a shotgun and had been penetrated by twenty-five to thirty buckshot pellets in his head, neck, back, and legs. He never saw his attacker, he said, and had not drawn his pistol until after having been hit by the first shotgun blast. He never got off a shot, however, since he couldn't locate his attacker. Sheriff Patterson testified that he had been informed that the shooter was hiding in the brick shed at the back of the First National Bank building and, when he kicked open the door, he discovered C. B. Berry hiding inside with his weapons, including a .12-gauge shotgun.

C. B. Berry took the stand in his own defense. He admitted shooting Sneed, but said he did so in self-defense. He claimed that Sneed had attempted to draw his pistol before he fired his shotgun the first time. Nobody else saw that. It was the third Paducah shooting episode in a row where the defendant testified that his adversary had attempted to draw a pistol before the defendant fired his first round. And it was the third trial in a row where there were no corroborating witnesses who saw the victim pull a pistol before being shot.

Nevertheless, Berry had another arrow in his quiver this time. He pled that at the time he fired the first shot he was in "real or apparent danger" of being killed by that known and experienced killer, John Beal Sneed. And he cited Beal's ambush-style killings of Colonel Boyce and Al Boyce, Jr. Berry testified:

> I shot to save my own life. I knew that Sneed was going to kill me.
> I just raised my gun and fired twice. I knew that he had threatened
> to kill me at the first opportunity. I knew how he had killed A. G.
> Boyce, Sr. and Al Boyce, Jr. and the methods he had resorted to in
> hunting them down. I just had to shoot, that was all.[28]

Testimony was concluded in one day. The jury began deliberating the next morning, February 29, 1924. The jurors returned to the courtroom thirty-five minutes later, finding C. B. Berry "not guilty."[29] It was apparent that juries in both the Sneed and Berry trials felt that the two dueling shootists came out about even and hence no judicial interventions were appropriate.

As time passed, Beal Sneed focused more of his time and boundless energy on his land-trading enterprise, leaving most of the farm management duties to Wood Barton—at least until Barton earned his comeuppance. Cottle County *deed records* prove that Sneed pursued his real estate ventures with his customary vigor and determination.

Meanwhile, the Cottle County *district court records* attest that Beal pursued that endeavor with his customary combativeness. From 1919 through 1924, in Cottle County alone, Sneed was involved, either as a plaintiff or as a defendant, in twenty-two civil lawsuits, some of which involved multiple parties.[30] Land-trading disputes were the subject of most.

Although in the first years after his return to Paducah most of his civil litigation seemed to turn out favorably for Beal Sneed, nevertheless, from 1922 through 1924, he suffered serious reversals, leading to the surmise that Beal's contentious and overbearing ways were at last beginning to wear pretty thin with the locals. Plus, it became increasingly obvious that his unending civil and criminal courthouse wrangling had just about drained Beal's financial well dry. In October 1922, a bank recovered a judgment against Beal in the Cottle County District Court for almost $8,000 on a past-due loan.[31] (The judgment was by default, meaning that Beal put up no defense.) Shortly thereafter a cottonseed company took another default judgment against Beal for almost $2,500 on another bad debt,[32] and in April 1924, P. M. Fields obtained a judgment against Beal whereby he won title to a ninety-acre tract of land and monetary damages of approximately $12,500 on delinquent notes.[33] Another default judgment for $2,118.16 was taken on March 6, 1923, in the Hardeman County District Court for the purchase in 1920 of seed wheat.[34]

All those Cottle County suits were small potatoes compared to a federal lawsuit filed by Nicholas Bilby against Sneed in 1921 in the U.S. District Court in Abilene, Texas.[35] Bilby, owner of the famous O Bar O Ranch, which encompassed more than a half million acres with headquarters near Spur, Texas, sued Beal to recover possession of approximately 100,000 acres of the ranch land plus damages of $1,212,435. He alleged that he had leased Beal the 100,000 acres beginning June 1, 1919, but Beal had not paid him any compensation for the use of the land through October 1, 1921, yet still retained possession of the land and refused to surrender it back to Bilby.

In what one may surmise was one of Beal's tried-and-true trial tactics, he attempted to assure courtroom success by bribing a juror.

The arrogant Beal Sneed, no doubt emboldened by past successes, must have felt he was bulletproof. His bribery efforts were crude and direct. He and his codefendant, Jack Renfro, lured a juror, H. J. Patterson, to Renfro's Abilene hotel room during the trial where they plied him with generous portions of whiskey before offering him $1,000 to hang the jury. He agreed. Although the corrupted juryman did succeed in causing a hung jury—eleven to one in Bilby's favor—nevertheless, Beal, for the first time, ended up getting himself indicted, tried, and convicted for bribing the juror[36] when Patterson had an attack of conscience and confessed his sin to the judge.[37] (Bilby, in a retrial of the civil suit, eventually succeeded in recovering possession of his land plus a $25,000 judgment against Sneed.)[38] In October 1922, Sneed and Renfro were each sentenced to two years in the federal penitentiary.[39] Patterson, the bribed juror who rolled over and testified for the prosecution, got off with a relatively light thirty-day jail sentence for contempt of court.[40] Of course, Beal Sneed did not give up. He appealed—first to the U.S. Fifth Circuit Court of Appeals in New Orleans and then to the U.S. Supreme Court—but lost.[41] Next he petitioned federal officials from U.S. Senator Morris Sheppard to the U.S. attorney general to intercede with President Calvin Coolidge, pleading for a pardon. But to no avail. Finally, in August 1924, after years of constant legal wrangling, Beal ran out of options and, at last, was shipped to the federal penitentiary in Leavenworth, Kansas.

The *Abilene Reporter*, in telling of Sneed's federal bribery trial, informed its readers (in what has to be a classic understatement) that John Beal Sneed was "well-known" throughout West Texas.[42] Actually, by this time, nearly everybody who was anybody in West Texas had either been shot at or sued by Beal Sneed—or vice versa. John Beal Sneed served only nine months' hard time of his two-year federal sentence for bribing a juror before being paroled. Considering all of Sneed's misdeeds, that brief stint behind bars seemed hardly more than a wrist slap to many . . . mighty light indeed.

In 1923, before his incarceration, Beal and Lena had packed their bags and departed Paducah (where Beal had undoubtedly worn out his welcome) and moved to Dallas. After his release from prison on parole in 1925, Sneed settled comfortably in an upscale neighborhood in North Dallas and promptly set about recouping his fortune. The irrepressible John Beal Sneed was a resounding success and soon became a wealthy independent Texas oilman, drilling in the fabulous East Texas oilfield and other oil-rich areas.[43]

For the next thirty-plus years, he and Lena lived together in style in North Dallas in what had to have been one of the most curious and symbiotic relationships of all time—lived together until Beal died of bone cancer on April 22, 1960.[44] Lena survived until March 6, 1966, when she died of heart failure.[45] Neither of their obituaries printed one word about the scandals, the killings, or the trials that had devastated the three pioneer Texas families almost a half century earlier.

Except for serving nine months on the federal bribery conviction, John Beal Sneed escaped punishment by the law, although, as one wag later pointed out, it cost him: he had succeeded in sentencing himself to life without parole . . . with Lena. Vengeance may have been John Beal Sneed's long suit, but apparently he didn't have a monopoly on it. He may have succeeded in forcing Lena to live with him until death did they part, but he couldn't force her to love him or like him, or to make life pleasant for him—whether she was sane or insane, morally or otherwise. As Clara Sneed, a great-niece of John Beal Sneed, reflected years later in recounting Sneed family lore: "[Lena], did not, by all accounts, give Beal an easy time of it."[46]

Beal and Lena—in peace, at long last—now rest, side by side, in the Hillcrest Cemetery in North Dallas.

All of the Boyce family is buried in the Llano Cemetery in Amarillo where Colonel Boyce and Al Boyce, Jr., have rested since 1912. Mrs. Boyce was the last of her family to die, having survived not only her husband but all of her children as well. Back in 1912, Annie Boyce must have agonized over a choice of words to carve on the gravestone of her son, Al Boyce, Jr. Finally, she settled on this plaintive epitaph: "Jesus knows all about our struggles."

GRAVESTONE OF ALBERT GALLATIN BOYCE, JR., (1875–1912) in the Llano Cemetery in Potter County, Texas. Epitaph selected by his mother, Annie Boyce, reads: "Jesus Knows All About Our Struggles." *Photograph by Allen Kimble in author's collection.*

GRAVESTONE OF ALBERT GALLATIN BOYCE, SR. (1842–1912), AND WIFE, ANNIE E. BOYCE (1850-1929) in the Llano Cemetery, Potter County, Texas. *Photograph by Allen Kimble in author's collection.*

✐ EPILOGUE

A. Snatching Victory from the Jaws of Defeat

Spin-Doctoring, Dirty Tricks, and Whatever Else It Takes

WHEN AT THE END of Sneed's second Fort Worth murder trial the jury shot back a "not guilty" verdict without even bothering to deliberate, much less to read the court's jury instructions, Judge Swayne was flabbergasted—*stunned* is perhaps a better word. Both Judge Swayne's words and his actions during and after the trial clearly demonstrated that he had no doubt—reasonable or otherwise—that John Beal Sneed had intentionally killed Colonel Boyce without any legal justification. How, he puzzled, could the jury have gotten it so wrong?

Better question was, how did the defense manage to snatch victory from the jaws of a seemingly certain defeat? How did McLean and company manage to lay the sins of the son at the feet of the father and then convince the jury that it was somehow necessary to slay Colonel Boyce in order to "protect the home" of the killer? And they did all of that despite the efforts of Judge Swayne during the second trial to rein in the excesses of the McLean team. Admittedly the judge was not entirely successful at that, but then what mortal judge could have totally repressed the combined aggression and forcefulness of McLean, Johnson, Scott, and John Beal Sneed himself—particularly when the prosecution lawyers did so little to assist him?

Besides the judge's helpful efforts, the prosecution had some ammunition that it didn't have during the first trial. Sneed's Amarillo neighbor, Ernest Thompson, testified he heard a very incriminating remark Sneed made shortly before the killing: he heard

Sneed grumble, "I ought to kill the old _____" (referring to Colonel Boyce). Then too, there was the fiasco of a key defense witness, W. A. Weaver, who imploded right in front of the jury. The defense had offered Weaver as an eyewitness to the killing of Colonel Boyce, and Weaver proceeded to give a very defense-friendly eyewitness account of the killing of Colonel Boyce—one carefully crafted to echo Beal Sneed's version. Trouble was, the prosecution demonstrated beyond doubt that Weaver was a liar and a fraud by proving that he wasn't even at or near the scene when the fatal shots were fired.

Also, Judge Swayne reversed his ruling from the first trial and allowed the prosecution to read to the jury the prior testimony of the late Ed Throckmorton giving his account of the killing— eyewitness testimony that depicted Sneed as a vengeful killer. In addition, at the time of the second trial Al Boyce was dead, thus depriving the defense of a potent jury argument it drove home before: send Sneed to prison and you will guarantee that Lena will marry that villainous Al Boyce, leaving poor, helpless Lena unprotected, and, worse yet, ensuring that Al Boyce would corrupt those defenseless little children. Finally, at the end of the trial Judge Swayne gave the jury a "blockbuster" jury charge that he believed would force the jurors to return a "guilty" verdict. Judge Swayne and the prosecution lawyers felt confident of victory this time. But, as it turned out, the game wasn't even close. It was a complete rout for the defense. The jury apparently ignored not only Judge Swayne's instructions but also all that extra ammunition that the prosecution believed would be so persuasive.

It is clear that Judge Swayne as well as the state's attorneys were puzzled by the jury's verdict. Yet the real puzzle is why they were puzzled by that outcome. It should have been obvious to any seasoned trial attorney that the prosecution was a lost cause even before the first witness took the stand at the second trial. The answers and comments given by prospective jurors during the jury selection process made it abundantly clear that almost—to a man—they had already boarded Bill McLean's "protecting the home" express even before that train ever pulled out of the station.

Again, why? What happened?

It can be summed up in four words: the prosecution got out-lawyered. Perhaps lulled into overconfidence in the belief that it had an airtight case, the prosecution was more comatose than combative—a fatal mistake for most any trial lawyer facing off against a pack of world-class attack-dog lawyers. The Boyces made a critical mistake when they employed Senators Hanger and Odell to assist the local prosecutor in the belief that popular politicians, especially when they are great orators, automatically make great trial lawyers. Seldom is that the case. Gifted politicians and gifted trial lawyers may be kissing cousins, but usually they are *not* identical twins. Both Odell and Hanger were reasonably good trial lawyers and had previously represented clients in several well-publicized cases, but neither was in the same league as Bill McLean.

Numerous and diverse qualities go into the making of a truly great lawyer such as Bill McLean. Intelligence, mental agility, audacity, a keen judge of human character, a quick read of people and of rapidly changing situations, a superb acting talent, an ability to articulate ideas and concepts succinctly and in down-to-earth language that connects—gut-level—with jurors, a personality and style that can, by turns, charm jurors yet intimidate hostile witnesses and courtroom opponents, plus an encyclopedic knowledge of criminal laws, and especially the laws of trial procedure and evidence. But beyond these skills there is something that can't be taught: a lawyer either has it or he doesn't—and very few possess it—and it is a born instinct for how to try a case before a jury. Vincent Bugliosi, the renowned trial lawyer who successfully prosecuted the famous Charles Manson murder case and who, when he was a prosecutor for the Los Angeles District Attorney's office won 105 of the 106 felony criminal cases he tried, described it this way:

> It is almost a feral instinct not only to survive, but to destroy . . . whatever obstacle that stands in your way . . . The instinct, like someone who has a natural instinct for the violin [or] a particular sport . . . enables the possessor to see and handle, very easily, matters that are difficult or even impossible

for others. It enables the possessor to take the facts of a case and
play with them in such a way that the point [he wants] to make
becomes irresistible.[1]

Bugliosi goes on to compare the facts of a criminal case with
the keys on a piano, saying that an ordinary pianist just "hacks out
a tune," but that Horowitz, working with the same piano keys, can
produce soaring, soul-touching music. There are two other factors
that must come into play before even the most talented of trial lawyers can produce a courtroom masterpiece: prior trial experience,
plus hundreds of hours of pretrial preparation.

The defense team, talented as it was to begin with, bolstered its
jury appeal in the Sneed case by reaching into a bag of tricks and coming up with trial tactics that would not be tolerated by most modern
judges who keep a tight rein on their court proceedings—trial tactics
such as allowing attorneys to constantly interrupt key adverse witnesses
with frivolous objections and then tack on caustic sidebar remarks or
allowing defendants to disrupt opposing counsel's jury arguments by
staging outrageous spectacles. No trial judge today would countenance
the maudlin trick the defense team pulled during final jury arguments
when it brought Sneed's two small children into the courtroom and
had them sit on his lap a few feet from the jury and encouraged them
to wail and weep and cling to the defendant every time a prosecutor
made any derogatory remark about their father.

The defense team added extra punch to its presentation by
taking full advantage of loose professional ethical standards that
are appalling by today's standards. Case in point being allowing
the defense to get away with a blatant conflict of interest by hiring
U.S. Attorney Will Atwell as Beal Sneed's private attorney—he who
ordered the Boyce mail intercepted and opened, he who used his
office to try to get Al Boyce indicted and extradited on the federal
white slavery charge, and he who later testified as a key witness in
Sneed's murder trial purporting to give an eyewitness account of
the events and conversations that allegedly transpired just before
the fatal encounter. Not so surprisingly, that account fit neatly into
the Sneed defense story line.

As shocking and as reprehensible as that was, the Sneed defense went far beyond that, dipping yet deeper into its arsenal of dirty tricks, this time bringing up tactics that were as illegal then as they are today, such as bribing a juror and knowingly sponsoring perjured testimony. And what about that very suspicious sudden death of a key prosecution witness, Ed Throckmorton, on the eve of the trial? Rules, laws, ethics be damned—creative skullduggery was the order of the day always welcomed and admired—a "no-holds-barred" game insofar as the McLean team was concerned. Their Bible contained only one commandment: "win—whatever it takes!" It was a core philosophy that mirrored that of their client, John Beal Sneed, an unprincipled and unrepentant liar and killer. Professional ethics today, as enforced by bar association disciplinary boards, have checked most but not all such egregious conduct.

From the very beginning of the first trial, another key part of the defense strategy began to unfold, although the trial judge and prosecutors seemed blissfully unaware of it. That was not so surprising since it was a relatively new tactic that only a few trial lawyers had ever resorted to in the past and then with only limited expertise. But Bill McLean and his fellows, including Beal Sneed, recognized its tremendous potential. Widely recognized and utilized today, it is called "spin-doctoring."

As we have seen, at the time the first Beal Sneed murder trial began, public sentiment was distinctly tilted in favor of the prosecution, and the local newspaper, the *Fort Worth Star-Telegram* (which was about the only media source available to folks in that area, including prospective jurors) printed stories that were objective. But that gradually began to change as the first trial progressed and as McLean began courting not only jurors but also the spectators, and most especially the news reporters. Stories of the trial were carried on the front page of the *Star-Telegram* every day, and it became obvious that the defenseward drift was more pronounced. As Lena informed Al in one of her letters written just after the first trial ended in a deadlock, public sentiment had shifted significantly in Sneed's favor. "All Texas is divided," she wrote, voicing her opinion that Beal Sneed would never be convicted. By the time the second trial got under way, it should have been apparent to any perceptive observer that the *Star-Telegram* had become a virtual mouthpiece for the defense. As a result, public opinion had shifted still further in Sneed's favor, and consequently the entire Tarrant County jury pool had been indoctrinated.

(Witness, for example, the answers the prospective jurors gave during the jury selection process voicing support of "protecting the home" and killing any scoundrel who "slandered" a man's wife.) Public opinion had indeed crystallized and probably to the extent that no prosecution team in the country could have reversed the trend. In retrospect, a "not guilty" verdict seemed inevitable as revealed by the *Star-Telegram's* take on prosecutor Odell's final jury argument. The reporter castigated Odell for being overzealous and characterized his plea for conviction as being a "merciless attack on a man on trial for his life and liberty." The reporter failed to mention anything about the defendant's merciless attack that took the life and liberty of an innocent and unarmed victim.

Insightful as is Vince Bugliosi's portrait of a super trial lawyer, he failed to emphasize one essential attribute a successful trial lawyer must possess: a keen awareness of what will resonate with the target audience and how to strike just the right chords—whether spin-doctoring the press or persuading the jurors. It was a gift that McLean possessed. In spades.

The prosecutors as well as Judge Swayne were startled by the "not guilty" verdict. Judge Swayne's straitlaced and rigid moral code coupled with his ironclad and unswerving dedication to the pursuit of justice under the written laws of Texas apparently blinded him to the more earthy if less noble inherited cultural creed of the jurors. He was simply unable to conceive how any jury could view the same set of facts and come to a different conclusion.

Bill McLean, on the other hand, was keenly aware before the first gavel sounded that to have any chance of winning a "not guilty" verdict for his client, he had to select a jury that would be receptive to his appeal to ignore the written laws of the State of Texas in favor of the "unwritten laws" of the Old South. McLean understood well the extent to which the patriarchal code of the Old South's Victorian culture still permeated the mind-set of many Anglo Texans in 1912: a belief that women were weak and worldly innocent creatures who had to be protected and their virtue defended by gallant, chivalrous men, and that fact, in turn, bestowed upon those gallant masculine champions the right to dominate their families and the right and duty to kill any scoundrel who disrupted their family relationships. A correlative belief posited that a man's honor had to be defended at all costs—that honor was more important than life itself. Furthermore, if a man's honor was besmirched, the courts could not adequately vindicate his honor. Only by direct, violent self-redressment of the wrong could a man's honor be restored. When future President Andrew Jackson was a small boy his proud southern-bred mother taught him this: "To go to the law for redress is to confess publicly that you have been wronged, and the demonstration of your vulnerability places your honor in jeopardy . . . The law affords no remedy that can satisfy the feelings of a true man."[2] Those honor-code beliefs undergirded the unwritten laws of an old South and the western frontier.[3]

Thomas J. Kernan, a colorful nineteenth-century judge—a southerner—once undertook the daunting task of reducing to writing the tenets of the unwritten law, and in a 1906 address to the American Bar Association he laid them out, two of which read as follows:

> Any man who commits adultery may be put to death with impunity by the injured husband, who shall have the right to determine the mode of execution, be it ever so cowardly.
>
> Any man who seduces an innocent girl may, without a hearing, be shot or stabbed to death by her, or any near relative of hers, and, if deemed necessary by the slayer, such shooting or stabbing may be done in the back, or while lying in wait.[4]

Although by 1912 the potency of the unwritten laws was waning,[5] there still existed a deeply rooted emotional dedication to its tenets among many native Anglo Texans as well as Anglo immigrants from other southern states—especially those who lived in the Fort Worth area, and more especially yet among the all-Anglo, all-male jury pool from which the Sneed jury was selected. By challenges for cause and by peremptory challenges, Bill McLean managed to weed out any prospective juror with a "northern attitude," and no prospective juror with roots north of the Mason-Dixon line made the final cut. In the end, Bill McLean ended up with a jury that was exactly what Bill McLean wanted. All were white married males with children. All were small farmers residing in rural Tarrant County. Five of the twelve were native Texans and the other seven were all natives of other southern states who had migrated to Texas.

Perfect. Just dead solid perfect . . . at least from the standpoint of the defense. And Bill McLean hesitated not a beat to take full advantage of the jury's deeply ingrained receptiveness to those unwritten laws—as was so dramatically showcased in the John Beal Sneed murder trial.

Yet there was still more to it than that: something that lay beneath the surface of the unwritten laws—something more than just preserving and vindicating a man's honor; something so viscerally discomforting to the prudish Victorian psyche of that culture that it could only be obliquely hinted at if mentioned at all: feminine sexuality. Or its flip side: masculine fear of female eroticism. Sons of the South were taught that women—at least "good" women—were not cursed with libido. Ladies only yielded their virtue to husbands in the privacy of the marital bed, and then only out of a sense of duty or to birth offspring for the family. Only "bad" women felt any erotic urges. That being the case, then how to explain why a properly reared lady—such as Lena, for instance—would suddenly kick over the traces, abandon home and hearth, and run off with some lustful Lothario? Was "moral insanity"—whatever that was—really the explanation? Or was there another, a much darker explanation? The Sneed jurors had, after all, heard doctors testifying for the prosecution pronounce Lena sane. Did that plant a nagging suspicion in the jurors' minds that nice girls might actually harbor secret erotic desires? As well as a nagging suspicion about their own wives? Was it possible that their own wives secretly harbored those nasty erotic urges and, therefore, unless closely monitored and kept in line, might succumb to the siren song of another, more attractive man? How humiliating that would be! How humiliating to be publicly dishonored plus have doubts cast on one's own manhood in that Victorian society. It was this fear that McLean and his associates skillfully cultivated and nourished—a fear coupled with a thinly veiled warning to each juryman. Hear their arguments: Cone Johnson saying, "May God protect every one of you good men, may the guardian angel protect your home," then adding that he hoped none of the jurors ever came home to hear his wife tell him that she was leaving him, that she had fallen in love with another.[6] McLean saying that the only verdict the jurors could be proud of was a "not guilty" verdict. That, and only that, he assured them, would send a message that "a man has the right to protect his home," adding that if "some scoundrel" entered the home of any of the jurors and "despoiled it while you were away attending to business, may you take your shotgun, go after him, get him, and I will defend you."[7] Cone Johnson again praising John Beal Sneed for "defying the miserable doctrine of free love," adding that "free love is what is the matter with society." And so on.

The repeated allusions to the creeping decadence going on in the North served to further incite and alarm those twelve white, rural, southern-born, married, male jurors. They had all heard rumors of the scandalous behavior that was taking root in northern society: free love, rampant promiscuity, easy divorces, frivolous women—scantily attired—gaily gadding about in public, smoking cigarettes, and making spectacles of themselves instead of staying home attending to their family duties. In 1912 anything "northern" was an anathema to most Anglos born below the Mason-Dixon. Although the last shot of the Civil War had been fired almost half a century earlier, still from their perspective—the survivors as well as their descendants—the psychic wounds of the horrendous slaughter, the humiliating defeat, and then the occupation of their war-ravaged homeland by the hated enemy, continued to fester and seethe barely below the surface. It would take the passing of many generations to dissipate that inherited bitterness. Predictably then, the McLean team adroitly portrayed John Beal Sneed as the holy champion of all things held dear to Anglo Texans and southerners—courageously standing up against another threatened invasion by the Yankees—this time in the form of all those noxious, northern modernistic notions.

How skillfully, how masterfully, did McLean, Johnson, Scott, and even Beal Sneed himself when he took the stand, play on those prejudices, those fears of female eroticism, which, unless decisively restrained, threatened their own manhood and honor, those fears that a northern encroachment of modernism was threatening their core values and their way of life. In the end, the only patriotic thing the jurors could do to protect the home of John Beal Sneed, and— even more importantly—to protect their own homes, and to protect the homes of all upright and right-thinking citizens of Texas was to send forth a clear and resounding message that this was not the North; that henceforth free love, promiscuity, female eroticism, lightness in women, easy divorces, as well as lustful libertines, and any other brand of northern modernism would not be tolerated. Henceforth Texas homes would be protected!

Because . . . well, after all, because this was Texas.

In the end, it seems more than probable that the jurors, at least the jurors in the second Fort Worth murder trial, didn't really believe that Lena was insane, didn't really buy into that "moral insanity" charade. But they were willing to give Beal Sneed a pass on that to salvage his tattered pride. What the jurors did buy into, however, was the "protecting the home" fiction that the McLean-Johnson-Sneed team orchestrated so masterfully to resonate so well with the jurors' inherited Victorian culture.

Somehow, somewhere along the way, in all that patriotic fervor to strike a blow for heritage preservation as well as for the protection of their homes and their own manly honor, the vision of the cowardly assassination of Colonel Boyce simply slipped below the jury's radar screen.

B. Reflections, Speculations, and Unsolved Mysteries

And What Happened to Lena's Baby?

One great mystery in this drama remains unsolved: what became of Lena's pregnancy, which she and Al Boyce supposedly planned and accomplished during their secret tryst in July 1912 in Dallas after Lena had returned to Beal? She had often expressed a wish to have

Al's child, and according to Lena's letter to Al on August 10, 1912, she became pregnant during that July tryst. Shortly after Al was killed on September 14, 1912, the *Fort Worth Star-Telegram* ran a story that seemed to confirm the fact that Lena was indeed pregnant. The reporter noted that Lena was "shortly to be a mother." (Beal Sneed must have read that story. There is no report of his reaction, but it couldn't have been one of unfettered joy at the news that he would soon be a proud papa. One thing can be posited with certainty: John Beal Sneed would never have allowed—not for one minute—Al and Lena's love child to toddle around his house.)

After the September 26, 1912, *Star-Telegram* article, there is no public report, official record, private paper, or personal report that has been discovered that mentions Lena being pregnant or that a child was born to her. If Lena became pregnant in July 1912 she would have come full term in her pregnancy in late March or April 1913, shortly after Beal Sneed was acquitted in February in his Vernon trial. At that time she was visiting her sister Pearl Perkins in Louisiana. Did she have a miscarriage? Did she have an abortion? It seems unlikely Lena would have destroyed her last physical link with her lover. Did she have the child with Pearl's doctor husband in attendance and give it up for adoption? Did Pearl take the baby as her own and raise it as her child? No birth records exist. Yet birth records in the early twentieth century were often lost or destroyed, if made at all. In that time if a birth amounted to a family embarrassment, it simply was not reported.

Clara Sneed in her *Panhandle-Plains Review* article reports that she investigated the mystery, but found no answers. She could find no birth or death records, and interviews with family descendants were fruitless. None of the Sneed relatives ever heard about such a pregnancy, and Pearl Snyder Perkins's grandson, A. J. Perkins, could account for all those buried in the Perkins plot in Lake Charles. Clara Sneed concluded that "silence is the only answer."[8]

But could there have been yet another possibility? Maybe Lena was not pregnant at all. She stated she was pregnant only two times. The first was in her August 10, 1912, letter to Al. Did she simply misrepresent the pregnancy to Al as a continuation of her hedge on the outcome of the impending showdown between Al and her husband? It would hardly have been the first time that Lena had been duplicitous in hedging her bets. Recall that at the beginning of her forced incarceration at the Allison asylum she wrote love letters to Beal telling how much she missed him, closing them with terms of endearment such as "Lovingly, Lena," and "Your girl, Lena." At the same time she dashed off a frantic note to Al: "For God's sake, come and take me away." The only other time Lena said she was pregnant was in her September 26, 1912, interview with the *Star-Telegram* reporter who noted that Lena would "shortly be a mother." If Lena had, in fact, become pregnant during the July 12 tryst, it seems highly unlikely that her pregnancy would have been apparent from her physical appearance two months later. Then why would Lena tell the reporter that she was pregnant if she wasn't? It is not difficult to conclude that in the aftermath of Beal's assassination of her lover two weeks earlier, Lena was furious. She had not only lost her lover and a chance finally to live the rest of her life with him, but now she was doomed to live the rest of her life with a man she despised. What better way to retaliate against the prideful Beal Sneed than to publicly pierce his inflated ego. Recall that Beal in his testimony in the previous murder trial had gone on record saying that he and Lena were not "living together as man and wife," but that he, the self-sacrificing hero, was only living with her so that he could care for her as he would a helpless, wounded child. Lena recognized and seized a wonderful opportunity to retaliate, and she must have taken great satisfaction in publicly humiliating Beal. She knew it would infuriate him. But what could he do about it? He couldn't give her the satisfaction of a divorce. He couldn't kill her. He couldn't publicly deny that Lena was pregnant without drawing more unwanted publicity, comment, and speculation.

Still, as plausible as that scenario sounds, it is speculation. And the mystery remains unsolved.

Another tantalizing unsolved mystery revolves around Lena's ultimate decision to return to Beal. What happened that caused Lena to change her mind between May 21, 1912, when Lena wrote

Al that she wished Beal were dead and that she would die before she would live with him again and a month later when she did just that—moved back in with Beal? Speculation as to Lena's motive, or motives, was conjectured in chapter eight, but again, no conclusive answer has ever surfaced.

On September 14, 1912, the first thing that Lynn Boyce did when he learned that John Beal Sneed had just killed his brother was to stalk the streets of Amarillo, Winchester in his hand and blood in his eye. Had he come within rifle range of Sneed that fateful September day in 1912, no one doubted but that the next murder trial would have featured Lynn Boyce as the defendant. Although Sneed scurried to the safety of the nearest jail that day—well knowing what would happen to him if he lost that race—still, everybody believed that sooner or later one of the surviving Boyce brothers would exact revenge. The next day's sensational headline in the *New York Times* warned: "Boyce-Sneed Feud Feared: Clans of Hostile Families Gather in Amarillo."

Yet even though Sneed subsequently walked away from the courthouse a free man after being tried for killing Al Boyce, and even though for years thereafter the Boyce and Sneed families (including John Beal Sneed) continued to live in the Amarillo area, none of the Boyce brothers attempted retaliation. The mystery: why? Texans, after all, had a long and bloody history of family feuds. As noted frontier historian C. L. Sonnichsen put it: "'Vengeance is Mine!' saith the Lord.' But in Texas He has always had plenty of help."[9] Sonnichsen went on to observe:

> In Texas the folk law of the frontier was reinforced by the unwritten laws of the South and produced a habit of self-redress more deeply ingrained, perhaps, than anywhere else in the country. The grievances and abuses of the bad days after the Civil War gave extraordinary scope for the application of the old ways of dealing justice.[10]

All of the Boyce family, as well as the Sneeds, were born and raised in that frontier Texas culture and imbued with those values. So, again the question begs an answer: why did the Boyce brothers forswear violent retribution against the man who had ambushed and killed their father and brother?

Two answers occur. First, and probably foremost, it was said that Annie Boyce forbade her sons to shed any more blood and thus perpetuate this awful feud and its tragic consequences, realizing that once a full-blown feud is started, it's almost impossible to put the brakes on it and stop the killings—at least for several generations. She simply had all of the hate, the killings, the funerals, and the loss she could bear.[11] Second, by 1912, the frontier feudist culture that was so ingrained in nineteenth-century Texas was beginning to wane as the new century and its values advanced.

Thanks in large part to Annie Boyce's wise counsel, no Sneed blood was ever shed by a Boyce, and therefore the Boyce-Sneed affair never escalated into a feud in the classic sense. Nevertheless, there existed much bad blood between the families and their supporters. Amarillo society was sharply divided, and everyone was forced to choose sides. Neutrality was hardly an option. Bitterness between the two factions ran so deep that party hosts had to carefully go over their invitation lists to ensure against a social catastrophe—or worse. Over the years the bitterness gradually subsided until at an Amarillo High School class reunion in 1985, one of the Sneed descendants finally had the nerve to approach a Boyce descendant, extend her hand, and say: "This thing has been going on a long time and neither of us had a thing to do with it. I think it's time it ended."[12] They shook hands, and that's how the Boyce-Sneed "feud" finally came to a close some seventy-three years after the last killing.

During all those years everyone—at least everyone in the upper echelon of Amarillo society—was well aware of the Boyce-Sneed affair, yet if it was mentioned at all, it was spoken of in hushed, guarded conversations. A code of silence prevailed—a code so typical of other nineteenth-century Texas communities where violent feuds broke out.[13]

Another unsolved mystery: Were Lena and Al sweethearts before she married Beal Sneed? On September 15, 1912, the day after Beal Sneed ambushed Al Boyce, the *Fort Worth Star-Telegram* carried the news story accompanied by a sidebar with this soap-opera headline:

"Pathetic Story of School Day Love of Two Men for Same Girl, Hate and Revenge, Revealed in Boyce-Sneed Tragedies." Under that attention grabber, the story gushed:

> Threads of pathos and tragedy of a love that time and the unrelenting hand of fate could not lessen are woven into the life history of Lena Sneed . . . John Beal Sneed, and Al Boyce, Jr.

The story then went on to tell that back in Georgetown Lena had:

> Smiled with the careless freedom of a schoolgirl upon those who sought her favor . . . yielding at last to the pleadings of John Beal Sneed . . . Al Boyce, who had been one of her most ardent suitors, passed out of her life.[14]

The *Star-Telegram,* however, did not quote a source for its tabloid style revelation. Colonel Boyce told others that there had been a romance between Al and Lena before she married Beal, that they had been childhood sweethearts. The ever-prideful John Beal Sneed, of course, denied it as did Lena's father, Tom Snyder, in one of his testimonial rants against Al Boyce. The credibility of Snyder's denial is called into question for the same reason that Beal's denial is suspect; however, Judge James D. Hamlin, a contemporary who knew all three families well, later recorded in his memoirs that Al and Lena had been childhood sweethearts.[15] In none of their recorded words or letters did either Al or Lena ever confirm or deny that there had been a childhood romance. Still, the passion and intensity of the romance that blossomed in the spring of 1911 hints that perhaps there really was an earlier "first love" attraction that kindled the torrid affair. Yet it remains another mystery unsolved.

The biggest mystery of all is John Beal Sneed himself. How could such a vicious, cold-blooded, and vindictive person have come from such solid stock—all devoutly religious people who kept their faith on a hostile and violent frontier. Most notable of these forebears was John Beal Sneed's own grandfather, the old circuit-riding preacher,

Parson Sneed, "the old Devil fighter," who ministered in the wilderness to black and white alike and founded several churches. The Snyders, the Sneeds, and the Boyce family—all faithful Methodists—were instrumental in 1875 in founding Southwestern University with its emphasis on Christian values. The mystery of how such an illustrious family tree could have yielded such bitter fruit as John Beal Sneed will doubtless remain unsolved—at least in this world.[16]

The Rest of the Tragic Story of Hugh D. Spencer

Miss Lillie Was a Rover

HUGH D. SPENCER was the district attorney who prosecuted Beech Epting and John Beal Sneed for the murder of Al Boyce, Jr. The Epting trial began on January 4, 1913. Some seven years later almost to the day—January 5, 1920—Hugh Spencer was a central figure in another sensational murder trial, this time in Decatur, Texas. The local newspaper, the *Wise County Messenger*, called the trial "one of the strangest in the annals of criminal jurisprudence."[1] It certainly lived up to its billing.

Although John Beal Sneed had no direct connection with the 1920 Decatur killing and its resulting murder trial, nevertheless the bizarre story of that killing and the murder trial begs to be told as a part of—and not merely as a footnote to—the equally bizarre Sneed story. While Spencer played a role in each, that was only the beginning of the similarities. The killings, the murder trials, the reactions of the jurors as well as the mind-set of the society of that time and place were almost a mirror image of each other. Eerily enough, the killing in the Decatur case was an identical twin, factually, to the assassination of Al Boyce, Jr.: a killer who fired three shots into his unsuspecting victim; a killer who readily admitted that he shot his victim with intent to kill; a killer who never denied that he shot his victim without a warning and without giving him a chance to defend himself; and a killer who was immediately identified and arrested.

Even though the facts of the Decatur case tracked the Sneed case insofar as the assassination of the victim was concerned, there were three significant differences. First, the Decatur killer admitted that prior to the execution, he had never seen, and did not know, his victim. Second, the killer's wife—with whom the killer assumed that the intended victim was having a torrid love affair—did not know, nor had she ever even seen her suspected lover. Finally, although Hugh Spencer was a central figure in the Decatur murder trial, he was neither the prosecutor, nor the defense attorney, nor the defendant, nor a witness in that case. Hugh D. Spencer was the victim.

There was yet another connection between the tragic tale of Hugh Spencer and the Beal Sneed story. Spencer's downward spiral began shortly after the 1913 Vernon murder trial of Sneed. When Spencer prosecuted the Vernon murder trial of Sneed in February 1913, the handsome thirty-eight-year-old bachelor was a bright and fast-rising star in the Texas Panhandle legal fraternity, serving his third two-year term as district attorney of the sprawling, ten-county Forty-Sixth Judicial District of Texas. His hometown newspaper described Spencer as being "pleasant, affable, and accommodating to the extreme, willing to do anything for his friends." [2] Never in his wildest imagination could Hugh Spencer have envisioned what a terrible and unlikely fate would befall him before the year of 1913 came to an end.

Spencer had grown to maturity in the north central Texas town of Decatur forty miles northwest of Fort Worth where his father served with distinction for years as the county judge.[3]

Starting at the bottom of the judicial ladder in his home county in 1898, he diligently worked his way up: two terms as justice of the peace, one term as city attorney of Decatur, and then two terms as county attorney of Wise County. It was during this period that the first history of Wise County was written, and the local historian had this to say of young Spencer:

> The continuous trust that the people have placed in him is evidence of his true worth. Mr. Spencer is an upright citizen in the private walks of life, and as a public official he has a record that

is absolutely beyond reproach . . . The people of Wise County have had few officers that have been as attentive to the interests of the people and that have enforced the laws of the state without fear or favor as has Mr. Spencer . . . he has made one of the best attorneys Wise County ever had.[4]

About that time Spencer, sensing the opportunities to the west after railroads had opened Texas Panhandle lands for settlement, moved to Memphis in Hall County and opened a law office. His legal talents as well as his sterling character and pleasing personality soon resulted in his election as district attorney, an office he held in 1913 when he headed the prosecution team in the Epting trial in Memphis and the Sneed trial in Vernon. At that time Hugh D. Spencer was not only a distinguished and prospering lawyer, he was also a happy bachelor.

Then came Lillie—pretty, young widow-lady Lillie Pierce.

Hugh Spencer fell in love with her and on August 22, 1913, some six months after the Sneed trial, he married her. And that is when Hugh D. Spencer's troubles began. Miss Lillie was a rover. The details of her escapade, or escapades, are not recorded. That the salacious nitty-gritty—whatever it was—went unreported publicly is hardly surprising considering that era's prudish, honor-sensitive values still so much attuned to the Old South's Victorian mindset: family scandals were customarily only whispered about within the community but rarely ever even hinted at in newspapers. Nevertheless, the January 24, 1919, edition of Spencer's hometown paper in Decatur, the *Wise County Messenger,* teetered on the brink of dropping a hint about Miss Lillie's naughtiness when it printed this cryptic report:

> Not one word was ever heard questioning the man's [Spencer's] honesty and integrity. He lived right and he stood for the best in this life. In the Memphis district he was recognized as one of the best and most successful attorneys, and up to the time of his marriage he was successful as a money-maker. Soon after his marriage he lost his health, and his accumulations of several years were swept away . . . A woman figures in the cause of the terrible tragedy.[5]

Whatever the details of "the terrible tragedy" were, sometime during the previous year (1918) Spencer abruptly left Memphis, abandoned his legal career, and returned to his ancestral home in Decatur to regain his health, and then, hopefully, to resume his legal career. Meanwhile, he and Lillie had separated, and she, taking their six-year-old son with her, moved to Waco. By this time, the United States was involved in World War I, and Waco was full of lonely soldiers from nearby Camp MacArthur. And Lillie was still young and pretty.

Sometime in 1918 Lillie brought their son, Hugh D. Spencer, Jr., to Decatur to visit his father. While there, a letter slipped out of Lillie's purse and Hugh, Sr., found it. That is how he discovered Lillie's latest escapade. Without benefit of a prior divorce, Lillie had married a soldier named Floyd Huff on July 24, 1918—just before he was shipped out to battle the Germans in the trenches of France. When confronted by Spencer, Lillie agreed to an uncontested divorce from Spencer plus granting him custody of the child. At the time of the confrontation, Lillie not only agreed to the divorce and custody arrangement but also agreed to leave Texas and never return. Spencer told her that to protect their child he would not expose her scandalous misbehavior if she would move back to Missouri where she had relatives—and stay there. Lillie agreed at first, but she soon reneged on her promise. She moved back to Waco. After all, that is where all the soldiers were stationed. As a contemporary, news report coyly phrased it: "She remained in Waco, posing as a young lady, and was sought after by soldiers. She is young and pretty."[6]

Back in Decatur, Spencer filed the divorce suit. As agreed, Lillie did not bother to contest it, and on January 6, 1919, the Wise County District Court granted a divorce to Spencer and awarded him custody of six-year-old Hugh D. Spencer, Jr. Thus it would appear that Spencer, now forty-three years old, would be done with Lillie—and all the troubles she had brought to his life—done with her once and for all. Now he could recover his health and fortune. Sadly, that was not to be.

Lillie, meanwhile, took a room in a boardinghouse run by a Mrs. McClain. In some idle girl-talk, Mrs. McClain's pretty young boarder happened to mention that she had an estranged husband back in Decatur named Hugh Spencer. Shortly thereafter the helpful Mrs. McClain took it upon herself to drop Spencer a little note informing him that Lillie was employed at Sanger's Department Store in Waco. And, oh yes, by the way, did you know that she is about to marry a Camp MacArthur soldier named Boland? [7]

Shortly after the divorce, Spencer's young son began missing his mother and begged Spencer to let him see Lillie. In response, Spencer wrote a letter to Lillie in an attempt to get her to come to Decatur, via rail connections through Fort Worth. The letter read as follows:

> Decatur, Texas, January 15, Lillie: Don't be afraid to write me. I want you to get off from Sanger's and come to Decatur. Tell them you have a sick brother in Fort Worth and you will not be back until Tuesday. Hugh Dickson cries everyday for his mother. Come Saturday night on [the] rear sleeper and I will meet you at [the] depot. Put on veil and no one will know you, and I will not mention your recent escapade. Don't fail to come. H. D. Spencer[8]

Mistakenly assuming that Lillie had by now married the soldier, he addressed the letter to "Lillie Boland" and sent it to her in care of Sanger's Department Store in Waco. But Lillie was not working there under the name "Boland." There was another woman working at Sanger's, however, whose last name was "Bolger "—a Mrs. W. M. Bolger. Although Mrs. Bolger's first name was Sallie, not Lillie, nevertheless the postal clerk at Sanger's mistakenly assumed the letter was intended for Mrs. Bolger and delivered it to her. Mrs. Bolger read the letter and realized that it was not intended for her. Unfortunately, however, she happened to mention the curious letter to her husband, and he read it. Mr. Bolger, a Waco merchant, was, unfortunately, an extremely jealous husband with a very suspicious mind. He immediately jumped to the conclusion that his wife was having a clandestine affair with this fellow Spencer from Decatur. No amount of denials by Mrs. Bolger could dissuade him. The more she denied having an affair, the more he believed that she really was having an affair, and the more enraged he became. It seemed not to have occurred to him that had his wife really been having an affair, she certainly would not have shown him the letter. Without further ado, W. M. Bolger grabbed his .38- caliber Iver Johnson double action revolver and caught the next train bound for Decatur.

The next day found him at the courthouse square in Decatur looking for a Mr. Hugh Spencer. He had never met the man and had no idea what he looked like. Bolger introduced himself to a stranger as Mr. Duncan and asked him if he knew Hugh Spencer.

If Hugh Spencer believed that his string of incredibly bad luck was over when he got rid of Lillie and won custody of his son, Hugh, Jr., he was sadly—tragically—mistaken. Just about the time that "Mr. Duncan" (a.k.a. W. M. Bolger) asked the stranger if he knew a Mr. Hugh Spencer, the star-crossed, ill-fated Hugh Spencer emerged from the Decatur post office and began walking across the lawn of the Wise County courthouse. The stranger pointed to Hugh Spencer and said, "Sure, that's Spencer." Bolger then walked up behind the man and called, "Spencer." The unsuspecting and unarmed victim turned around to answer, but before he could say anything, Bolger shot him three times. A fourth bullet went wild and hit a bystander, but did little damage to him. As Spencer fell, another bystander, Ira Maley, heard Bolger growl, "Damn you, you'll never break up another home!" [9] Mortally wounded, Spencer was rushed to a Fort Worth hospital where he died two days later, January 20, 1919. Before he died, he told officials that he did not know, and had never before seen, his assailant, and that he had no idea why the man shot him.

Bolger was arrested on the spot. On his person was found Spencer's letter addressed to "Lillie Boland." While in jail Bolger soon learned of his tragic mistake and begged to be taken to Spencer to apologize. But it was too late. Spencer was already dead—forever forty-three years old.

W. M. Bolger was promptly indicted for murder and tried in the Forty-Third Judicial District Court of Wise County, Texas, in Decatur. He never denied killing Spencer. Instead, he relied on the unwritten law defense, code-worded "protecting the home." To buttress

HUGH D. SPENCER. This 1907 picture depicts a young Hugh Spencer. Later as district attorney of the Forty-sixth Judicial District he prosecuted Beech Epting and John Beal Sneed in 1913 for the murder of Al Boyce, Jr. Still later, on January 18, 1919, in a tragic case of mistaken identity, Spencer was shot and killed in Decatur, Texas, by a man he had never seen before. *Photograph taken from* History of Wise County: From Red Men to Railroads—Twenty Years of Intrepid History *by Cliff D. Cates compiled under the auspices of the Wise County Old Settlers' Association, Decatur, Texas, 1907.*

that unwritten law defense, Bolger's attorney had the court instruct the jury on the "insulting conduct" statutory law:

> Insulting conduct by the deceased towards a female relative of the defendant is deemed in law an adequate cause to produce a degree of anger, rage or sudden resentment in a person of ordinary temper sufficient to render the mind incapable of cool reflection.[10]

Under the Texas law, even if all the above were true, that statute only served to reduce the offense from murder to manslaughter—not to exonerate the defendant from guilt. However, as observed before, when defense attorneys got through massaging that statute

around before a jury it always seemed to amount to a justification
for the killing.

In the end, even though Bolger shot a completely innocent and
unarmed man—one he had never seen before that instant—and
shot him three times without giving him a chance to answer any
accusations of misconduct, the Wise County jury must have been
persuaded that W. M. Bolger really believed in the righteousness of
his mission—really believed that he was attempting to "protect his
home"—when he killed Spencer. The jury did, however, on January 14, 1920, end up finding Bolger guilty of manslaughter, but it
assessed only probation—a five-year suspended sentence.[11] Five
years later, on May 27, 1925, Bolger, not having violated the terms of
his probation or blown away any other innocent victims during the
interim, came back to the Wise County District Court and petitioned
the court to clear him entirely. Accordingly, the court obliged him,
and the indictment was dismissed with prejudice so that it could
never be filed again. The end result was that Bolger never served a
day in a Texas prison for killing an innocent victim, and his criminal
record was expunged.

Timeline

1839	"Parson" Joseph Perkins Sneed, Tennessee circuit-riding Methodist preacher, migrates to Texas and settles in Central Texas area north of Austin.
1839	Tennessee native James Boyce migrates to Texas and settles in the same Central Texas area.
May 8, 1842	Albert Gallatin Boyce, son of James Boyce, is born near Austin.
1854	Dudley H. Snyder, Mississippi native, migrates to Texas at the age of twenty-one and settles a short distance north of Austin.
1856	John Wesley Snyder, younger brother of Dudley H. Snyder, migrates to Texas, soon followed by a third Snyder brother, Thomas Shelton Snyder. All settle in the same Central Texas area.
July 24, 1875	Al Boyce, Jr., son of Colonel Albert G. Boyce and wife, Annie Boyce, is born.
Dec. 30, 1877	John Beal Sneed, son of Joseph Tyre Sneed and wife, Lillian Beal Sneed, and grandson of Joseph Perkins Sneed, the Methodist parson, is born.
Aug. 15, 1879	Lenora (Lena) Snyder, daughter of Thomas Shelton Snyder, is born.
Mid-1880s	Famous three-million-acre XIT Ranch carved out of Texas Panhandle is granted by the State of Texas to a Chicago consortium named the "Capitol Syndicate" in consideration for construction of a capitol building in Austin.
1885	Colonel Albert G. Boyce drives a herd of D. H. and J. W. Snyder's cattle to the XIT Ranch and is hired as an XIT cowboy.

1887	Colonel Boyce is promoted to general manager of the XIT Ranch.
1887	Joseph Tyre Sneed, son of Parson Joseph Perkins Sneed, and father of John Beal Sneed and J. T. Sneed, Jr., buys a large block of land in Cottle County, Texas, some 130 miles southeast of Amarillo and approximately eleven miles south of Paducah, Texas.
1890s	Al Boyce, Jr., John Beal Sneed, and Lena Snyder, childhood friends, attend college at Southwestern University in Georgetown, Texas, a short distance north of Austin.
Oct. 17, 1900	John Beal Sneed marries Lenora (Lena) Snyder, daughter of Thomas Shelton Snyder.
1904	John Beal Sneed and wife, Lena Snyder Sneed, move to Amarillo.
1905	Colonel Boyce retires as manager of XIT Ranch; he and his family move to Amarillo.
Fall 1910	Al Boyce, son of Albert Boyce, liquidates his cattle herd in far West Texas and moves to the family home in Amarillo.
1911	
May	Al Boyce and Lena Sneed begin an affair.
July 22	Mrs. Annie Boyce, Colonel Boyce's wife and mother of Al Boyce, has conversation with Lena Sneed about the affair.
Oct. 13	Lena confronts her husband, John Beal Sneed, and demands a divorce so she can marry Al Boyce, Jr.
Oct. 17	John Beal Sneed takes Lena to Fort Worth and has her committed to a mental institution–the Arlington Heights Sanitarium
Oct. 28	Lena writes Al a letter: "Take me away!"
Nov. 2	Al receives Lena's letter and heads for Fort Worth.
Nov. 8	Al and Lena elope, fleeing to Winnipeg, Canada.
Nov. 9	Sneed hires Burns Detective Agency to find Lena and Al.
Nov. 11	Sneed files criminal charges in Fort Worth state court charging Al with abducting Lena.

Nov. 27	Sneed buys a .32-caliber pistol in Fort Worth under name of "John Smith."
Dec. 26	Al and Lena are discovered in Winnipeg and arrested by Canadian authorities for entering Canada under false names.
Dec. 27	Sneed leaves for Winnipeg.
Dec. 30	At Sneed's behest, the Fort Worth grand jury returns indictments against Al Boyce for abduction, kidnapping, and rape.
1912	
Jan. 1	Sneed arrives in Winnipeg.
Jan. 2	Canadian authorities at Sneed's behest deport Lena but refuse to deport Al.
Jan. 13	Sneed takes Lena back to Fort Worth sanitarium and again has her committed.
Jan. 13	Colonel Boyce succeeds in getting Fort Worth authorities to dismiss the state indictments against his son Al.
Jan. 13	Later the same day, Sneed kills Colonel Boyce in lobby of Metropolitan Hotel in Fort Worth in presence of Colonel Boyce's friend Ed Throckmorton.
Jan. 16	At Sneed's behest, U.S. Attorney Will Atwell has federal grand jury impaneled to consider a federal white slavery indictment against Al. Lena summoned to testify.
Jan. 17	Sneed indicted for the murder of Colonel Boyce, with trial set for Jan. 29, 1912.
Jan. 19	Lena files habeas corpus suit in Fort Worth state court to have herself declared sane and discharged from mental institution. Judge Simmons declares Lena sane and orders her released.
Jan. 24	Sneed, under arrest for killing Colonel Boyce, files habeas corpus action to have bond set for his release. He succeeds and is released on $35,000 bond.
Jan. 26	Prosecution's key witness in Sneed murder trial, Ed Throckmorton, mysteriously stricken with convulsions.
Jan. 29	Murder trial of Sneed for killing Colonel Boyce begins in Judge J. W. Swayne's court in Fort Worth.

Feb. 1	Ed Throckmorton dies, claiming that he's been "doped."
Feb. 9	Lena leaves Fort Worth and goes to live with her sister Pearl in Lake Charles, Louisiana.
Feb. 29	Trial ends with hung jury. Judge Swayne declares mistrial.
March 6	Joseph Tyre Sneed, Sr., John Beal Sneed's father, shot and killed in Georgetown by disgruntled tenant farmer.
March 6	Lena writes to Al in Canada warning him that if he returns to Texas, Beal won't hesitate to shoot him in the back.
March 18	Lena decides to make a fresh start by moving to California, apparently hoping to rendezvous with Al there, but Beal sends his paid spy, Nellie Steele, to accompany Lena.
May 4	Lena, lonely and ill, returns to Texas and checks herself into Johnson's Sanitarium (hospital) in Fort Worth
May 21	Lena writes Al informing him that U.S. Attorney Will Atwell was "forced to dismiss" the federal White Slavery indictment against him.
June 20	Lena checks out of Johnson's Sanitarium and reunites with Beal Sneed.
June 24	Earl McFarland writes letter to Beal Sneed complaining that Beal's attorneys, Cone Johnson and Walter Scott, haven't paid him for all expenses he incurred as per their agreement to bribe a juror in Beal Sneed's first trial for killing Colonel Boyce.
July 8	Beal, Lena, and their children are living in a rented flat at 4523 Reiger Street in Dallas.
July 21	While Beal is away, Al and Lena have a secret tryst in the Reiger Street apartment in Dallas. Lena allegedly becomes pregnant.
Aug. 10	Lena's last letter to Al, informing him that she is pregnant with their child.
Sept. 14	John Beal Sneed ambushes and kills Al Boyce, Jr., in Amarillo and then surrenders to Potter County sheriff.
Sept. 23	Beal Sneed's bail bond hearing in Amarillo. Judge Browning denies bail, but his order is overturned on appeal. Beal posts bond and is released.

Nov. 11	Second trial of Beal Sneed for murdering Colonel Boyce begins in Fort Worth.
Dec. 3	Fort Worth jury finds Beal Sneed not guilty of murdering Colonel Boyce.
1913	
Jan. 6	Trial of Beech Epting, Beal Sneed's accomplice in the killing of Al Boyce, begins in Memphis, Texas.
Jan. 23	Jury finds Beech Epting not guilty.
Feb. 11	Trial of Beal Sneed for the killing of Al Boyce begins in Vernon, Texas.
Feb. 25	Beal Sneed found not guilty of murdering Al Boyce.
March	Beal Sneed, Lena, and daughters move to Beal's farm near Paducah, Texas.
1920	
Jan. 18	Wood Barton, Beal Sneed's farm manager and son-in-law (married to daughter Georgia), gets into argument with farmer A. G. Green. Barton attacks Green.
Jan. 19	Green files assault charges against Wood Barton. Barton is tried, convicted, sentenced to two years in prison, but appeals. Conviction is reversed and returned for retrial.
1921	
Oct. 1	Nicholas Bilby, owner of the 500,000-acre O Bar O Ranch in West Texas sues John Beal Sneed in U.S. District Court in Abilene, Texas, alleging that he leased 100,000 acres out of the ranch to Beal Sneed in 1919 but that Sneed has never paid any lease money yet refuses to vacate the leased premises. Bilby also wants $1.2 million in damages.
November	When the Bilby case comes to trial in the federal court in Abilene, Sneed bribes a juror who hangs the jury—eleven for Bilby, one for Sneed—thus preventing Bilby from winning a verdict.
1922	
October	Beal Sneed is convicted in federal court in Abilene for bribing a juror in the Bilby civil suit and sentenced to two years in the federal penitentiary. He appeals.

Nov. 11	Wood Barton gets into argument with another Paducah farmer, C. B. Berry. Berry shoots and kills Wood Barton.
1923	
March 7	Beal Sneed (free on appeal from his federal bribery conviction) shoots C. B. Berry five times on downtown street in Paducah but Berry survives.
July 2	C. B. Berry shoots Beal Sneed on downtown street in Paducah, but Sneed survives.
July 10	C. B. Berry tried in Seymour, Texas, for murder of Wood Barton but found not guilty.
1923	Beal (out of jail pending appeal of his federal bribery conviction) and Lena move from Paducah to a luxurious home in North Dallas.
1924	
Feb. 27	John Beal Sneed (still out on appeal from his federal conviction) tried in Benjamin, Texas, for attempted murder of C. B. Berry but found not guilty.
Feb. 29	C. B. Berry tried for attempted murder of John Beal Sneed in Benjamin, Texas, but found not guilty.
August	All appeals finally exhausted, Sneed sent to federal prison for two years for bribing juror in the Bilby case.
May 1925	Beal Sneed released from prison on parole after serving nine months of his federal sentence.
1925–1960	John Beal Sneed regains his fortune as an independent oilman beginning with discoveries in the East Texas oil field.
1960	
Aug. 22	John Beal Sneed, age eighty-two, dies of cancer in Dallas, Texas.
1966	
March 16	Lena Snyder Sneed, age eighty-six, dies of a heart attack, still living in that luxurious North Dallas home. She is buried beside her husband in Hillcrest Memorial Park in Dallas, Texas.

⨋ ENDNOTES

Preface

1. Clara Sneed, "Because This is Texas: An Account of the Sneed-Boyce Feud," *Panhandle-Plains Historical Review* 72 (1999): 78.

2. Ibid.

3. *Fort Worth Star-Telegram*, February 25, 1912. The *New York Times* and the *St. Louis Post-Dispatch* closely followed the developing story as did the *Winnipeg Saturday Press* and the *Manitoba Free Press* in Canada.

4. Ibid., February 29, 1912.

5. *Amarillo Daily News*, February 26, 1913.

Chapter One

1. James D. Hamlin, *The Flamboyant Judge: The Story of Amarillo and the Development of the Great Ranches of the Texas Panhandle,* a biography as told to J. Evetts Haley and William Curry Holden (Canyon, Texas: Palo Duro Press, 1972), 95; *Fort Worth Star-Telegram,* February 14, 1912.

2. *New Handbook of Texas*, Ron Tyler, ed., s.v. "Sneed, Joseph Perkins," by Norman W. Spellmann (Austin: Texas State Historical Society, 1996), 5:1123–24.

3. John M. Sharp, "Experiences of a Texas Pioneer," and D. H. Snyder, "Made Early Drives," both in J. Marvin Hunter, ed., *The Trail Drivers of Texas* (n.p.: Cokesbury Press, 1925; repr. Austin: University of Texas Press, 1985), 721–29, and 1029–31.

4. In a 1933 interview, Tom Snyder recalled finding the dying Sam Bass, *Waco News Tribune,* December 3, 1933.

5. Tyler, s.v. "Boyce, Albert Gallatin," 1:681; Hunter, "Colonel Albert G. Boyce," *Trail Drivers of Texas,* 672.

6. Tyler, s.v. "Wilbarger, Josiah Pugh," 6:965; J. W. Wilbarger, *Indian Depredations in Texas* (Repr., Austin: Statehouse Books, 1985), 7–14. Wilbarger County, Texas, was named in honor of Josiah Wilbarger.

7. J. B. Pumphrey and R. B. Pumphrey, "The Pumphrey Brothers' Experience on the Trail," Hunter, *Trail Drivers of Texas,* 27–30; Wilbarger, *Indian Depredations in Texas,* 277–79.

8. Hunter, "Colonel Albert G. Boyce," 672–73; Tyler, s.v. "Boyce, Albert Gallatin," 1:681.

9. T. R. Fehrenbach, *Lone Star: A History of Texas and Texans* (New York: Macmillan, 1968), 393–409; Ernest Wallace, *Texas in Turmoil: The Saga of Texas, 1849–1875* (Austin: Steck-Vaughn Company, 1965), 139–59.

10. Fehrenbach, *Lone Star,* 554–58; Wayne Gard, *The Chisholm Trail* (Norman: University of Oklahoma Press, 1954), 12; James M. Smallwood, *The Feud That Wasn't: The Taylor Ring, Bill Sutton, John Wesley Hardin and Violence in Texas* (College Station: Texas A&M University Press, 2008), 4.

11. Rupert Norval Richardson, *Texas: The Lone Star State* (New York: Prentice-Hall, 1943), 310–14.

12. Sharp, "Experiences of a Texas Pioneer," and Snyder, "Made Early Drives," in Hunter, *Trail Drivers of Texas*, 721–29, 1029–31.

13. Tyler, s.v. "Boyce, Albert Gallatin," 1, 681.

14. Hunter, "Colonel Albert G. Boyce," 672.

15. Edwin James, "Account of an Expedition from Pittsburgh to the Rocky Mountains, Performed in the Years 1819 and '20 . . . under Command of Major Stephen H. Long," in *Early Western Travels*, ed. R. G. Thwaites (Cleveland: Arthur H. Clark, 1905), quote from 95; John Miller Morris, *El Llano Estacado: Exploration and Imagination on the High Plains of Texas and New Mexico, 1536–1860* (Austin: Texas State Historical Association, 1997), 202–4; J. Evetts Haley, *The XIT Ranch of Texas and the Early Days of the Llano Estacado* (Chicago: Capitol Reservation Lands, 1929; repr. Norman: University of Oklahoma Press, 1967, 1985), 16–17. See also W. Eugene Hollon, *The Great American Desert: Then and Now* (New York: Oxford University Press, 1966).

16. Randolph B. Marcy, letter from the Secretary of War George W. Crawford, Feb. 21, 1850, "Route from Fort Smith to Santa Fe," H. Exec. Doc. 45, 31st Cong., 1st Sess., p. 41; Morris, *El Llano Estacado*, 261; Paul H. Carlson, *Amarillo: The Story of a Western Town* (Lubbock: Texas Tech University Press, 2006), 14–15; Ernest R. Archambeau, "The Fort Smith-Santa Fe Trail Along the Canadian River in Texas," *Panhandle-Plains Historical Review* 27 (1954): 1–26.

17. Viewing those sweeping vistas, high clarity, and "wonderful emptiness" of the high plains, Georgia O'Keeffe discovered a new vision for her art, a way to magnify in brilliant pinks and yellows and pastels the beauty found in the spare commonplace, and thus the eccentric, unconventional, and controversial O'Keeffe became a major modernist artist. Llano Estacado, she would later recall, was "the only place where I have ever felt that I really belonged; that I felt really at home." Carlson, *Amarillo*, 74–76; James L. Haley, *Texas: From Spindletop through World War II* (New York: St. Martin's Press, 1993), 81–87. Also see Jeffrey Hogrefe, *O'Keeffe: The Life of an American Legend* (New York: Bantam Books, 1992).

18. For a gripping account of the loneliness and desolation experienced by many West Texas settlers see their journals and letters collected by Louis Fairchild, *The Lonesome Plains: Death and Revival on an American Frontier* (College Station: Texas A&M University Press, 2002). See also the classic novel by Dorothy Scarborough, *The Wind* (Repr., Austin: University of Texas Press, 1979).

19. Rupert Norval Richardson, *The Comanche Barrier to South Plains Settlement* (Glendale, Calif.: Arthur H. Clark, 1933).

20. Fred Rathjen, *The Texas Panhandle Frontier*, rev. ed. (Lubbock: Texas Tech University Press, 1998), 115–39.

21. Ibid., 171–75.

22. Frederick Nolan, *Tascosa: Its Life and Gaudy Times* (Lubbock: Texas Tech University Press, 2007), 87.

23. Ibid., 101.

24. Ibid., 67–86, 268–74.

25. Carlson, *Amarillo*, 19–31.

26. Rathjen, *Texas Panhandle Frontier*, 186–91.

27. Haley, *XIT Ranch of Texas*, 59. In 1881 Austin was also chosen by the state as the location of The University of Texas, and classes began on September 15, 1883. See also *New Handbook of Texas*, Ron Tyler, ed., s.v. "University of Texas at Austin," by William James Battle (Austin: Texas State Historical Association, 1996), 6:643–44.

28. Haley, *XIT Ranch of Texas*, 81–83, 217; Lewis Nordyke, *Cattle Empire: The Fabulous Story of the 3,000,000 Acre XIT* (New York: William Morrow, 1949), 159–73.

29. Haley, *XIT Ranch of Texas*, 82–83.

30. Ibid., 149–50.

31. Ibid., 214–15.

32. Ibid., 217; Nordyke, *Cattle Empire*, 247; Hamlin, *Flamboyant Judge*, 94.

33. Hamlin, *Flamboyant Judge*, 95.

34. Joe Sneed, Jr., later became president of the Texas and Southwestern Cattle Raisers Association and much later he served as chairman of the board of directors of Texas Tech University in Lubbock. *Cattleman*, Fort Worth, April 1953; *Amarillo Daily News*, April 16, 1933; Hamlin, *Flamboyant Judge*, 95.

35. Hamlin, *Flamboyant Judge*, 94–96.

36. Carlson, *Amarillo*, 28–31, 53; Rathjen, *Texas Panhandle Frontier*, 192–93; Haley, *XIT Ranch of Texas*, 204–5.

37. Carlson, *Amarillo*, 41–42, 54–55. Also see B. Byron Price and Frederick W. Rathjen, *The Golden Spread: An Illustrated History of Amarillo and the Texas Panhandle* (Northridge, Calif.: Windsor Publications, 1986).

38. Carlson, *Amarillo*, 73.

39. Editors of Time-Life Books, *This Fabulous Century: Vol. II, 1910–1920* (New York: Time, Inc., 1969), 86–98.

40. Amarillo's streetcar system was established in 1908. Paving of city streets commenced in 1911. Della Tyler Key, *In the Cattle Country: History of Potter County, 1887–1966*, 2nd ed. (Quanah: Nortex Offset Publications, 1972), 169, 214.

41. Hamlin, *Flamboyant Judge*, 127, 201–3; Key, *In the Cattle Country*, 178.

42. Editors of Time-Life Books, *This Fabulous Century: Vol. II, 1910–1920*, p. 30.

43. See *Los Angeles Times*, September 12, 1910, story reprinted in Gordon Morris Bakken and Brenda Farrington, *Learning California History* (Wheeling, Ill.: Harlan Davidson, 1999), 64.

44. Editors of Time-Life Books, *This Fabulous Century, Vol. II, 1910–1920*, pp. 116–18.

45. Charles F. Robinson II, "Legislated Love in the Lone Star State: Texas and Miscegenation," *Southwestern Historical Quarterly* 108, no. 1 (July 2004): 79. See also Blaine A. Brownell, "The Urban South Comes of Age, 1900–1920," in *The City in Southern History*, eds. Blaine A. Brownell and David R. Goldfield (Port Washington, N.Y.: National University Publications, 1977), 148–49.

46. Editors of Time-Life Books, *This Fabulous Century, Vol. II, 1910–1920*, p. 23.

47. Clara Sneed, "Because This is Texas: An Account of the Sneed-Boyce Feud," *Panhandle-Plains Historical Review* 72 (1999): 7.

48. Mary Kate Tripp, former book editor and columnist for the *Amarillo News Globe*, a letter dated November 27, 1993, to author Clara Sneed recounting gossip that Thomas Thompson, former editor of the *Amarillo News Globe*, heard from Lena's neighbors, quoted in Sneed, "Because This is Texas," 7.

49. *Fort Worth Star-Telegram*, January 1, 1912.

50. Lena Sneed to Al Boyce, letter dated April 23, 1912, quoted in "Because This is Texas," 39 (Lena's emphasis).

Chapter Two

1. *Fort Worth Star-Telegram*, February 10, 1912.

2. Lena Snyder Sneed to Albert G. Boyce, Jr., letter dated April 6, 1912, quoted in Clara Sneed, "Because This is Texas: An Account of the Sneed-Boyce Feud," *Panhandle-Plains Historical Review* 72 (1999): 16–17. Correspondence between Lena Sneed and Al Boyce, Jr., hereafter cited as "Lena to Al" or "Al to Lena." (Lena's emphasis.)

3. *Fort Worth Star-Telegram*, February 9, 1912.

4. *John Beal Sneed v. State of Texas*, Cause No. 1535 in the Forty-seventh Judicial District Court of Potter County, Texas, transcript of a writ of habeas corpus hearing (hereafter cited as "habeas corpus hearing transcript"), testimony of John Beal Sneed, September 23, 1912.

5. Peter W. Bardaglio, *Reconstructing the Household: Families, Sex, and the Law in the Nineteenth-Century American South* (Chapel Hill: University of North Carolina Press, 1995), 40.

6. Ibid., 42.

7. Habeas corpus hearing transcript, testimony of John Beal Sneed, 209.

Chapter Three

1. Article 562, *Texas Penal Code* (1856) provides: "A homicide is justifiable when committed by the husband upon the person of any one taken in the act of adultery with his wife; provided the killing takes place before the parties to the act of adultery have separated." Also see Paul Kens, "Don't Mess Around in Texas: Adultery and Justifiable Homicide in the Lone Star State," in Gordon Morris Bakken, ed., *Law in the Western United States* (Norman: University of Oklahoma Press, 2000), 114–17.

2. *Infante Institute* (1797); Fred R. Shapiro, ed., *The Yale Book of Quotations* (New Haven, Conn.: Yale University Press, 2006), 560n54.

3. See Articles 574.031, 574.034, and 574.035 of *Texas Mental Health Code* (1991). Among other requirements, the code provides that the hearing must be open to the public, that a record be made of the proceedings, that the patient must be present and is entitled to a jury unless waived, that the *Texas Rules of Evidence* apply and

must be followed during the hearing, and that the party seeking the commitment bears the burden of proof by "clear and convincing evidence" that the patient is mentally ill as that term is defined by the statute.

4. Lawrence H. Officer and Samuel H. Williamson, "Purchasing Power of Money in the United States from 1774 to 2010," Measuring Worth, 2006, *http://www.measureing worth.com/ppowerus/*.

5. Habeas corpus hearing transcript, testimony John Beal Sneed, 218.

6. *Fort Worth Star-Telegram*, February 14, 1912.

7. Ibid.

8. Ibid., February 17, 1912.

9. Ibid., December 27, 1911.

10. For reports of the criminal charges filed by Beal Sneed see the following accounts: *Fort Worth Star-Telegram*, December 27, 29, 30, 31, 1911, and January 2, 1912, and February 20, 1912; *Amarillo Daily News*, December 31, 1911, and January 1, 1912; *Manitoba Free Press*, December 27, 28, 29, 31, 1911, and January 1, 3, 4, 10, 13, 15, 1912; Sneed habeas corpus hearing transcript, 249; and Sneed, "Because This is Texas," 22–24.

11. *Manitoba Free Press*, date uncertain but probably January 2, 1912.

12. Lena to Al, undated letter but most probably December 31, 1911, quoted in Sneed, "Because This is Texas," 24.

13. Ibid.

14. *Manitoba Free Press*, January 15, 1912.

15. Lena to Al, undated letter but written while Al was in Canada, quoted in Sneed, "Because This is Texas," 39.

16. Al to Lena, letter dated January 13, 1912, quoted in Sneed, "Because This is Texas," 27; habeas corpus hearing transcript, 249.

17. *Winnipeg Saturday*, January 6, 1912.

Chapter Four

1. *Fort Worth Star-Telegram*, December 31, 1911.

2. Ibid.

3. Ibid., February 19, 1912.

4. Lena to Henry Boyce, telegram dated January 12, 1912, quoted in Sneed, "Because This is Texas," 27.

5. Lena to Al, letter dated March 10, 1912, quoted in Sneed, "Because This is Texas," 38n82.

6. *Fort Worth Star-Telegram*, February 2, 1912.

7. Lena to Al, letter dated February 9, 1912, quoted in Sneed, "Because This is Texas," 89n148.

8. *Fort Worth Star-Telegram*, February 17, 1912.

9. See David Langum, *Crossing Over the Line: Legislating Morality and the Mann Act* (Chicago: University of Chicago Press, 1994).

10. *Fort Worth Star-Telegram*, February 9, 1912.

11. Ibid., February 2, 1912.

12. Ibid., February 23, 1912.

13. Ibid.

14. *Dallas Dispatch*, February 5, 1912.

15. *Manitoba Free Press*, January 15, 1912.

16. Al to Lena, letter dated January 13, 1912, quoted in Sneed habeas corpus hearing, 251–252; Sneed, "Because This is Texas," 29.

17. Ibid.

18. *Manitoba Free Press*, January 18 or 19, 1912.

Chapter Five

1. "Wild Bill's" father, Judge William Pinckney McLean, was a major in the Confederate army. After the Civil War, Major McLean served as a member of the Texas Legislature, as a U.S. Congressman, as a member of the convention that adopted the Texas Constitution of 1876 (still in force today, though much amended), as a member of the Texas Railroad Commission when it was first established, as a judge of the Fifth Judicial District Court of Texas, and finally as a private practitioner in partnership with his son "Wild Bill" McLean in Fort Worth from 1894 until his death in 1925.

2. *Fort Worth Star-Telegram*, January 19, 1912.

3. Carolyn A. Conley, *The Unwritten Law: Criminal Justice in Victorian Kent* (New York: Oxford University Press, 1991), 173–201. The author argues that "Victorian justice was shaped by three central concerns of Victorian society: respectability, public order, and class," 173.

4. Kenneth Lamott, *Who Killed Mr. Crittenden? Being a True Account of the Notorious Murder That Stunned San Francisco—The Laura D. Fair Case* (New York: David McKay, 1963), 6. See also Robert M. Ireland, "Frenzied and Fallen Females," *Journal of Women's History* 3 (Winter 1992): 95–117; and Gordon Morris Bakken and Brenda Farrington, *Women Who Kill Men* (Lincoln: University of Nebraska Press, 2009), 19–39.

5. Dr. John P. Gray, "The Trial of Mary Harris," *American Journal of Insanity* 22 (1865–1866); J. D. Lawson, ed. "The Trial of Mary Harris for the Murder of Adoniram J. Burroughs," *The American State Trials* 17 (1865), 233–375. Although the jury acquitted Mary Harris, finding her insane due to suffering from PMS aggravated by being "crossed in love," she apparently made a remarkable recovery because after the trial her fearless defense attorney, Joseph H. Bradley, Sr., married her. Allen D. Spiegel, Ph.D., and Merrill S. Spiegel, J.D., "Not Guilty of Murder by Reason of Paroxysmal Insanity: The 'Mad' Doctor vs. 'Common Sense' Doctors in an 1865 Trial," *Psychiatric Quarterly* 62, no. 1 (Spring 1991): 51–66.

6. Douglas O. Linder, "The Trial of Charles Guiteau: An Account," 2007, *http://www.law.umkc.edu/faculty/projects/ftrials/guiteau/guiteauaccount.html*, 1–13.

7. John Ellard, "The History and Present Status of Moral Insanity," *Australian and New Zealand Journal of Psychiatry* 22 (1988): 386.

8. Linder, "The Trial of Charles Guiteau," *supra.*

9. *Fort Worth Star-Telegram,* January 20, 1912.

10. Ibid.

11. Lena to Al, letter dated February 2, 1912, quoted in Sneed, "Because This is Texas," 30.

12. *Fort Worth Star-Telegram,* January 20, 1912.

13. Al to Lena, letter dated January 18, 1912, quoted in Sneed, "Because This is Texas," 30, 88; Sneed habeas corpus hearing transcript, 255.

14. *Fort Worth Star-Telegram,* January 23, 1912.

15. Ibid.

16. Ibid.

17. Richard F. Selcer, *Hell's Half Acre* (Fort Worth: Texas Christian University Press, 1991).

18. Jerry Flemmons, "Smiting a Sinful World," in *Plowboys, Cowboys, and Slanted Pigs* (Fort Worth: Texas Christian University Press, 1984), 75–90; Jerry Flemmons, "Smiting a Sinful World," in Judy Alter and James Ward Lee, eds. *Literary Fort Worth* (Fort Worth: Texas Christian University Press, 2002), 180–193. The leading crusader against Hell's Half Acre was the flamboyant demagogue, the Reverend J. Frank Norris, pastor of the First Baptist Church of Fort Worth. In the above article, Jerry Flemmons wrote that once J. Frank Norris "spied the venerable Hell's Half Acre [he] fell on that sinful Eden with the enthusiasm of a prospector finding the mother lode." Among other of J. Frank Norris's favorite targets were Catholics, booze drinkers, booze peddlers, gamblers, card players, Sunday picture show operators, dancers, evolutionists, "kooch show" operators, modernists, or, as Flemmons put it, nearly anyone else suspected of having a good time. Once during a two-hour tirade against evolutionists, Norris turned loose a herd of screeching monkeys that raced up and down the church aisles while the reverend denounced them as "Darwin's cousins."

19. Selcer, *Hell's Half Acre,* 83.

Chapter Six

1. *Fort Worth Star-Telegram,* February 25, 1912.

2. Ibid., February 10, 1912. *The Fort Worth Star-Telegram* covered the John Beal Sneed trial story with daily reports from January 31, 1912, through February 29, 1912. The author has relied primarily on that source for this story. Any quotes in text of the following story that are not directed to an endnote source were obtained from a *Star-Telegram* story.

3. *State of Texas v. John Beal Sneed,* Cause No. 19,777 in the Seventeenth Judicial District Court of Tarrant County, Texas.

4. Richard F. Selcer, *Fort Worth Characters* (Denton: University of North Texas Press, 2009), 230. Judge Swayne's finest hour came in 1913 when he stood on the steps of the Tarrant County jail and faced down a lynch mob that had laid siege to the jail and was threatening to break in and seize a black man who had killed a white police officer and another man who had wounded four others. He ordered the sheriff to

fire into the mobsters if all else failed to disperse them. The mob dispersed. Later, he called a grand jury and ordered it to indict the mob leaders. Although several indictments were returned, all-white Fort Worth juries failed to convict anybody.

5. *Fort Worth Star-Telegram*, February 2, 1912.

6. *Dallas Dispatch*, February 2, 1912; *Fort Worth Star-Telegram*, February 2, 1912.

7. Lena to Al, letter dated February 2, 1912, quoted in Sneed, "Because This is Texas," 34.

8. Article 562, *Texas Penal Code* (1856).

9. A good place to start research on the issue of justice and the unwritten law is Alison Dendes Renteln and Alan Dundes, eds., *Folk Law: Essays in Theory and Practice of Lex Non Scripta*, 2 vols. (Madison: University of Wisconsin Press, 1994).

10. F. G. Fontain, *Trial of the Hon. Daniel E. Sickles for Shooting Philip Barton Key, Esq.* (New York: R. M. DeWitt, Publisher, 1859); John D. Lawson, "Trial of Daniel E. Sickles for the Murder of Philip Barton Key," in *American State Trials*, 17 vols., edited by John D. Lawson (St. Louis: 1914–1936), 12: 530–32; *Washington Evening Star*, March 5, 1859; Hendrick Hartog, "Lawyering, Husband's Rights and the Unwritten Law in Nineteenth-Century America," *Journal of American History* 84, no. 1 (June 1997): 67–96.

11. Robert M. Ireland, "The Libertine Must Die: Sexual Dishonor and the Unwritten Law in Nineteenth-Century United States," *Journal of Social History* 23 (Fall 1989): 32.

12. Ibid., 32–33.

13. *Fort Worth Star-Telegram*, July 26, 1913.

14. Ibid., February 7, 1912.

15. Lena to Al, letter dated February 9, 1912, quoted in Sneed, "Because This is Texas," 38.

16. *Fort Worth Star-Telegram*, February 6, 1912.

17. Ibid., February 9, 1912. Wiley Holder Fuqua, noted Amarillo banker and businessman, was a self-made, rags-to-riches, wheeler-dealer. The Fuqua family's fortune was lost after the Civil War, and, virtually penniless, they moved from Mississippi to East Texas in 1877 when W. H. Fuqua was fifteen years old, and settled in Ennis. Young Fuqua worked his way through East Texas University in Tyler doing odd jobs. Afterward he established his own country school and divided his time between teaching students, working in cotton fields, and trading horses and cattle. In 1889 Fuqua and his young wife decided to take a round trip by train to Clayton, New Mexico, but they never reached their destination. They got off the train in Amarillo, liked what they saw, and there they stayed. First Fuqua purchased a livery stable and operated horse-drawn streetcars. Then he opened a stage line to Plainview and Crosbyton. Following that he established a retail coal business and ended up owning all the coal yards in Amarillo.

When the First National Bank of Amarillo opened in January 1890, Fuqua was among its stockholders. In 1896 he bought all the stock and became its sole owner. In time he acquired stock in forty-three other Panhandle banks, including controlling stock in seven. At one time he owned about 560 sections of farm and ranch land in the Texas Panhandle, New Mexico, and Missouri, as well as various real estate properties in Amarillo and other town sites. Fuqua was president of the Texas Bankers Association in 1910–11 and president of the Amarillo Chamber of Commerce in 1912. H. Allen Anderson, "Fuqua, Wiley Holder," in *New Handbook of Texas*, 6 vols. Ron Tyler, ed. (Austin: Texas State Historical Society, 1996), 3:34.

18. Will Atwell had a long and colorful legal career. After his service as a U.S. District Attorney, he, in 1922, was appointed by President Warren G. Harding as judge of the U.S. District Court for the Northern District of Texas where he presided until he retired some thirty-two years later at age eighty-five. His greatest national fame came late in his career when he handed down salty-tongued decisions bucking the U.S. Supreme Court's school integration decision (*Brown v. Board of Education*). He resisted integration of the Dallas school system as long as he was on the bench. "It would be unthinkably and unbearably wrong to make white students get out of Dallas schools so as to let in colored students." Although a strict disciplinarian in court, Judge Atwell bordered on the eccentric in his personal life. He enjoyed playing poker and chewing tobacco; he had his formal, black, "old school" suits custom made with no pockets at all, only two slits in his jacket (one for his glasses and one for a hand-kerchief); he never carried money; and, as a commissioner of the Dallas zoo, he also enjoyed "checking out" a lion or two and taking them for a ride in his automobile on sunny Sunday afternoons. *Fort Worth Star-Telegram*, December 23, 1961.

19. *Fort Worth Star-Telegram*, February 10, 1912.

20. Ibid., February 12, 1912.

21. Ibid.

22. Ibid., February 10, 1912.

23. Ibid., February 14, 1912.

24. Ibid.

25. Ibid.

26. Ibid.

27. Ibid., February 15, 1912.

28 Ibid.

29. Ibid., February 14, 1912.

30. Ibid.

31. Ibid.

32. Ibid.

33. Ibid.

Chapter Seven

1. *Fort Worth Star-Telegram*, February 17, 1912.

2. Ibid., February 16, 1912.

3. Ibid., February 19, 1912.

4. Ibid.

5. Ibid.

6. Ibid.

7. Ibid., February 22, 1912.

8. Ibid., February 23, 1912.

9. Ibid., February 22, 1912.

10. Ibid., February 23, 1912.

11. Ibid., February 24, 1912.

12. Ibid.

13. Ibid., February 25, 1912.

14. Ibid., February 19, 1912. Some two years later, in yet another of Crazy Mary's endless courtroom squabbles, she returned to Judge Swayne's court with another pistol—a six-shooter she had concealed "in her bosom" as the newspaper account so delicately phrased it. Before anyone could stop her, she yanked it out of her bosom and fired off a shot at Judge Swayne. Fortunately, her aim was off, but only slightly. The bullet slammed into the wall just above Judge Swayne's head. Only the quick action of Mary's own attorney, Durward McDonald, saved the judge. Grabbing Mary's arm, he forced it up so that Mary's remaining five rounds all hit the ceiling. Later, Mary was convicted of attempted murder, but never had to serve any time for that caper. Richard F. Selcer, *Fort Worth Characters* (Denton: University of North Texas Press, 2009), 229.

15. *Fort Worth Star-Telegram*, February 25, 1912. Senator Hanger never made any bones about his racial views. A decade later, in 1922, when there was a national resurgence of the Ku Klux Klan, Hanger was the leader of a pro-Klan political action movement in Fort Worth. Ken Anderson, *Dan Moody: Crusader for Justice* (Georgetown, Tex.: Georgetown Press, 2008), 16–19; David M. Chalmers, *Hooded Americanism: The History of the Ku Klux Klan*, 2nd ed. (New York: New Viewpoints, 1981), 2–5, 39–48.

16. *Fort Worth Star-Telegram*, February 23, 1912. Some sixteen years later, in 1928, Cone Johnson—a rural, Protestant, prohibitionist southerner—was a Texas delegate to the National Democratic Convention that nominated Al Smith—an urban, Catholic, anti-prohibition politician with ties to New York city's Tammany Hall—as the Democratic nominee for president. It was a nomination that the Texas delegation fought against. When Smith won the nomination, the victorious pro-Smith delegates paraded through the convention hall. Cone Johnson later penned this recollection of the event: "I sat by the central aisle while the parade passed following Smith's nomination and the faces I saw in that mile-long procession were not American faces. I wondered where were the Americans?" *Dallas Morning News*, July 4, 1928; Norman D. Brown, *Hood, Bonnet, and Little Brown Jug: Texas Politics, 1921–1928* (College Station: Texas A&M University Press, 1984), 9.

17. *Fort Worth Star-Telegram*, February 23, 1912.

18. Ibid.

19. Ibid.

20. Ibid., February 23, 1912 (emphasis mine).

21. Ibid., February 24, 1912.

22. Ibid., February 22, 1912.

23. Ibid., February 23, 1912.

24. *Dallas Morning News*, February 23, 1912 (emphasis mine).

25. *Fort Worth Star-Telegram*, February 25, 1912.

26. Ibid., February 24, 1912.

27. Ibid.

28. Ibid., February 25, 1912.

29. Ibid.

30. Ibid.

31. Ibid.

32. Ibid.

Chapter Eight

1. Lena to Al, letter dated March 2, 1912, quoted in Sneed, "Because This is Texas," 71.

2. Lena to Al, letter dated March 27, 1912, quoted in Sneed, "Because This is Texas," 71.

3. Sneed, "Because This is Texas," 21, 48.

4. Lena to Al, letter dated March 10, 1912, quoted in Sneed, "Because This is Texas," 48.

5. Sneed, "Because This is Texas," 43; Lena to Al, letter dated March 21, 1912, quoted in Sneed, "Because This is Texas," 93n215.

6. Hamlin, *The Flamboyant Judge*, 96.

7. Lena to Al, letter dated April 6, 1912, quoted in Sneed, "Because This is Texas," 50.

8. Lena to Al, letter dated May 18, 1912, quoted in Sneed, "Because This is Texas," 50.

9. *State of Texas v. John Beal Sneed* in Cause No. 1535 in the Forty-seventh Judicial District Court of Potter County, Texas, habeas corpus hearing transcript (hereafter cited as "habeas corpus hearing transcript"), testimony of Billie Steele, September 23, 1912, p. 121.

10. Pearl Snyder Perkins to Lena, letter dated July 19, 1912, quoted in Sneed, "Because This is Texas," 59.

11. Lena to Al, letter dated August 10, 1912, quoted in Sneed, "Because This is Texas," 56.

12. Lena to Al, undated letter but probably about December 28, 1911, quoted in Sneed, "Because This is Texas," 58.

13. Lena to Al, undated letter but probably about January 2, 1912, quoted in Sneed, "Because This is Texas," 58.

14. Lena to Al, letter dated April 6, 1912, quoted in Sneed, "Because This is Texas," 50.

15. *Fort Worth Star-Telegram*, September 18, 1912.

16. Habeas corpus hearing transcript, testimony of Joe Barr, 140; habeas corpus hearing transcript, testimony of John Blanton, 160.

17. *Fort Worth Star-Telegram*, February 20, 1913.

18. Sneed, "Because This is Texas," 60.

19. Habeas corpus hearing transcript, testimony of O. K. Gilvin, 66–67.

20. Sneed, "Because This is Texas," 60n307.

21. *Fort Worth Star-Telegram*, February 15, 1913.

22. Habeas corpus hearing transcript, testimony of Potter County Sheriff W. M. Burwell, 14–15.

23. Ibid., testimony of Ernest Robinson, 25–26

24. Ibid., 27.

25. Ibid., 31.

26. Ibid., testimony of Earl Jackson, 34.

27. Ibid.

28. Ibid., testimony of John F. Speed, 191.

29. Ibid., testimony of A. F. Lumpkin, 22–24.

30. Ibid., testimony of C. J. Collier, 194.

31. Ibid., testimony of Mrs. Maria Kindred, 47.

32. Roxana Robinson, *Georgia O'Keeffe, A Life* (New York: Harper & Row, 1989), 88–89; Lisle Laurie, *Portrait of an Artist: A Biography of Georgia O'Keeffe* (New York: Seaview Books, 1980), 51–52; Sneed, "Because This is Texas," 61.

33. Habeas corpus hearing transcript, testimony of C. J. Collier, 193; *Fort Worth Star-Telegram*, February 19, 1913.

34. *St. Louis Post-Dispatch*, September 15, 1912.

Chapter Nine

1. *Ex parte Sneed*, Cause No. 1535 in the Forty-seventh Judicial District Court of Potter County, Texas.

2. *Ex parte Sneed* (on appeal to the Texas Court of Criminal Appeals), 150 S.W. 1197 (Tex.Ct.Crim. App., 1912) (emphasis mine).

3. *Fort Worth Star-Telegram*, November 11, 1912.

4. Charles E. Coombes, *The Prairie Dog Lawyer* (Dallas: Texas Folklore Society and University Press of Dallas, 1945), 270–71.

5. Keith Carter, "The Texas Court of Criminal Appeals," *Texas Law Review* 11 (1933), 196. Because of slavish adherence to hypertechnical rules of practice and procedure inherited from the English common law system, almost *any* trial error was deemed a reversible error. Over the years, due to remedial legislation and appellate court opinions, Texas has adopted a "harmless error" rule recognizing that a trial court error or errors should be disregarded on appeal unless the error or errors were so substantial that they were calculated to deprive the defendant of his right to a fair trial. As numerous appellate courts and legal scholars have since observed,

the U.S. and state constitutions were never intended to guarantee defendants a *perfect* trial, only a *fair* trial. Yet that often raises another thorny issue: at what point does two or more "harmless errors" become weighty enough to turn an *imperfect* trial into an *unfair* trial?

6. Richard F. Selcer, *Fort Worth Characters* (Denton: University of North Texas Press, 2009), 226.

7. *Fort Worth Star-Telegram*, November 17, 1912. The second Fort Worth murder trial of John Beal Sneed lasted from November 9, 1912, through December 3, 1912. The *Star-Telegram* covered each day's proceedings, and the author has relied primarily on those accounts to tell the story of the daily events of this trial. Quotes set out in the text of the story that are not documented by endnotes came from *Star-Telegram* stories.

8. *Fort Worth Star-Telegram*, November 15, 1912.

9. Ibid., November 20, 1912.

10. Ibid., November 24, 1912.

11. *Dallas Morning News*, November 26, 1912.

12. *Fort Worth Star-Telegram*, November 28, 1912.

13. Ibid., November 26, 1912.

14. Ibid., November 29, 1912. The *Fort Worth Star-Telegram* carried daily reports of the final jury arguments in the Beal Sneed murder trial, and they are found in the November 29 and 30, and the December 1 and December 2, 1912, editions, with the jury verdict and its aftermath being reported in the December 3, 1912, edition. Except as otherwise noted in the text, the account of the jury arguments and the verdict have been taken from those editions and will not be separately noted.

15. *Fort Worth Star-Telegram*, December 1, 1912 (emphasis mine).

16. *Dallas Dispatch*, December 3, 1912.

17. In first-degree murder cases in Texas in which the death penalty is an option, the district attorney has the sole discretion to determine whether or not to seek the death penalty. District attorneys had this discretion during the time of the Sneed murder trials as well as today (Article 37.071, *Texas Code of Criminal Procedure*). At the time of the Sneed trials, if a criminal case were tried before a jury, then it was also up to the jury to fix punishment and do so in the same verdict—presuming, of course, that the jury found the defendant guilty. Nowadays, however, Texas law provides for a "bifurcated" or two-part criminal trial (Article 37.07 *Texas Code of Criminal Procedure*). The first trial focuses solely on the issue of guilt or innocence. If the defendant is found guilty, then the jury is recalled and hears evidence relevant to the issue of punishment. This change prevents an unnecessary and illogical retrial on the guilt-innocence issue in cases where the jury finds the defendant guilty but subsequently deadlocks on punishment.

Had the bifurcated trial statue been in effect during the Sneed murder trials, it would have made an enormous difference in the evidence, which the jury would have been allowed to hear in the first (guilt-or-innocence) trial and very likely would have affected the outcome. The only issue the Sneed jury would have had to resolve was: did John Beal Sneed intentionally kill Colonel Boyce? (Judge Swayne had ruled that evidence hadn't raised the issue of self-defense.) During the guilt or innocence phase, the defense would not have been entitled to run wild and introduce all that extraneous testimony about the love triangle, or Lena's supposed moral insanity, or Beal's self-portrait as the self-righteous, long-suffering, unselfish martyr, or the heart-rending story of the bleak 1911 Christmas at Bowman's house, or Beal's self-pitying letter to his friend Fuqua, or Captain Snyder's rants about Al, that "cigarette and whiskey-drinking fiend," and so on. If the bifurcated law had been in effect, and had Judge Swayne reined in the defense team's excesses and kept them within the evidentiary boundaries, McLean would have been prevented from kidnapping the jury's emotions with all the melodrama. Had that happened, it is difficult to see how the jury could have returned a verdict other than "guilty."

18. *Dallas Morning News*, December 4, 1912.

19. *Dallas Dispatch*, December 3, 1912.

20. *Amarillo Daily News*, December 4, 1912.

21. How the concept of honor was perceived by diverse groups during Arizona's Rim Country War of the 1880s is explored by historian Daniel Justin Herman in his recent book, *Hell on the Range: A Story of Honor, Conscience, and the American West* (New Haven, Conn.: Yale University Press, 2010). The web of conflict in the Rim Country War involved Mormons, Texas cowboys, New Mexican sheepherders, Jewish merchants, and mixed-blood ranchers. Herman notes that Hispanic Americans and American southerners shared an emphasis on patriarchy, extended family, concern over "outward appearances," and an orientation toward honor. Men in both groups glorified and defended the chastity and fidelity of their women. Finally, honor included the male prerogatives of gambling, drinking, and fighting (72). Most Texan imports to the Rim Country also shared southern notions of honor although the Texas cowboys tended to be less interested in lineage and family and were more individualists. Like southerners they measured success via old rites of manliness, rites of courage, excess, and exuberance, but first and foremost they were creatures of honor. And they were more violent; cowboy honor begat cowboy violence. Bad men would have to die. As in Texas, where lynching was rampant, the culture of honor—with its emphasis on assertion, violence, and shaming—would have to be served (96–99, 180–187). Yet the author notes that there was another type of Texas cowboy import to the Rim Country—much in the minority, to be sure—but ones who, while holding a man's honor dear, nevertheless also held dear an unswerving evangelical Protestant creed that forbade drinking, gambling, cursing, and most any form of frivolity (171–177). In disputes with gentiles over territorial rights, Mormons were motivated more by a sense of self-righteousness than by injury to their sense of honor. Mormons defined their enemies as sinners, criminals, defilers. God-sanctioned "conscience," the Mormons believed, gave them the right to expand, whereas sinfulness denied their enemies the right to resist (79). Also see Jacqueline M. Moore, *Cow Boys and Cattle Men: Class and Masculinities on the Texas Frontier, 1865–1900* (New York: New York University Press, 2009), 64–65.

Chapter Ten

1. *State of Texas v. John Beal Sneed and Beech Epting*, Cause No. 1534 in the Forty-seventh Judicial District Court of Potter County, Texas.

2. *State of Texas v. Beech Epting*, Cause No. 412 in the Forty-sixth Judicial District Court of Hall County, Texas.

3. *State of Texas v. John Beal Sneed*, Cause No. 2087 in the Forty-sixth Judicial District Court of Wilbarger County, Texas.

4. *Fort Worth Star-Telegram*, January 6, 1913. The author has relied primarily on the daily accounts of the Beech Epting trial published in the *Star-Telegram* to tell this story. Any quotes in this chapter not specifically documented came from those *Star-Telegram* reports. The trial began on January 6, 1913, and concluded on January 23, 1913.

5. *Fort Worth Star-Telegram*, January 9, 1913.

6. Ibid., January 12, 1913.

7. Al to Lena, letter dated January 13, 1912, quoted in Sneed, "Because This is Texas," 29; habeas corpus hearing transcript, 251–52.

8. Al to Lena, letter dated January 15, 1912, quoted in Sneed, "Because This is Texas," 21; habeas corpus hearing transcript, 253.

9. *Fort Worth Star-Telegram*, January 18, 1913.

10. Ibid., January 22, 1913.

11. Ibid.

12. Ibid.

13. Ibid.

14. Ibid.

15. Article 38.05, *Texas Code of Criminal Procedure* provides: "In ruling on the admissibility of evidence, the judge shall not discuss or comment upon the weight of the same or its bearing on the case, but shall simply decide whether or not it is admissible; nor shall he, at any stage of the proceeding previous to the return of a verdict, make any remark calculated to convey to the jury his opinion of the case."

Chapter Eleven

1. *State of Texas v. John Beal Sneed*, Cause No. 2087 in the Forty-sixth Judicial District Court of Wilbarger County, Texas.

2. *Fort Worth Star-Telegram*, February 13, 1913. The Vernon, Texas, murder trial of John Beal Sneed began February 11, 1913, and concluded on February 25, 1913. This chapter is based primarily on the daily reports published in the *Fort Worth Star-Telegram*.

3. *Fort Worth Star-Telegram*, February 15, 1913.

4. Ibid., February 21, 1913.

5. Ibid.

6. *Fort Worth Star-Telegram*, February 20, 1913; Sneed, "Because This is Texas," 59.

7. *Fort Worth Star-Telegram*, February 19, 1913.

8. Ibid.

9. Ibid., February 20, 1913.

10. Ibid., February 19, 1913

11. Ibid., February 20, 1913

12. Ibid.

13. Ibid.

14. Ibid.

15. Ibid.

16. Ibid., February 22, 1913.

17. Ibid.

18. Ibid.

19. Ibid., February 23, 1913.

20. Ibid.

21. Ibid., February 24, 1913.

22. Ibid.

23. Ibid.

24. Carmen Taylor Bennett, *Our Roots Grow Deep: A History of Cottle County* (Floydada, Texas: Blanco Offset Printing, 1970), 74–75.

Chapter Twelve

1. Carmen Taylor Bennett, *Our Roots Grow Deep: A History of Cottle County* (Floydada, Texas: 1970), 175–76; Jim Wheat, *More Ghost Towns of Texas* (Garland, Texas: Lost and Found, 1971); Charles G. Davis, "Sneedville, Texas," *Handbook of Texas Online*, *http://tshaonline.org/handbook/online/articles/hrs53* (accessed November 6, 2010).

2. *Wichita [Falls] (TX) Daily Times*, July 11, 1923.

3. Ibid.

4. *State of Texas v. Wood Barton*, Cause No. 847 in the District Court of Cottle County, Texas.

5. *Wichita Daily Times*, July 11, 1923.

6. Ibid.

7. Ibid.

8. *Paducah Post*, November 16, 1922.

9. *Paducah Post*, March 8, 1923.

10. *Quanah Tribune-Chief*, March 9, 1923.

11. Red Burton (ex-Texas Ranger), oral history interview, 1969, Mart, Texas, Southwest Collection/Special Collections, Texas Tech University, Lubbock, Texas.

12. *Paducah Post*, July 5, 1923.

13. *Wichita Daily Times*, February 28, 1924.

14. *State of Texas v. C. B. Berry*, Cause No. 1038 in the District Court of Cottle County, and Cause No. 1529 in the District Court of Baylor County.

15. *State of Texas v. John Beal Sneed*, Cause No. 1043 in the District Court of Cottle County, and Cause No. 1520 in the District Court of Knox County.

16. *State of Texas v. C. B. Berry*, Cause No. 1074 in the District Court of Cottle County, and Cause No. 1537 in the District Court of Knox County.

17. *Wichita Daily Times*, July 11, 1923.

18. *Quanah Tribune-Chief*, July 12, 1923.

19. For reports of the trial of C. B. Berry for the killing of Wood Barton see *Wichita Daily Times*, July 11, 1923; *Quanah Tribune-Chief*, July 12 and 17, 1923; and *Foard County News*, July 20, 1923.

20. *Wichita Daily Times*, July 11, 1923

21. Ibid.

22. Ibid.

23. *Quanah Tribune-Chief*, July 17, 1923.

24. *Wichita Daily Times*, February 27, 1924.

25. Ibid.

26. Ibid.

27. For reports of the trial of C. B. Berry for the attempted murder of John Beal Sneed, see *Wichita Daily Times*, February 28 and 29, 1924.

28. *Wichita Daily Times*, February 29, 1924.

29. Ibid.; *Paducah Post*, March 6, 1924. Also see Carmen Taylor Bennett, *Our Roots Grow Deep: A History of Cottle County* (Floydada, Texas: Blanco Offset Printing, 1970), 89–91.

30. Civil cases in which John Beal Sneed was either the plaintiff or defendant from 1919 through 1924 in the Cottle County District Court appear under the following Cause Nos.: 404, 427, 436, 437, 441, 609, 614, 615, 623, 649, 651, 673, 790, 797, 805, 821, 980, 1013, 1030, 1048, 1058, and 1191.

31. *First National Bank of Shiner, Texas v. John Beal Sneed*, Cause No. 1013 in the Cottle County District Court.

32. *Acala Cotton Seed Co. v. John Beal Sneed*, Cause No. 1030 in the Cottle County District Court.

33. *P. M. Fields v. John Beal Sneed*, Cause No. 1058 in the Cottle County District Court.

34. *Quanah Mill & Elevator Co. v. John Beal Sneed*, Cause No. 1551 in the Hardeman County District Court.

35. *Nicholas Bilby v. John Beal Sneed*, Cause No. 559 on the civil docket of the U.S. District Court for the Northern District of Texas, Abilene Division.

36. *United States v. John Beal Sneed*, Cause No. 785 on the criminal docket of the U.S. District Court for the Northern District of Texas, Abilene Division.

37. *Abilene Reporter*, October 6, 1923.

38. *Fort Worth Star-Telegram*, October 16, 1921.

39. *Abilene Reporter,* October 8, 1922; *Fort Worth Star-Telegram,* October 8, 1922.

40. *Fort Worth Star-Telegram,* October 16, 1922.

41. *Sneed, et al. v. The United States,* Cause No. 3994 in the U.S. Fifth Circuit Court of Appeals in New Orleans, 298 F. Supp. 911, 1924; appeal aff'd, Lexis No. 2729, 37 A.L.R. 722 (1924).

42. *The Abilene Reporter,* October 8, 1922.

43. Ron Tyler, ed., s.v. "Boyce-Sneed Feud," *Handbook of Texas* (Austin: Texas State Historical Assn., 1996), 1:682.

44. *Dallas Morning News,* April 23, 1960.

45. *Dallas Morning News,* March 7, 1966.

46. Sneed, "Because This is Texas," 78.

Epilogue

1. Vincent Bugliosi, *Outrage: The Five Reasons Why O. J. Simpson Got Away With Murder* (New York: Bantam Doubleday Dell, 1996), 445–46.

2. Edward L. Ayers, *Vengeance and Justice: Crime and Punishment in the Nineteenth-Century American South* (New York: Oxford University Press, 1984), 18; Michael P. Rogin, *Fathers and Children: Andrew Jackson and the Subjugation of the American Indian* (New York: Vintage Books, 1976), 58.

3. How the unwritten law's "honor" defense was successfully asserted in six celebrated Texas murder trials from 1896 to 1977 in cases where the murder victim was killed by the defendant because of some real or perceived sexual misconduct, see Bill Neal, *Sex, Murder, and the Unwritten Law: Courting Judicial Mayhem, Texas Style* (Lubbock: Texas Tech University Press, 2009). Author Daniel Justin Herman, in his lively account of Arizona's Rim Country War of the 1880s, explores a web of conflict involving Mormons, Texas cowboys, New Mexican sheepherders, and others and argues that at the heart of Arizona's range war was the conflict between the cowboy code of honor—an outgrowth of southern culture—and a Mormon code of conscience born of Puritanism, the Enlightenment, and religious revival. Daniel Justin Herman, *Hell on the Range: A Story of Honor, Conscience, and the American West* (New Haven, Conn.: Yale University Press, 2010). Also see Paul H. Carlson, "Cowboys and Sheepherders," in Paul H Carlson, ed., *The Cowboy Way: An Exploration of History and Culture* (Lubbock: Texas Tech University Press, 2006), 109–18.

4. Thomas J. Kernan, "The Jurisprudence of Lawlessness," *American Bar Association Report,* 1906, 451–53.

5. For a discussion of the waning of the unwritten law and of the waxing of the statutory law as the nineteenth century turned into the twentieth century and the frontier culture of the American South and West matured, see Neal, *Sex, Murder, and the Unwritten Law,* 239–48. Also see Herman, *Hell on the Range,* 255–91.

6. *Fort Worth Star-Telegram,* December 1, 1912.

7. *Dallas Dispatch,* December 3, 1912.

8. Sneed, "Because This is Texas," 74.

9. C. L. Sonnichsen, *Ten Texas Feuds: "Vengeance Is Mine!" Saith the Lord. But in Texas He has always had plenty of help!* (Albuquerque: University of New Mexico Press, 1971).

10. C. L. Sonnichsen, *I'll Die Before I'll Run: The Story of the Great Feuds of Texas* (Lincoln: University of Nebraska Press, 1988), 8.

11. Sneed, "Because This is Texas," 75.

12. Ibid., 78.

13. Sonnichsen, *I'll Die Before I'll Run,* 10.

14. *Fort Worth Star-Telegram,* September 15, 1912.

15. James D. Hamlin, *The Flamboyant Judge: The Story of Amarillo and the Development of the Great Ranches of the Texas Panhandle,* a biography as told to J. Evetts Haley and William Curry Holden (Canyon, Texas: Palo Duro Press, 1972), 95.

16. Historian Stephen L. Hardin is a spellbinder of a storyteller who believes it does history no harm to write it sans "academic vernacular" so folks will enjoy reading it. But he is also a scrupulous historian who admonishes other historians not to revise history to fit their agenda. In his recent book, *Texian Macabre: The Melancholy Tale of a Hanging in Early Houston* (Abilene, Texas: State House Press, 2007), 257, Professor Hardin says this:

> . . . writers of history need guard against . . . "present mindedness": the pernicious practice of judging long dead people by current trends. It disregards professional methodology, is arrogant, and, ultimately, dishonest. The historian's responsibility is to understand and explain the past, not condemn those who lived it.

When I reread the last paragraph of my book wherein I had condemned John Beal Sneed as being "vicious, cold-blooded, and vindictive," Professor Hardin's admonishment flashed back into my consciousness. So I went back and reread his exhortation. I was relieved when I read the rest of Hardin's statement. After warning against "judging long dead people by current trends," he added this:

> This is not to say, however, that the living should view the past only as mute observers. Even by 1830s standards, Francis Moore, Jr., was a sanctimonious prig. Chauncey Goodrich was a cheap thug, and John Kirby Allen was a snake oil salesman. Moreover, any historian would have to be pitifully mealy-mouthed not to say so.

Following Professor Hardin's counsel, I concluded that I would have been mealy-mouthed indeed to describe John Beal Sneed as anything less than "vicious, cold-blooded, and vindictive."

Appendix One

1. *Wise County Messenger,* January 24, 1919.

2. *Decatur News,* January 24, 1919. The Forty-Sixth Judicial District of Texas was created in 1889 shortly after the Fort Worth and Denver City Railway completed laying tracks from Fort Worth to Amarillo. It initially comprised ten sparsely populated

counties, five of which were organized counties (Donley, Greer, Childress, Hardeman, and Wilbarger) and five of which were unorganized counties (Hall, Collingsworth, Cottle, Briscoe, and Armstrong). However, after Oklahoma became a state in 1907, the U.S. Supreme Court declared that Greer County—located in the southwest corner of that state—was actually a part of Oklahoma. Consequently, it was no longer a part of the Forty-Sixth Judicial District of Texas.

3. Rosalie Gregg, ed., *Wise County History: A Link with the Past* (Austin: Nortex Press, 1987), 62.

4. Cliff D. Cates, *Pioneer History of Wise County: From Red Men to Railroads—Twenty Years of Intrepid History* (Decatur, Texas: Wise County Old Settlers' Association, 1907), 383–84.

5. *Wise County Messenger*, January 24, 1919. The account of the killing of Hugh Spencer by W. M. Bolger and the pretrial hearing is reported in the January 24, 1919, and January 31, 1919, editions of the *Wise County Messenger* printed in Decatur, Texas. For a brief account of the incident and the result of the trial, also see Jim Tom Barton, *Eighter From Decatur: Growing Up in North Texas* (College Station: Texas A&M University Press, 1980), 89–90. This account, recalled by a Wise County native years later from family legends passed down to him, contains several factual errors.

6. *Wise County Messenger*, January 24, 1919

7. Ibid.

8. Ibid.; *Fort Worth Star-Telegram*, January 24, 1919.

9. *Fort Worth Record*, January 10, 1920.

10. *State v. W. M. Bolger*, Cause No. 2146 in the Forty-Third Judicial District Court of Wise County, Texas.

11. *Fort Worth Star-Telegram*, January 14, 1920.

✍ BIBLIOGRAPHY

BOOKS

Alter, Judy, and James Ward Lee, eds. *Literary Fort Worth*. Fort Worth: Texas Christian University Press, 2002.

Anderson, Ken. *Dan Moody: Crusader for Justice*. Georgetown, Texas: Georgetown Press, 2008.

Ayers, Edward L. *Vengeance and Justice: Crime and Punishment in the Nineteenth-Century American South*. New York: Oxford University Press, 1984.

Bakken, Gordon Morris, and Brenda Farrington. *Women Who Kill Men*. Lincoln: University of Nebraska Press, 2009.

————. *Learning California History*. Wheeling, Ill.: Harlan Davidson, 1999.

Bardaglio, Peter. *Reconstruction of the Household: Families, Sex and the Law in the Nineteenth-Century South*. Chapel Hill: University of North Carolina Press, 1995.

Barton, Tom. *Eighter From Decatur: Growing Up in North Texas*. College Station: Texas A&M University Press, 1980.

Beckham, Diane Burch, ed. *Criminal Laws of Texas, 2001–2003*. Austin: Texas District & County Attorneys Association, 2001.

Bennett, Carmen Taylor. *Our Roots Grow Deep: A History of Cottle County*. Floydada, Texas: Blanco Offset Printing, 1970.

Brown, Norman D. *Hood, Bonnet, and Little Brown Jug: Texas Politics, 1921–1938*. College Station: Texas A&M University Press, 1984.

Brownell, Blaine A. "The Urban South Comes of Age, 1910–1920." In *The City in Southern History*, edited by Blaine A. Brownell and David R. Goldfield. Port Washington, N.Y.: National University Publications, 1977.

Bugliosi, Vincent. *Outrage: The Five Reasons Why O. J. Simpson Got Away with Murder*. New York: Bantam Doubleday Dell Publishing Group, 1996.

Carlson, Paul H. *Amarillo: The Story of a Western Town*. Lubbock: Texas Tech University Press, 2006.

————. "Cowboys and Sheepherders." In *The Cowboy Way: An Exploration of History and Culture*, edited by Paul H. Carlson. Lubbock: Texas Tech University Press, 2006.

Cates, Cliff D. *Pioneer History of Wise County: From Red Men to Railroads—Twenty Years of Intrepid History*. Decatur, Texas: Wise County Old Settlers' Association, 1907.

Chalmers, David M. *Hooded Americanism: The History of the Ku Klux Klan*. 2nd ed. New York: New Viewpoints, 1981.

Coombes, Charles E. *The Prairie Dog Lawyer*. Dallas: Texas Folklore Society and University Press of Dallas, 1945.

Conley, Carolyn A. *The Unwritten Law*. New York: Oxford University Press, 1991.

Fairchild, Louis. *The Lonesome Plains: Death and Revival on an American Frontier*. College Station: Texas A&M University Press, 2002.

Fehrenbach, T. R. *Lone Star: A History of Texas and the Texans*. New York: Macmillan, 1968.

Gard, Wayne. *The Chisholm Trail.* Norman: University of Oklahoma Press, 1954.

Haley, James L. *Texas: From Spindletop Through World War II.* New York: St. Martin's Press, 1993.

Haley, J. Evetts. *The XIT Ranch of Texas: and the Early Days of the Llano Estacado.* Norman: University of Oklahoma Press, 1967.

Hamlin, James D. *The Flamboyant Judge.* Canyon, Texas: Palo Duro Press, 1972.

Hardin, Stephen L. *Texian Macabre: The Melancholy Tale of a Hanging in Early Houston.* Abilene, Texas: State House Press, 2007.

Herman, Daniel Justin. *Hell on the Range: A Story of Honor, Conscience, and the American West.* New Haven, Conn.: Yale University Press, 2010.

Hogrefe, Jeffrey. *O'Keeffe: The Life of an American Legend.* New York: Bantam Books, 1992.

Hollon, W. Eugene. *The Great American Desert: Then and Now.* New York: Oxford University Press, 1966.

Hunter, J. Marvin, ed. *The Trail Drivers of Texas.* Austin: University of Texas Press, 1985.

Jones, Billy M. *The Search for Maturity: The Saga of Texas, 1875–1900.* Austin, Texas: Steck-Vaughn, 1965.

Kens, Paul. "Don't Mess Around in Texas: Adultery and Justifiable Homicide in the Lone Star State." In *Law in the Western United States,* edited by Gordon Morris Bakken. Norman: University of Oklahoma Press, 2000.

Key, Della Tyler. *In the Cattle Country: History of Potter County, 1887–1966.* 2nd ed. Quanah, Texas: Nortex Offset Publications, 1972.

Lamott, Kenneth. *Who Killed Mr. Crittenden?* New York: David McKay, 1963.

Langum, David. *Crossing Over the Line: Legislating Morality and the Mann Act.* Chicago: University of Chicago Press, 1994.

McKay, Seth S., and Odie B. Faulk. *Texas After Spindletop: The Saga of Texas: 1901–1965.* Austin, Texas: Steck-Vaughn, 1965.

Moore, Jacqueline M. *Cow Boys and Cattle Men: Class and Masculinities on the Texas Frontier, 1865–1900.* New York: New York University Press, 2009.

Morris, John Miller. *El Llano Estacado: Exploration and Imagination on the High Plains of Texas and New Mexico, 1536–1860.* Austin: Texas State Historical Association, 1997.

Murrah, David J. *Oil, Taxes, and Cats: A History of the Devitt Family and the Mallet Ranch.* Lubbock: Texas Tech University Press, 1994.

Neal, Bill. *Sex, Murder, and the Unwritten Law: Courting Judicial Mayhem, Texas Style.* Lubbock: Texas Tech University Press, 2009.

Nolan, Frederick. *Tascosa: Its Life and Gaudy Times.* Lubbock: Texas Tech University Press, 2007.

Nordyke, Lewis. *Cattle Empire: the Fabulous Story of the 3,000,000 Acre XIT.* New York: William Morrow, 1949.

Price, B. Byron, and Frederick W. Rathjen. *The Golden Spread: An Illustrated History of Amarillo and the Texas Panhandle.* Northridge, California: Windsor Publications, 1986.

Rathjen, Frederick W. *The Texas Panhandle Frontier,* revised ed. Lubbock: Texas Tech University Press, 1998.

Richardson, Rupert Norval. *The Comanche Barrier to South Plains Settlement.* Glendale, California: Arthur H. Clark, 1973.

———. *Texas: The Lone Star State.* New York: Prentice-Hall, 1947.

Rogin, Michael P. *Fathers and Children: Andrew Jackson and the Subjugation of the American Indian.* New York: Vintage Books, 1976.

Scarborough, Dorothy. *The Wind.* Austin: University of Texas Press, 1979.

Selcer, Richard F. *Fort Worth Characters.* Denton, Texas: University of North Texas Press, 2009.

———. *Hell's Half Acre.* Fort Worth: Texas Christian University Press, 1991.

Shapiro, Fred R., ed. *The Yale Book of Quotations.* New Haven, Conn.: Yale University Press, 2006.

Shirley, Glenn. *Temple Houston: Lawyer With A Gun.* Norman: University of Oklahoma Press, 1968.

Smallwood, James M. *The Feud That Wasn't: The Taylor Ring, Bill Sutton, John Wesley Hardin, and Violence in Texas.* College Station: Texas A&M University Press, 2008.

Sonnichsen, C. L. *I'll Die Before I'll Run: The Story of the Great Feuds of Texas.* Lincoln: University of Nebraska Press, 1988.

———. *Ten Texas Feuds.* Albuquerque: University of New Mexico Press, 1971.

Thwaites, R. G., ed. *Early Western Travels.* Cleveland: Arthur H. Clark, 1905.

Time-Life Books. *This Fabulous Century: 1910–1920,* Vol. II. New York: Time, 1969.

Tyler, Ron, ed. *The New Handbook of Texas.* Austin: Texas Historical Society, 1996, s.vv. "Boyce, Albert Gallatin," "Boyce-Sneed Feud," "Goodnight, Charles," "Sneed, Joseph Perkins," "Wilbarger, Josiah Pugh."

Wallace, Ernest. *Texas in Turmoil: The Saga of Texas, 1849–1875.* Austin: Steck-Vaughn Company, 1965.

Webb, Walter Prescott. *The Great Plains.* New York: Grosset & Dunlap, 1931.

Wheat, Jim. *More Ghost Towns of Texas.* Garland, Texas: Lost and Found, 1971.

Wilbarger, J. W. *Indian Depredations in Texas.* Austin: Statehouse Books, 1985.

ARTICLES

Archambeau, Ernest R. "The Fort Smith-Santa Fe Trail Along the Canadian River in Texas." *Panhandle-Plains Historical Review* 27 (1954): 1–26.

Carter, Keith. "The Texas Court of Criminal Appeals." *Texas Law Review* 11 (1933): 185–196.

Ellard, John. "The History and Present Status of Moral Insanity." *Australian and New Zealand Journal of Psychiatry* 22 (1988): 386.

Ireland, Robert M. "Frenzied and Fallen Females." *Journal of Women's History* 3 (Winter 1992): 95–117.

Gray, Dr. John P. "The Trial of Mary Harris." *American Journal of Insanity* 22 (1865–1866): 67–83.

Lawson, J. D., ed. "The Trial of Mary Harris for the Murder of Adoniram J. Burroughs," *American State Trials* 17 (1865): 233–375.

Linder, Douglas O. "The Trial of Charles Guiteau: An Account." *http://www.law. umkc.edu/faculty/projects/ftrials/guiteau/guiteauaccount.html.*

Robinson, Charles F., II. "Legislated Love in the Lone Star State: Texas and Misce-
    genation," *Southwestern Historical Quarterly* 108, no. 1 (July 2004): 79.
Sneed, Clara. "Because This Is Texas: An Account of the Sneed-Boyce Feud."
    Panhandle-Plains Historical Review 72 (1999): 1–100.
Spiegel, Allen D., and Merrill S. Spiegel. "Not Guilty of Murder by Reason of
    Paroxysmal Insanity: The 'Mad' Doctor vs. 'Common Sense' Doctors in an
    1865 Trial," *Psychiatric Quarterly* 62, no. 1 (Spring 1991): 51–66.

NEWSPAPERS

Abilene Reporter-News
Amarillo Daily News
Cattleman
Dallas Dispatch
Dallas Morning News
Decatur News
Foard County News
Fort Worth Record
Fort Worth Star-Telegram

Los Angeles Times
Manitoba (Canada) Free Press
New York Times
Quanah Tribune-Chief
St. Louis Post-Dispatch
Wichita [Falls] (Texas) Daily Times
Winnipeg (Manitoba) Saturday
Wise County Messenger

OFFICIAL RECORDS

John Beal Sneed v. State of Texas, Cause No. 1535, Forty-seventh Judicial District Court,
    Potter County, Texas. Habeas corpus hearing.
State of Texas v. John Beal Sneed, Cause No. 1534, Forty-seventh Judicial District Court,
    Potter County, Texas.
State of Texas v. John Beal Sneed, Cause No. 19,777, Seventeenth Judicial District
    Court, Tarrant County, Texas.
State of Texas v. John Beal Sneed, Cause No. 412, Forty-sixth Judicial District Court,
    Hall County, Texas.
State of Texas v. John Beal Sneed, Cause No. 2087, Forty-sixth Judicial District Court,
    Wilbarger County, Texas.
State of Texas v. Beech Epting, Cause No. 412, Forty-sixth Judicial District Court, Hall
    County, Texas.
State of Texas v. John Beal Sneed, Cause No. 1520, Fiftieth Judicial District Court, Knox
    County, Texas.
State of Texas v. C. B. Berry, Cause No. 1537, Fiftieth Judicial District Court, Knox
    County, Texas.
State of Texas v. John Beal Sneed, Cause No. 1529, Fiftieth Judicial District Court, Bay-
    lor County, Texas.
Letter from U.S. Secretary of War George W. Crawford to Randolph B. Marcy dated
    February 21, 1850, styled "Route from Fort Smith to Santa Fe." H. Exec. Doc.
    45, 31st Cong., 1st Sess., pg. 41.
Ex Parte Sneed, 150 S.W. 1197 (Tex.Ct.Crim.App., 1912). Habeas corpus appeal.
State of Texas v. W. M. Bolger, Cause No. 2146, Forty-third Judicial District Court,
    Wise County, Texas.

First National Bank of Shiner, Texas v. John Beal Sneed, Cause No. 1013, Cottle County District Court.

Acala Cotton Seed Co. v. John Beal Sneed, Cause No. 1030, Cottle County District Court.

P. M. Fields v. John Beal Sneed, Cause No. 1058 in the Cottle County District Court.

Quanah Mill & Elevator Co. v. John Beal Sneed, Cause No. 1551, Hardeman County District Court.

Nicholas Bilby v. John Beal Sneed, Cause No. 559 on the civil docket of the U.S. District Court for the Northern District of Texas, Abilene Division.

United States v. John Beal Sneed, Cause No. 785 on the criminal docket of the U.S. District Court for the Northern District of Texas, Abilene Division.

Sneed, et al v. The United States, Cause No. 3994 in the U.S. Fifth Circuit Court of Appeals in New Orleans, 298 F. Supp. 911, 1924; appeal aff'd Lexis No. 2729, 37 A.L.R. 722 (1924).

CORRESPONDENCE AND INTERVIEWS

Boyce, Albert, Jr., to Lena Snyder Sneed. Letters. In Sneed, "Because This is Texas."

Burton, Red (ex-Texas Ranger). Interview, Mart, Texas, 1969. Oral history collection, Southwest Collection/Special Collection Library, Texas Tech University, Lubbock, Texas.

Sneed, Lena Snyder, to Albert Boyce, Jr. Letters. In Sneed, "Because This is Texas."

Sneed, Lena Snyder, to Pearl Snyder Perkins. Letter. In Sneed, "Because This is Texas."

LIBRARIES

Abilene Public Library, Abilene, Texas.

Fort Worth Public Library, Fort Worth, Texas.

J. Evetts Haley History Center, Midland, Texas.

Panhandle-Plains Historical Museum Archives, Canyon, Texas.

Rupert Richardson Library, Hardin-Simmons University, Abilene, Texas.

Southwest Collection/Special Collection Library, Texas Tech University, Lubbock, Texas.

University of Texas at Arlington Library, Arlington, Texas.